AA004128

SEMAPRO 2020

The Fourteenth International Conference on Advances in Semantic Processing

October 25 - 29, 2020

SEMAPRO 2020 Editors

Tim vor der Brück, FFHS, Lucerne University of Applied Sciences and Arts, Switzerland

Printed from e-media with permission by:

Curran Associates, Inc.
57 Morehouse Lane
Red Hook, NY 12571

Some format issues inherent in the e-media version may also appear in this print version.

Printed with permission by Curran Associates, Inc. (2020)

International Academy, Research, and Industry Association (IARIA)
412 Derby Way
Wilmington, DE 19810

Phone: (408) 893-6407
Fax: (408) 527-6351

petre@iaria.org

Additional copies of this publication are available from:

Curran Associates, Inc.
57 Morehouse Lane
Red Hook, NY 12571 USA
Phone: 845-758-0400
Fax: 845-758-2633
Email: curran@proceedings.com
Web: www.proceedings.com

Table of Contents

SEMAPRO 2020

Forward

The Fourteenth International Conference on Advances in Semantic Processing (SEMAPRO 2020), held on October 22-29, 2020, continued a series of events that were initiated considering the complexity of understanding and processing information. Semantic processing considers contextual dependencies and adds to the individually acquired knowledge emergent properties and understanding. Hardware and software support and platforms were developed for semantically enhanced information retrieval and interpretation. Searching for video, voice and speech [VVS] raises additional problems to specialized engines with respect to text search. Contextual searching and special patterns-based techniques are current solutions.

With the progress on ontology, web services, semantic social media, semantic web, deep web search /deep semantic web/, semantic deep web, semantic networking and semantic reasoning, SEMAPRO 2020 constituted the stage for the state-of-the-art on the most recent advances.

The conference had the following tracks:

- Basics on semantics
- Domain-oriented semantic applications
- Semantic applications/platforms/tools

We take here the opportunity to warmly thank all the members of the SEMAPRO 2020 technical program committee, as well as all the reviewers. The creation of such a high quality conference program would not have been possible without their involvement. We also kindly thank all the authors that dedicated much of their time and effort to contribute to SEMAPRO 2020. We truly believe that, thanks to all these efforts, the final conference program consisted of top quality contributions.

We also gratefully thank the members of the SEMAPRO 2020 organizing committee for their help in handling the logistics and for their work that made this professional meeting a success.

We hope that SEMAPRO 2020 was a successful international forum for the exchange of ideas and results between academia and industry and to promote further progress in the field of semantic processing.

SEMAPRO 2020 General Chair

Sandra Sendra, Universitat Politecnica de Valencia, Universidad de Granada, Spain

SEMAPRO 2020 Steering Committee

Fabio Grandi, University of Bologna, Italy
Sandra Lovrenčić, University of Zagreb, Croatia

Michele Melchiori, Università degli Studi di Brescia, Italy
Wladyslaw Homenda, Warsaw University of Technology, Poland
Tim vor der Brück, Lucerne University of Applied Sciences and Arts, Switzerland
Els Lefever, LT3 | Ghent University, Belgium
Sofia Athenikos, Twitter, USA

SEMAPRO 2020 Publicity Chair

Daniel Andoni Basterrechea, Universitat Politecnica de Valencia, Spain

SEMAPRO 2020

COMMITTEE

SEMAPRO 2020 General Chair

Sandra Sendra, Universitat Politecnica de Valencia, Universidad de Granada, Spain

SEMAPRO Steering Committee

Sandra Lovrenčić, University of Zagreb, Croatia
Michele Melchiori, Università degli Studi di Brescia, Italy
Fabio Grandi, University of Bologna, Italy
Sofia Athenikos, Twitter, USA
Wladyslaw Homenda, Warsaw University of Technology, Poland
Tim vor der Brück, Lucerne University of Applied Sciences and Arts, Switzerland
Els Lefever, LT3 | Ghent University, Belgium

SEMAPRO 2020 Publicity Chair

Daniel Andoni Basterrechea, Universitat Politecnica de Valencia, Spain

SEMAPRO 2020 Technical Program Committee

Witold Abramowicz, Poznan University of Economics, Poland
Riccardo Albertoni, Istituto per la Matematica Applicata e Tecnologie Informatiche "Enrico Magenes" - Consiglio Nazionale delle Ricerche (IMATI-CNR), Italy
Jose María Alvarez Rodríguez, Carlos III University of Madrid, Spain
Sofia Athenikos, Twitter, USA
Giuseppe Berio, Université de Bretagne Sud | IRISA, France
Loris Bozzato, Fondazione Bruno Kessler, Trento, Italy
Zouhaier Brahmia, University of Sfax, Tunisia
Okan Bursa, Ege University, Turkey
Ozgu Can, Ege University, Turkey
Rodrigo Capobianco Guido, São Paulo State University (UNESP), Brazil
Damir Cavar, Indiana University, USA
Julio Cesar Duarte, Instituto Militar de Engenharia, Rio de Janeiro, Brazil
David Chaves-Fraga, Universidad Politécnica de Madrid, Spain
Christos Christodoulopoulos, Amazon, UK
Ioannis Chrysakis, FORTH-ICS, Greece / Ghent University, Belgium
Ademar Crotti Junior, Trinity College Dublin, Ireland
Cláudio de Souza Baptista, Federal University of Campina Grande, Brazil
Christian Dirschl, Wolters Kluwer Deutschland GmbH, Germany
Milan Dojchinovski, InfAI | Leipzig University, Germany / Czech Technical University in Prague, Czech Republic
Enrico Francesconi, IGSG - CNR, Italy
Panorea Gaitanou, Greek Ministry of Justice, Athens, Greece

Bilel Gargouri, MIRACL Laboratory | University of Sfax, Tunisia
Fabio Grandi, University of Bologna, Italy
Damien Graux, ADAPT Centre - Trinity College Dublin, Ireland
Bidyut Gupta, Southern Illinois University, USA
Shun Hattori, Muroran Institute of Technology, Japan
Tobias Hellmund, Fraunhofer Institute of Optronics, System Technologies and Image Exploitation IOSB, Germany
Tracy Holloway King, Amazon, USA
Wladyslaw Homenda, Warsaw University of Technology, Poland
Tzung-Pei Hong, National University of Kaohsiung, Taiwan
Thomas Hubauer, Siemens AG Corporate Technology, Germany
Sergio Ilarri, University of Zaragoza, Spain
Agnieszka Jastrzebska, Warsaw University of Technology, Poland
Young-Gab Kim, Sejong University, Korea
Stasinos Konstantopoulos, Institute of Informatics and Telecommunications, NCSR "Demokritos", Greece
Petr Kremen, Czech Technical University in Prague, Czech Republic
Jaroslav Kuchař, Czech Technical University in Prague, Czech Republic
André Langer, Chemnitz University of Technology, Germany
Kyu-Chul Lee, Chungnam National University, South Korea
Els Lefever, LT3 | Ghent University, Belgium
Antoni Ligęza, AGH-UST Kraków, Poland
Johannes Lipp, Fraunhofer Institute for Applied Information Technology FIT, Germany
Giuseppe Loseto, Polytechnic University of Bari, Italy
Sandra Lovrenčić, University of Zagreb, Croatia
Federica Mandreoli, Universita' di Modena e Reggio Emilia, Italy
Miguel A. Martínez-Prieto, University of Valladolid, Segovia, Spain
Miguel Felix Mata Rivera, UPIITA-IPN, Mexico
Michele Melchiori, Università degli Studi di Brescia, Italy
Dimitri Metaxas, Rutgers University, USA
Mohamed Wiem Mkaouer, Rochester Institute of Technology, USA
Luis Morgado da Costa, Nanyang Technological University, Singapore
Fadi Muheidat, California State University San Bernardino, USA
Yotaro Nakayama, Technology Research & Innovation Nihon Unisys, Ltd., Tokyo, Japan
Nikolay Nikolov, SINTEF Digital, Norway
Fabrizio Orlandi, ADAPT Centre | Trinity College Dublin, Ireland
Peera Pacharintanakul, TOT, Thailand
Peteris Paikens, University of Latvia - Faculty of Computing, Latvia
Panagiotis Papadakos, FORTH-ICS | University of Crete, Greece
Silvia Piccini, Institute Of Computational Linguistics "A. Zampolli" (CNR-Pisa), Italy
Vitor Pinheiro de Almeida, Pontifícia Universidade Católica do Rio de Janeiro (PUC-Rio), Brazil
Livia Predoiu, Otto-von-Guericke-Universität *Magdeburg*, Germany
Matthew Purver, Queen Mary University of London, UK
Irene Renau, Pontificia Universidad Católica de Valparaíso, Colombia
Tarmo Robal, Tallinn University of Technology, Estonia
Christophe Roche, University Savoie Mont-Blanc, France
Michele Ruta, Politecnico di Bari, Italy
Minoru Sasaki, Ibaraki University, Japan
Wieland Schwinger, Johannes Kepler University Linz (JKU) | Inst. f. Telekooperation (TK), Linz, Austria

Floriano Scioscia, Polytechnic University of Bari, Italy
Congyu "Peter" Wu, University of Texas at Austin, USA
Carlos Seror, Independent Researcher, Spain
Saeedeh Shekarpour, University of Dayton, USA
George Tambouratzis, Institute for Language and Speech Processing, Athena R.C., Greece
Christos Tryfonopoulos, University of the Peloponnese, Greece
Jouni Tuominen, University of Helsinki / Aalto University, Finland
Taketoshi Ushiama, Kyushu University, Japan
Sirje Virkus, Tallinn University, Estonia
Daiva Vitkute-Adzgauskiene, Vytautas Magnus University, Lithuania
Tim vor der Brück, Lucerne University of Applied Sciences and Arts, Switzerland
Heba Wageeh, British University in Egypt, Cairo, Egypt
Rita Zaharah Wan-Chik, Universiti Kuala Lumpur, Malaysia
Wai Lok Woo, Northumbria University, UK
Roberto Yus, University of California, Irvine, USA
Martin Zelm, INTEROP-VLabBrussels, Belgium
Shuai Zhao, New Jersey Institute of Technology, USA
Qiang Zhu, University of Michigan - Dearborn, USA

Copyright Information

For your reference, this is the text governing the copyright release for material published by IARIA.

The copyright release is a transfer of publication rights, which allows IARIA and its partners to drive the dissemination of the published material. This allows IARIA to give articles increased visibility via distribution, inclusion in libraries, and arrangements for submission to indexes.

I, the undersigned, declare that the article is original, and that I represent the authors of this article in the copyright release matters. If this work has been done as work-for-hire, I have obtained all necessary clearances to execute a copyright release. I hereby irrevocably transfer exclusive copyright for this material to IARIA. I give IARIA permission or reproduce the work in any media format such as, but not limited to, print, digital, or electronic. I give IARIA permission to distribute the materials without restriction to any institutions or individuals. I give IARIA permission to submit the work for inclusion in article repositories as IARIA sees fit.

I, the undersigned, declare that to the best of my knowledge, the article is does not contain libelous or otherwise unlawful contents or invading the right of privacy or infringing on a proprietary right.

Following the copyright release, any circulated version of the article must bear the copyright notice and any header and footer information that IARIA applies to the published article.

IARIA grants royalty-free permission to the authors to disseminate the work, under the above provisions, for any academic, commercial, or industrial use. IARIA grants royalty-free permission to any individuals or institutions to make the article available electronically, online, or in print.

IARIA acknowledges that rights to any algorithm, process, procedure, apparatus, or articles of manufacture remain with the authors and their employers.

I, the undersigned, understand that IARIA will not be liable, in contract, tort (including, without limitation, negligence), pre-contract or other representations (other than fraudulent misrepresentations) or otherwise in connection with the publication of my work.

Exception to the above is made for work-for-hire performed while employed by the government. In that case, copyright to the material remains with the said government. The rightful owners (authors and government entity) grant unlimited and unrestricted permission to IARIA, IARIA's contractors, and IARIA's partners to further distribute the work.

Word Sense Disambiguation Using Graph-based Semi-supervised Learning

Rie Yatabe
Major in Computer and Information Sciences
Graduate School of Science and Engineering,
Ibaraki University
19nm732r@vc.ibaraki.ac.jp
4-12-1, Nakanarusawa, Hitachi, Ibaraki, 316-8511, Japan

Minoru Sasaki
Dept. of Computer and Information Sciences
Faculty of Engineering, Ibaraki University
minoru.sasaki.01@vc.ibaraki.ac.jp
4-12-1, Nakanarusawa, Hitachi, Ibaraki, 316-8511, Japan

Abstract— **Word Sense Disambiguation (WSD) is a well-known problem in the natural language processing. In recent years, there has been increasing interest in applying neural networks and machine learning techniques to solve WSD problems. However, these previous approaches often suffer from the lack of manually sense-tagged examples. Moreover, most supervised WSD methods suffer from small differences of examples within the overall training data or within each of the two sense labels. In this paper, to solve these problems, we propose a semi-supervised WSD method using graph convolutional neural network and investigate what kind of features are effective for this model. Experimental results show that the proposed method performs better than the previous supervised method and the morphological features obtained by the UniDic short-unit dictionary is effective for the semi-supervised WSD method. Moreover, the Jaccard coefficient is the most effective measure among three measures to construct a graph structure.**

Keywords- word sense disambiguation; graph convolutional neural network; semi-supervised learning.

I. INTRODUCTION

In human languages, many words have multiple meanings, depending on the context in which they are used. Identifying the sense of a polysemous word within a given context is a fundamental problem in natural language processing. For example, the English word "bank" has different meanings as "a commercial bank" or "a land along the edge of a river,", etc. Word Sense Disambiguation (WSD) is the task of deciding the appropriate meaning of a target ambiguous word in its context [1].

Among various approaches to the WSD task used over the past two decades, a supervised learning approach has been the most successful. In the supervised learning method, bag-of-words features extracted from a wide context window around the target word are used. However, a common problem of this approach is the lack of sufficient labelled training examples of specific words due to costly annotation work [2].

Moreover, most supervised WSD methods suffer from small differences of examples within the overall training data or within the two sense labels in the whole sense labels. For example, the following two example sentences of the Japanese word "教える (oshieru)" (word ID "5541") have a similar context, but they are used as different meanings.

1. 「そして、仕かけを工夫して、釣り方を教える。」(Sense Label : 5541-0-0-1) ("Then, they teach their customers how to fish using creative fish traps.")
2. 「1『エルマーのぼうけん』『おばけちゃん』のクイズ大作戦のやり方を教えよう。」(Sense Label : 5541-0-0-2) ("1. I'll show you how to conduct a big plan to take quizzes about the picture books 'My Father's Dragon' and 'Obake-chan'.")

For these examples, surrounding words can be extracted from the two words, on either side of the target word as follows:

1. "方", "を", "教える", "。"
2. "方", "を", "教えよう", "。"

As you can see from these obtained sets of words, almost the same words are contained in both sets. When the difference between the two meanings is small, it is difficult to classify them properly using the existing method. Therefore, if we can distinguish between such example sentences, we can consider improving the performance of WSD systems.

In order to overcome the above problem, semi-supervised learning has been applied successfully to word sense disambiguation. The semi-supervised methods requires only a small amount of sense labelled training examples and can take advantage of unlabelled examples to improve performance. We consider that the semi-supervised learning method is suitable for WSD because a huge amount of unlabelled examples are easily available and the supervised learning methods require a lot of manually sense labelled data. In the semi-supervised learning, we focus on semi-supervised classification method with graph convolutional neural network. This method can jointly train the embedding of an example to predict the sense label of the example and the neighbours in the graph. By using the proposed method, it is possible to incorporate information obtained from unlabelled examples without assigning a sense label to unlabelled examples. Moreover, by learning graph embeddings, it is possible to distinguish between two similar examples with different sense labels to construct a better classifier for WSD. However, it is not clear what kind of features are effective in WSD using the graph convolutional neural network.

In this paper, we investigate what kind of features are effective for graph-based semi-supervised WSD. If we can explore effective features, we consider that it is possible to build a high precision graph-based WSD system. Therefore, this paper aims to find effective features for training WSD classifier using a graph convolutional neural network. Then, we compared the performance for each of the five types of features that include surrounding words and their part of speech in a given window size, local collocations in the context and syntactic properties and so on.

This paper makes mainly two contributions for graph-based semi-supervised WSD as follows:

(1) We employ a graph convolutional neural network for semi-supervised WSD system to incorporate information obtained from unlabelled examples.
(2) We show that it is possible to distinguish between two similar examples with different sense labels using the proposed method.

The rest of this paper is organized as follows. Section 2 is devoted to the related works in the literature. Section 3 describes the proposed semi-supervised WSD method. In Section 4, we describe an outline of experiments and experimental results. Finally, we discuss the results in Section 5 and concludes the paper in Section 6.

II. Related Works

This section is a literature review of previous work on semi-supervised WSD and various related methods using a neural network.

In recent years, there has been increasing interest in applying neural networks and machine learning techniques to solve WSD problems. [3] employed a Bidirectional Long Short-Term Memory (Bi-LSTM) to encode information of both preceding and succeeding words within the context of a target word. [4] used an LSTM language model to obtain a context representation from a context layer for the whole sentence containing a target word. The context representations were compared to the possible sense embeddings for the target word. Then, the word sense whose embedding had maximal cosine similarity was assigned to classify a target word. [5] considered WSD as a neural sequence labelling task and constructed a sequence learning model for all-words WSD. These approaches are characterized by their high performance, simplicity, and ability to extract a lot of information from raw text.

In recent years, semi-supervised learning has been used in WSD tasks. Semi-supervised learning is a technique that makes use of a small number of sense-labelled examples with a large amount of unlabelled examples. [6] proposed a bootstrapping model that only has a small set of sense-labelled examples that gradually assigns appropriate senses to unlabelled examples. [4] and [7] proposed a semi-supervised WSD method to use word embeddings of surrounding words of the target word and showed that the performance of WSD could be increased by taking advantage of word embeddings.

[8] proposed a semi-supervised WSD method that automatically obtains reliable sense labelled examples using example sentences from the Iwanami Japanese dictionary to expand the labelled training data. Then, this method employs a maximum entropy model to construct a WSD classifier for each target word using common morphological features (surrounding words and POS tags) and topic features. Finally, the classifier for each target word predicts the sense of the test examples. They showed that this method is effective for the SemEval-2010 Japanese WSD task.

Some research in the field of WSD has taken advantage of graph-based approaches. [9] proposed a label propagation-based semi-supervised learning algorithm for WSD, which combines labelled and unlabelled examples in the learning process. [4] also introduced a Label Propagation (LP) for semi-supervised classification and LSTM language model. An LP graph consists of vertices of examples and edges that represent semantic similarity. In this graph, label propagation algorithms can be efficiently used to apply sense labels to examples based on the annotation of their neighbours.

In this paper, we use a semi-supervised learning method that incorporates knowledge from unlabelled examples by using graph convolutional neural network.

III. WSD Method Using Graph-based Semi-supervised Learning

In this section, we describe the details of the proposed semi-supervised WSD method using a graph convolutional neural network.

A. Overview of the Proposed Method

Our WSD method is used to select the appropriate sense for a target polysemous word in context. WSD can be viewed as a classification task in which each target word should be classified into one of the predefined existing senses. Word senses were annotated in a corpus in accordance with "Iwanami's Japanese Dictionary (The Iwanami Kokugo Jiten)" [10]. It has three levels for sense Ids, and the middle-level sense is used in this task.

The proposed semi-supervised WSD method requires a corpus of manually labelled training data to construct classifiers for every polysemous word and a graph between labelled and unlabelled examples. For each labelled and unlabelled example, features are extracted from a context around the target word, and the feature vector is constructed. Given a graph structure and feature vectors, we learn an embedding space to jointly predict the sense label and neighbourhood similarity in the graph using Planetoid [11] which is a semi-supervised learning method based on graph embeddings. When the WSD classifier is obtained, we predict one sense for each test example using this classification model.

B. Preprocessing

To implement the proposed WSD system, we extracted features from training data and test data of a target word, unlabelled examples from the Balanced Corpus of Contemporary Written Japanese (BCCWJ) corpus [12], and example sentences extracted from Iwanami Japanese Dictionary [10]. To segment a sentence into words, we use popular Japanese morphological analyser MeCab with the morphological dictionary UniDic or ipadic.

In this paper, we use the following twenty features (BF) for the target word w_i, which is the i-th word in the example sentence.

e1: the word w_{i-2}
e2: part-of-speech of the word w_{i-2}
e3: subcategory of the e2
e4: the word w_{i-1}
e5: part-of-speech of the word w_{i-1}
e6: subcategory of the e5
e7: the word w_i

e8: part-of-speech of the word w_i
e9: subcategory of the e8
e10: the word w_{i+1}
e11: part-of-speech of the word w_{i+1}
e12: subcategory of the e11
e13: the word w_{i+2}
e14: part-of-speech of the word w_{i+2}
e15: subcategory of the e14
e16: word that contains dependency relation with the w_i
e17: thesaurus ID number of the word w_{i-2}
e18: thesaurus ID number of the word w_{i-1}
e19: thesaurus ID number of the word w_{i+1}
e20: thesaurus ID number of the word w_{i+2}

To obtain the thesaurus ID number of each word, we use five-digit semantic classes obtained from a Japanese thesaurus "Bunrui Goi Hyo" [13]. When a word has multiple thesaurus IDs, e17, e18, e19, and e20 contain multiple thesaurus IDs for each context word. As additional local collocation (LC) features, we use bi-gram, tri-gram, and skip-bigram patterns in the three words on either side of the target word like IMS [14]. Skip-bigram is any pair of words in an example order with arbitrary gaps. Then, we can represent a context of word w_i as a vector of these features, where the value of each feature indicates the number of times the feature occurs.

To obtain additional example sentences from a dictionary, we use the same extraction method as in the previous work of [8]. In [8], sentences that include an exact match of Iwanami's example for each sense of headword are collected.

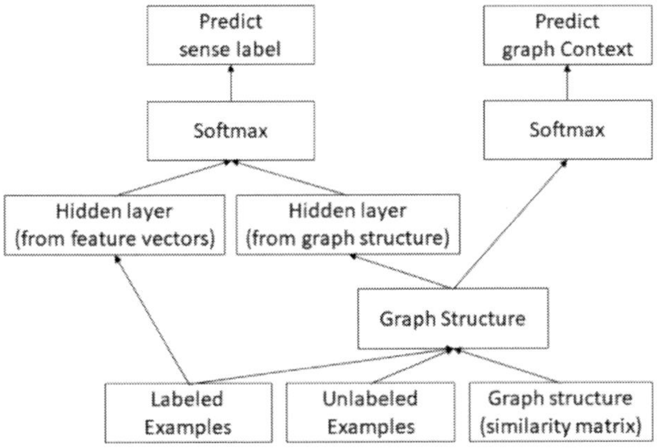

Figure 1. WSD model using graph convolutional neural network

C. Graph-based Semi-supervised Learning

We employ the Planetoid for the WSD model and predicts the sense of target word. In this method, as shown in Figure 1, we use a set of training examples, unlabelled examples and a graph structure representing the relationship between examples as input and learn a WSD classifier and graph context simultaneously. The classifier predicts the sense of the target word for unknown example.

The training examples and unlabelled examples are represented by feature vectors. The graph structure is constructed from the similarity between the obtained vectors. We learn a WSD model from the training data vector and the graph structure.

Planetoid utilizes stochastic gradient descent (SGD) in the mini-batch mode to train the WSD model. The mini-batch SGD is the popular optimization method for training deep neural networks. The mini-batch SGD is a first order optimization technique which computes the gradient of loss function $L(w)$ with respect to a certain subset of the data points. Using the learning rate ε and the loss function $L(w)$ of class label and node embedding prediction, the optimal model parameters are obtained by taking the following gradient steps.

$$\boldsymbol{w} = \boldsymbol{w} - \varepsilon(\partial L(\boldsymbol{w})/\partial \boldsymbol{w}). \quad (1)$$

Finally, we predict the appropriate sense label of the target word for the unknown examples using the optimized WSD model.

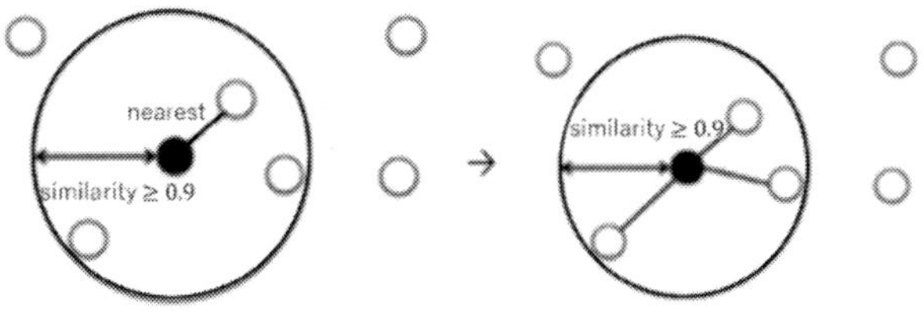

Figure 2. How to connect edges between examples

D. Input Graph Structure

The input graph structure is constructed by the relation between the training data and the unlabelled data. In the graph structure, each node is an example and an edge is the similarity between nodes. The similarity between nodes is calculated by using the following calculation method between two vectors of examples. In the proposed method, nodes with the highest similarity and nodes that have a similarity greater than the threshold are connected by edge. Figure 2 shows how the edges are connected.

The similarity calculation method between nodes uses Jaccard similarity J or cosine similarity. Jaccard similarity J is the ratio of the number of words in common between the two sets. Given a set of word vectors A and B, the similarity J is represented as follows:

$$J(A,B) = |A \cap B|/|A \cup B|, (0 \leq J(A,B) \leq 1). \quad (2)$$

Moreover, we use a mutual k-nearest neighbour graph to construct a graph structure. The mutual k-nearest neighbour graph is defined as a graph that connects edge between two nodes if each of the nodes belongs to the k-nearest neighbours of the other. In this method, the edges with the highest similarity between nodes are also added to the graph structure obtained by the mutual k-nearest neighbour graph. In our experiments, we use k=3 for the number of neighbours that have been provided by the user.

IV. EXPERIMENTS

To evaluate the efficiency of the proposed WSD method using a graph convolutional neural network, we conducted some experiments to compare the results to the baseline system. In this section, we describe an outline of the experiments.

A. Data Set

We used the Semeval-2010 Japanese WSD task data set, which includes 50 target words comprising 22 nouns, 23 verbs, and 5 adjectives [15]. In this data set, there are 50 training and 50 test instances for each target word.

As unlabelled example data for the construction of a graph structure, we used the BCCWJ developed by the National Institute for Japanese Language and Linguistics. The BCCWJ corpus comprises 104.3 million words covering various genres.

B. Settings

In our experiments, to construct a graph for all examples, two nodes that represent two examples are linked if they are nearest and if their similarity (based on the Jaccard coefficient) is not less than a specified threshold value of 0.9, which is the highest precision in parameter estimation. The basic idea behind this is that two nodes tend to have a high similarity if the corresponding contexts of the target word are similar.

For learning the graph-based neural network, optimization of the loss function of class label prediction is repeated for 11,000 iterations, and optimization of the loss function of graph context prediction is repeated for 1,000 iterations. Then, the obtained model is used to classify new examples of the target word into semantic classes.

In our experiments, we considered five types of features as follows:

- ipadicBF : word segmentation using dictionary "ipadic" for extracting BF features
- UniDicBF : word segmentation using dictionary "UniDic" for extracting BF features
- UniDicBF+IWA : UniDicBF and additional examples from Iwanami's dictionary
- UniDicBF+LC : UniDicBF and additional local collocation features
- UniDicBF+LC+IWA : UniDicBF, additional local collocation features and additional examples from Iwanami's dictionary

For the Japanese lexical sample WSD task, we compared our method with two previous methods. Firstly, we compared our method with the supervised SVM classifier approach [15]. Secondly, we compared our method with the semi-supervised WSD method that combines automatically labelled data expansion and semi-supervised learning [8].

V. RESULTS

Table I shows the results of the experiments of applying the proposed method and the two existing methods described in the previous section. The best result per column is printed in bold. As shown in Table I, the proposed method is the highest precision when UniDicBF is used as features. When UniDicBF is used as features, the proposed method is higher than the SVM classifier. However, when we use UniDicBF+IWA, it performs worse than the SVM classifier.

TABLE I. EXPERIMENTAL RESULTS APPLYING THE PROPOSED METHOD AND THE TWO EXISTING METHODS

Features	Proposed Method	SVM	(Fujita et al., 2011)
ipadicBF	77.24	77.28	-
UniDicBF	**77.76**	76.8	76.56
UniDicBF+IWA	76.68	**77.84**	**76.76**
UniDicBF+LC	75.88	75.72	74.92
UniDicBF+LC+IWA	76.28	77.36	76.52

TABLE II. EXPERIMENTAL RESULTS WHEN CHANGING THE GRAPH MAKING METHOD

Jaccard Coefficient	Cosine Similarity	Mutual k-Nearest Neighbour graph
77.76	77.24	77.56

TABLE III. CLASSIFICATION PRECISION IN SEMI-SUPERVISED NN AND MAXIMUM ENTROPY AND (FUJITA ET AL., 2011)

Proposed Method	Maximum Entropy	(Fujita et al., 2011)
77.76	76.52	79.2

Table II shows the results of precision among three measurements, the cosine similarity, the Jaccard coefficient, and the mutual k-nearest neighbour using the proposed method with UniDicBF. The results indicate that the Jaccard coefficient measure is the most effective one among all similarity measures with 77.76% precision.

Table III shows the experimental results of both the proposed method with the highest precision and the conventional semi-supervised method [8].

As shown in Table III, the proposed method performs worse than a previous semi-supervised method because the previous method uses the Hinoki Sensebank with UniDicBF+IWA to train a classifier. The Hinoki Sensebank consists of the Lexeed Semantic Database of Japanese [15] and corpora annotated with syntactic and semantic information. Therefore, for a fair comparison, we employed the UniDicBF+IWA features for both methods. As shown in Table I, the proposed method performs better than the previous method.

VI. DISCUSSIONS

Experimental results show that the proposed method performs better than the SVM classifier. This result was obtained by using the proposed method based on the graph-based semi-supervised learning in addition to the conventional supervised method. Therefore, we consider that the proposed method is efficient because it can cope with the lack of labelled data for WSD.

When we use UniDicBF+IWA, the proposed method performs worse than SVM classifier. Example sentences of the Iwanami's Japanese dictionary tend to be connected to short example sentences in the corpus. Therefore, examples of Iwanami's Japanese dictionary tend not to be effective in constructing a graph structure. However, using the SVM classifier, examples of Iwanami's Japanese dictionary are effective for WSD. When we construct a graph structure, we develop a method to utilize the example sentences of the Iwanami's Japanese dictionary effectively in the future.

As shown in Table I, the proposed method using the UniDicBF+LC+IWA performs worse than that using UniDicBF+IWA. The SVM classifier using the UniDicBF+LC+IWA also performs worse. Many examples of the Iwanami's Japanese dictionary are short so that the LC features are not so effective for both methods.

Comparing the features of ipadicBF and the features of UniDicBF, the features of UniDicBF are more effective than the features of ipadicBF. By using UniDic, it is possible to obtain more consistent word segmentation for Japanese sentences of many genres than using ipadic. Therefore, we consider that it is possible to construct an effective graph structure with the UniDic features.

Among the three measurements, the cosine similarity, the Jaccard coefficient, and the mutual k-nearest neighbour, the Jaccard coefficient measure is the most effective of all similarity measures. Thus, if available features are small and dense, the Jaccard coefficient is considered to be suitable for the construction of the graph structure.

Comparing the proposed method with the previous semi-supervised method [8], the proposed method performs worse than the previous method. The previous method uses the basic form (lemma) of the word and the Hinoki Sensebank in addition to the BF features without thesaurus IDs. However, the proposed method does not use the basic form of the word as features (word segmentation) and the Hinoki Sensebank that has 35,838 sentences in 158 senses. Because the features used in the proposed method differ from those used in the previous method, we consider that the features used in the previous method are more effective in comparison to the features used in the proposed method. Therefore, using the UniDicBF+IWA features for both methods for a fair comparison, the proposed method performs better than the previous method. From these results, we consider that the proposed method is more effective in terms of semi-supervised learning for the WSD task.

For the target word "教える (oshieru)," there exist five examples that have similar context, but they have different meanings in the test data. Using the SVM classifier, the classifier could not classify these examples correctly. However, the proposed method was able to classify one test example correctly out of the five examples. To construct the graph structure, the proposed method connects these five examples by the edge. We consider that it is possible to distinguish two examples because the edge between these two examples has been deleted by repeating training with the training examples.

VII. Conclusion

In this paper, we proposed a semi-supervised method using a graph convolutional neural network for the WSD task. The efficiency of the proposed method was evaluated on the Semeval-2010 Japanese WSD task dataset. Experimental results show that the proposed method performs better than the previous supervised method and the morphological features obtained by the UniDic short-unit dictionary is effective for the semi-supervised WSD method. Moreover, the Jaccard coefficient is the most effective measure among three measures to construct a graph structure. Moreover, for the problem with small difference such as examples that have similar context but have different meanings, the proposed method improved the performance of WSD. When the difference between two meanings is small, it is difficult to classify them properly using the existing method for examples that have similar context but have different meanings. Therefore, if we can distinguish such example sentences, we consider the performance of WSD systems improved.

In the future, we would like to explore methods to construct an effective graph structure by using paraphrase information, and the dependency analysis technique, the effective filtering method for unlabelled data. In addition, we would like to develop a method to use the example sentences of the Iwanami's Japanese dictionary effectively.

Acknowledgment

This work was supported by JSPS KAKENHI Grant Number 18K11422.

References

[1] R. Navigli, "Word sense disambiguation: A survey", ACM Comput. Surv. vol. 41, no. 2, article 10, pp. 1–69, February 2009.

[2] H. Shinnou et al., "Classification of Word Sense Disambiguation Errors Using a Clustering Method", Journal of Natural Language Processing vol. 22, no. 5, pp. 319–362, 2015.

[3] M. Kågebäck and H. Salomonsson, "Word Sense Disambiguation using a Bidirectional LSTM", Proceedings of the 5th Workshop on Cognitive Aspects of the Lexicon (CogALex-V), pp. 51–56, 2016.

[4] D. Yuan, J. Richardson, R. Doherty, C. Evans, and E. Altendorf, "Semi-supervised Word Sense Disambiguation with Neural Models". Proceedings of the 26th International Conference on Computational Linguistics (COLING2016), pp. 1374–1385, 2016.

[5] A. Raganato, C. Delli Bovi, and R. Navigli, "Neural sequence learning models for word sense disambiguation", Proceedings of the 2017 Conference on Empirical Methods in Natural Language Processing, pp. 1156–1167, 2017.

[6] D. Yarowsky, "Unsupervised Word Sense Disambiguation Rivaling Supervised Methods", Proceedings of the 33rd Annual Meeting of the Association for Computational Linguistics pp. 189–196, 1995.

[7] K. Taghipour and H. T. Ng, "Semi-Supervised Word Sense Disambiguation Using Word Embeddings in General and Specific Domains", Proceedings of the 2015 Conference of the North American Chapter of the Association for Computational Linguistics: Human Language Technologies (HLT-NAACL2015), pp. 314–323, 2015.

[8] S. Fujita and A. Fujino, "Word Sense Disambiguation by Combining Labeled Data Expansion and Semi-Supervised Learning Method", ACM Transactions on Asian Language Information Processing, vol. 12, no. 2, article 7, pp. 676–685, June 2013.

[9] Z. Niu, D. Ji, and C. L. Tan, "Word Sense Disambiguation Using Label Propagation Based Semi-Supervised Learning", Proceedings of the 43rd Annual Meeting on Association for Computational Linguistics, pp. 395—402, 2005.

[10] M. Nishio, E. Iwabuchi and S. Mizutani, "Iwanami Kokugo Jiten Dai Go Han", Iwanami Publisher, 1994.

[11] Z. Yang, W. W. Cohen and R. Salakhutdinov, "Revisiting Semi-Supervised Learning with Graph Embeddings", Proceedings of the 33rd International Conference on International Conference on Machine Learning - Volume 48 (ICML'16), pp. 40–48, 2016.

[12] K. Maekawa et al., "Balanced Corpus of Contemporary Written Japanese", Language Resources and Evaluation (LREC2014), pp. 345–371, 2014.

[13] National Institute for Japanese Language, "Bunrui Goi Hyo (enlarged and revised version)", Dainippon Tosho, 2004.

[14] Z. Zhong and H. T. Ng, "It Makes Sense: A Wide-Coverage Word Sense Disambiguation System for Free Text", Proceedings of the ACL 2010 System Demonstrations, pp.78–83, 2010.

[15] M. Okumura, K. Shirai, K. Komiya and H. Yokono, "SemEval-2010 task: Japanese WSD", Proceedings of the 5th International Workshop on Semantic Evaluation (SemEval '10), Association for Computational Linguistics, pp. 69–74, 2010.

[16] K. Kasahara et al., "Construction of a Japanese semantic lexicon: Lexeed". SIG-NL-159, IPSJ, Japan, pp. 75–82, 2004.

Large Scale Legal Text Classification Using Transformer Models

Zein Shaheen
ITMO University
St. Petersburg, Russia
shaheen@itmo.ru

Gerhard Wohlgenannt
ITMO University
St. Petersburg, Russia
gwohlg@corp.ifmo.ru

Erwin Filtz
Vienna University of Economics and Business (WU)
Vienna, Austria
erwin.filtz@wu.ac.at

***Abstract*—Large multi-label text classification is a challenging Natural Language Processing (NLP) problem that is concerned with text classification for datasets with thousands of labels. We tackle this problem in the legal domain, where datasets, such as JRC-Acquis and EURLEX57K labeled with the EuroVoc vocabulary were created within the legal information systems of the European Union. The EuroVoc taxonomy includes around 7000 concepts. In this work, we study the performance of various recent transformer-based models in combination with strategies such as generative pretraining, gradual unfreezing and discriminative learning rates in order to reach competitive classification performance, and present new state-of-the-art results of** 0.661 **(F1) for JRC-Acquis and** 0.754 **for EURLEX57K. Furthermore, we quantify the impact of individual steps, such as language model fine-tuning or gradual unfreezing in an ablation study, and provide reference dataset splits created with an iterative stratification algorithm.**

Keywords–multi-label text classification; legal document datasets; transformer models; EuroVoc.

I. INTRODUCTION

Text classification, i.e., the process of assigning one or multiple categories from a set of options to a document [1], is a prominent and well-researched task in Natural Language Processing (NLP) and text mining. Text classification variants include simple binary classification (for example, decide if a document is spam or not spam), multi-class classification (selection of one from a number of classes), and multi-label classification. In the latter, multiple labels can be assigned to a single document. In *Large Multi-Label Text Classification (LMTC)*, the label space is typically comprised of thousands of labels, which obviously raises task complexity. The work presented here tackles an LMTC problem in the legal domain.

LMTC tasks often occur when large taxonomies or formal ontologies are used as document labels, for example in the medical domain [2] [3], or when using large open domain taxonomies for labelling, such as annotating Wikipedia with labels [4]. A common feature of many LMTC tasks is that some labels are used frequently, while others are used very rarely (few-shot learning) or are never used (zero-shot learning). This situation is also referred to by *power-law* or *long-tail* frequency distribution of labels, which also characterizes our datasets and which is a setting that is largely unexplored for text classification [3]. Another difficulty often faced in LMTC datasets [3] are long documents, where finding the relevant areas to correctly classify documents is a needle in a haystack situation.

In this work, we focus on LMTC in the legal domain, based on two datasets, the well-known JRC-Acquis dataset [5] and the new EURLEX57K dataset [6]. Both datasets contain legal documents from Eur-Lex [7], the legal database of the European Union (EU). The usage of language in the given documents is highly domain specific, and includes many legal text artifacts such as case numbers. Modern neural NLP algorithms often tackle domain specific text by fine-tuning pretrained language models on the type of text at hand [8]. Both datasets are labelled with terms from the the European Union's multilingual and multidisciplinary thesaurus *EuroVoc* [9].

The goal of this work is to advance the state-of-the-art in LMTC based on these two datasets which exhibit many of the characteristics often found in LMTC datasets: power-law label distribution, highly domain specific language and a large and hierarchically organized set of labels. We apply current NLP transformer models, namely BERT [10], RoBERTa [11], DistilBERT [12], XLNet [13] and M-BERT [10], and combine them with a number of training strategies such as gradual unfreezing, slanted triangular learning rates and language model fine-tuning. In the process, we create new standard dataset splits for JRC-Acquis and EURLEX57 using an iterative stratification approach [14]. Providing a high-quality standardized dataset split is very important, as previous work was typically done on different random splits, which makes results hard to compare [15]. Further, we make use of the semantic relations inside the EuroVoc taxonomy to infer reduced label sets for the datasets. Some of our main evaluation results are the Micro-F1 score of 0.661 for JRC-Acquis and 0.754 for EURLEX57K, which sets new states-of-the-art to the best of our knowledge.

The main findings and contributions of this work are: (i) the experiments with BERT, RoBERTa, DistilBERT, XLNet, M-BERT (trained on three languages), and AWD-LSTM in combination with the training tricks to evaluate and compare the performance of the models, (ii) providing new standardized datasets for further investigation, (iii) ablation studies to measure the impact and benefits of various training strategies, and (iv) leveraging the EuroVoc term hierarchy to generate variants of the datasets for which higher classification performance can be achieved.

The remainder of the paper is organized as follows: After a discussion of related work in Section II, we introduce the EuroVoc vocabulary and the two datasets (Section III), and then present the main methods (AWD-LSTM, BERT, RoBERTa, DistilBERT, XLNet) in Section IV. Section V contains extensive evaluations of the methods on both datasets as well as ablation studies, and after a discussion of results (Section VI) we conclude the paper in Section VII.

II. Related Work

In connection with the *JRC-Acquis* dataset, Steinberger et al. [16] present the "JRC EuroVoc Indexer JEX", by the Joint Research Centre (JRC) of the European Commission. The tool categorizes documents using the EuroVoc taxonomy by employing a profile-based ranking task; the authors report an F-score between 0.44 and 0.54 depending on the document language. Boella et al. [17] manage to apply a support vector machine approach to the problem by transforming the multi-label classification problem into a single-label problem. Liu et al. [18] present a new family of Convolutional Neural Network (CNN) models tailored for multi-label text classification. They compare their method to a large number of existing approaches on various datasets; for the EurLex/JRC dataset however, another method (SLEEC), provided the best results. SLEEC (Sparse Local Embeddings for Extreme Classification) [19], creates local distance preserving embeddings which are able to accurately predict infrequently occurring (tail) labels. The results on precision for SLEEC applied in Liu et al. [18] are P@1: 0.78, P@3: 0.64 and P@5: 0.52 – however, they use a previous version of the JRC-Acquis dataset with only 15.4K documents.

Chalkidis et al. [6] recently published their work on the new EURLEX57K dataset. The dataset will be described in more detail (incl. dataset statistics) in the next sections. Chalkidis et al. also provide a strong baseline for LMTC on this dataset. Among the tested neural architectures operating on the full documents, they have best results with BIGRUs with label-wise attention. As input representation they use either GloVe [20] embeddings trained on domain text, or ELMO embeddings [21]. The authors investigated using only the first zones of the (long) documents for classification, and show that the title and recitals part of each document leads to almost the same performance as considering the full document [6]. This helps to alleviate BERT's limitation of having a maximum of 512 tokens as input. Using only the first 512 tokens of each document as input, BERT [10] archives the best performance overall. The work of Chalkidis et al. is inspired by You et al. [22] who experimented with RNN-based methods with self attention on five LMTC datasets (RCV1, Amazon-13K, Wiki-30K, Wiki-500K, and EUR-Lex-4K). Similar work has been done in the medical domain, Mullenbach et al. [2] investigate label-wise attention in LMTC for medical code prediction (on the MIMIC-II and MIMIC-III datasets).

In this work, we experiment with BERT, RoBERTa, DistilBERT, XLNet, M-BERT and AWD-LSTM. We provide ablation studies to measure the impact of various training strategies and heuristics. Moreover, we provide new standardized datasets for further investigation by the research community, and leverage the EuroVoc term hierarchy to generate variants of the datasets.

III. Datasets and EuroVoc Vocabulary

In this section, we first introduce the multilingual EuroVoc thesaurus which is used to classify legal documents published by the institutions of the European Union. The EuroVoc thesaurus is also used as a classification schema for the documents contained in the two legal datasets we use for our experiments, the *JRC-Acquis V3* and *EURLEX57K* datasets which are described in this section.

```
@prefix rdf: <http://www.w3.org/1999/02/22-rdf-syntax-ns
    #type> .
@prefix skos: <http://www.w3.org/2004/02/skos/core#> .
@prefix dcterms: <http://purl.org/dc/terms/> .
@prefix ev: <http://eurovoc.europa.eu/> .
@prefix evs: <http://eurovoc.europa.eu/schema#> .
<http://eurovoc.europa.eu/100142>
    rdf:type evs:Domain ;
    skos:prefLabel "04 POLITICS"@en .
<http://eurovoc.europa.eu/100166>
    rdf:type evs:MicroThesaurus ;
    skos:prefLabel "0421 parliament"@en ;
    dcterms:subject ev:100142 ;
    skos:hasTopConcept ev:41 .
<http://eurovoc.europa.eu/41>
    rdf:type evs:ThesaurusConcept ;
    skos:prefLabel "powers of parliament"@en ;
    skos:inScheme ev:100166 .
<http://eurovoc.europa.eu/1599>
    rdf:type evs:ThesaurusConcept ;
    skos:prefLabel "legislative period"@en ;
    skos:inScheme ev:100166
    skos:broader ev:41 .
```

Figure 1. EuroVoc example

A. EuroVoc

The datasets we use for our experiments contain legal documents from the legal information system of the European Union (Eur-Lex) and are classified into a common classification schema, the EuroVoc [9] thesaurus published and maintained by the Publications Office of the European Union since 1982. The EuroVoc thesaurus has been introduced to harmonize the classification of documents in the communications across EU institutions and to enable a multilingual search as the thesaurus provides all its terms in the official language of the EU member states. It is organized based on the *Simple Knowledge Organization System (SKOS)* [23] , which encodes data using the *Resource Description Format (RDF)* [24] and is well-suited to represent hierarchical relations between terms in a thesaurus like EuroVoc. EuroVoc uses SKOS to hierarchically organize its concepts into 21 domains, for instance *Law, Trade* or *Politics*, to name a few. Each domain contains multiple microthesauri (127 in total), which in turn have in total around 600 top terms. About 7K terms (also called *descriptors, concepts* or *labels*) are assigned to one or multiple microthesauri and connected to top terms using the predicate `skos:broader`.

All concepts in EuroVoc have a *preferred* (`skos:prefLabel`) label and *non-preferred* (`skos:altLabel`) label for each language; the label language is indicated with language tags. Figure 1 illustrates with an example serialized in Turtle (TTL) [25] format how the terms are organized in the EuroVoc thesaurus. Our example is from the domain *04 POLITICS* and we show only the English labels of the concepts. The domain *04 POLITICS* has the EuroVoc ID `ev:100142` and is of `rdf:type evs:Domain`. Each domain has microthesauri as the next lower level in the hierarchy. In this example, we can see that a `evs:Microthesaurus` named *0421 parliament* is assigned to the *04 POLITICS* domain using (`dcterms:subject ev:100142`) and is also connected to the next lower level of top terms. The top term *powers of parliament* (`ev:41`) is linked to the microthesaurus using `skos:inScheme`. Finally, the lowest level in this example is the concept *legislative period* (`ev:1599`) which is linked to its (`skos:broader`) top term *powers of parliament* (`ev:41`), and is also directly linked to the microthesaurus *0421 parliament* to which it belongs to using `skos:inScheme`.

The legal documents are annotated with multiple EuroVoc classes typically on the lowest level which results in a huge amount of available classes a document can be potentially classified in. In addition, this also comes with the disadvantage of the power-law distribution of labels such that some labels are assigned to many documents whereas others are only assigned to a few documents or to no documents at all. The advantages of using a multilingual and multi-domain thesaurus for document classification are manifold. Most importantly, it allows us to reduce the numbers of potential classes by going up the hierarchy, which does not make classification incorrect but only more general. Reducing the number of labels allows to compare the efficiency of the model for different label sets, which vary in size and sparsity. In this line, we use a class reduction method to generate datasets with a reduced number of classes by replacing the original labels with the *top terms*, *microthesauri* or *domains* they belong to. For the top terms dataset, we leverage the `skos:broader` relations of the original descriptors, for the microthesauri dataset we follow `skos:inScheme` links to the microthesauri, and the domains dataset is inferred via the `dcterms:subject` links of the microthesauri. This process creates three additional datasets (*top terms, microthesauri, domains*) [26]. Furthermore, such a thesaurus would also allow to incorporate potentially more fine-grained national thesauri of member states which could be aligned with EuroVoc and therefore enable multilingual search in an extended thesarus.

B. Legal Text Datasets

In this work we focus on legal documents collected from the Eur-Lex [7] database serving as the official site for retrieving European Union law, such as *Treaties*, *International agreements* and *Legislation*, and case law of the European Union (EU). Eur-Lex provides the documents in the official languages of the EU member states. As discussed in previous work [26] the documents are well structured and written in domain specific language. Furthermore, legal documents are typically longer compared to texts often taken for text classification task such as the Reuters-21578 dataset containing news articles.

In this paper, we use the English versions of the two legal datasets *JRC-AcquisV3* [27] and *EURLEX57K* [28]. The *JRC-Acquis V3* dataset has been compiled by the Joint Research Centre (JRC) of the European Union with the *Acquis Communautaire* being the applicable EU law and contains documents in XML format. Each JRC document is divided into body, signature, annex and descriptors. The *EURLEX57K* dataset has been prepared by academia [6] and is provided in JSON format structured into several parts, namely the header including title and legal body, recitals (legal background references), the main body (organized in articles) and the attachments (appendices, annexes). Furthermore and in contrast to JRC-Acquis, the EURLEX57K dataset is already provided with a split into train and test sets.

Table I shows a comparison of the dataset characteristics. *EURLEX57K* contains almost three times as many documents as the *JRC-Acquis V3* dataset, but the documents are comparable in their minimum number of tokens, median and mode of tokens per document. The large difference in the maximum number of tokens per document impacts the standard deviation and the mean number of tokens. The reason for this difference is that JRC-Acquis also includes documents dealing with the budget of the European Union, comprised of many tables. As both datasets originate from the same source, but with different providers, we analyzed the number of documents contained in both datasets and found an overlap of approx. 12%.

TABLE I. DATASET STATISTICS FOR JRC-ACQUIS AND EURLEX57K.

	JRC-Acquis	EURLEX57K
#Documents	20382	57000
Max #Tokens/Doc	469820	3934
Min #Tokens/Doc	21	119
Mean #Tokens/Doc	2243.43	758.46
StdDev #Tokens/Doc	7075.94	542.86
Median #Tokens/Doc	651.0	544
Mode #Tokens/Doc	275	275

Table II provides an overview of label statistics for both datasets. We created different versions based on the original descriptors (DE), top terms (TT), microthesauri (MT) and domains (DO) and present the numbers for all versions. The maximum number of labels assigned to a single document is similar for both datasets. The average number of labels per document in the original (DE) version is 5.46 (JRC-Acquis) and 5.07 (EURLEX57). Due to the polyhierarchy in the geography domain a label may be assigned to multiple *Top Terms*, therefore the number of *Top Term* labels is higher than that of the original descriptors.

Figure 2 visualizes the power-law (long tail) label distribution, where a large portion of EuroVoc descriptors is used rarely (or never) as document annotations. In the JRC-Acquis dataset only 50% of the labels available in EuroVoc are used to classify documents. Only 417 labels are used frequently (used on more than 50 documents) and 3,3147 labels have a frequency between 1–50 (few-short). The numbers for the EURLEX57K dataset are similar [6], with 59.31% of all EuroVoc labels being actually present in EURLEX57K. From those labels, 746 are frequent, 3,362 have a frequency between 1–50, and 163 are only in the testing, but not in the training, dataset split (zero-shot). The high number of infrequent labels obviously is a challenge when using supervised learning approaches.

IV. METHODS

In this section we describe the methods used in the LMTC experiments presented in the evaluation section, and the general training process. Furthermore, we discuss important related points such as language model pretraining and fine-tuning, and discriminative learning rates, and other important foundations for the evaluation section like dataset splitting and multilingual training.

A. General Training Strategy and Implementation

In accordance with common NLP practice, as first introduced by Howard and Ruder for text classification [29], we

TABLE II. DATASET STATISTICS – NUMBER OF LABELS PER DOCUMENT.

	JRC-Acquis				EURLEX57K			
Label	DE	TT	MT	DO	DE	TT	MT	DO
Max	24	30	14	10	26	30	15	9
Min	1	1	1	1	1	1	1	1
Mean	5.46	6.04	4.74	3.39	5.07	5.94	4.55	3.24
StdDev	1.73	3.14	1.92	1.17	1.7	3.06	1.82	1.04
Median	6	5	5	3	5	5	4	3
Mode	6	4	4	3	6	4	4	3

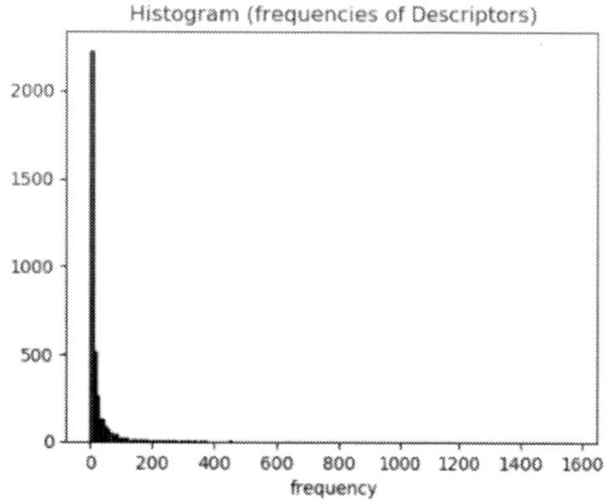

Figure 2. Power-law distribution of descriptors in the JRC-Acquis dataset.

train our models in two steps: first we fine-tune the language modeling part of the model to the target corpus (JRC-Acquis or EURLEX57K), and then we train the classifier on the training-split of the dataset.

The baseline model (AWD-LSTM) and the transformer models are available with pretrained weights, trained with language modelling objectives on large corpora such as Wikitext or Webtext – a process that is computationally very expensive. Fine-tuning allows to transfer the language modeling capabilities to a new domain [29].

Our implementation makes use of the FastAI library [30], which includes the basic infrastructure to apply training strategies like gradual unfreezing or slanted triangular learning rates (see below). Moreover, for the transformer models, we integrate the Hugging Face transformers package [31] with FastAI.

Our implementation including the evaluation results, is available on GitHub [32]. The repository also includes the reference datasets created with iterative splitting, which can be used by other researchers as reference datasets – in order to have a fair comparison of different approaches in the future.

B. Tricks for Performance Improvement (within FastAI)

In their Universal Language Model Fine-tuning for Text Classification (ULMFiT) approach, Howard and Ruder [29] propose a number of training strategies and tricks to improve model performance, which are available within the FastAI libary. Firstly, based on the idea that early layers in a deep neural network capture more general and basic features of language, which need little domain adaption, *discriminative fine-tuning* applies different learning rates depending on the layer; earlier layers use smaller learning rates compared to later layers. Secondly, *slanted triangular learning rates* quickly increase the learning rate at the beginning of a training epoch up to the maximal learning rate in order to find a suitable region of the parameter space, and then slowly reduce the learning rate to refine the parameters. And finally, in *gradual unfreezing* the training process is divided into multiple cycles, where each cycle consists of several training epochs. Training starts after freezing all layers except for the last few layers in cycle one, during later cycles more layers are unfrozen gradually (from last to first layers). The intuition is that, in fine-tuning a deep learning model (similar to discriminative fine-tuning), that later layers are more task and domain specific and need more fine-tuning. In the evaluation section, we provide details about our unfreezing strategy (Table IV).

C. Baseline Model

We use **AWD-LSTM** [33] as a baseline model. Merity et al. [33] investigate different strategies for regularizing word-level LSTM language models, including the *weight-dropped LSTM* with its recurrent regularization, and they introduce NT-ASGD as a new version of average stochastic gradient descent in AWD-LSTM.

In the ULMFiT approach [29] of FastAI, AWD-LSTM is used as encoder, with extra layers added on top for the classification task.

For any of the models (AWD-LSTM and transformers) we apply the basic method discussed above: a) fine-tune the language model on all documents (ignoring the labels) of the dataset (JRC-Acquis or EURLEX57K), and then b) fine-tune the classifier using the training-split of the dataset.

D. Transformer Models

In the experiments we study the performance of BERT, RoBERTa, DistilBERT and XLNet on the given text classification tasks. BERT is an early, and very popular, transformer model, RoBERTa is a modified version of BERT trained on a larger corpus, DistilBERT is a distilled version of BERT and thereby with lower computational cost, and finally, XLNet can be fed with larger input token sequences.

BERT: BERT [10] is a bidirectional language model which aims to learn contextual relations between words using the transformer architecture [34]. We use an official release of the pre-trained models, details about the specific hyperparameters are found in Section V-A.

The input to BERT is either a single text (a sentence or document), or a text pair. The first token of each sequence is the special classification token [CLS], followed by WordPiece tokens of the first text A, then a separator token [SEP], and (optionally) after that WordPiece tokens for the second text B.

In addition to token embeddings, BERT uses positional embeddings to represent the position of tokens in the sequence. For training, BERT applies Masked Language Modeling (MLM) and Next Sentence Prediction (NSP) objectives. In MLM, BERT randomly masks 15% of all WordPiece tokens in each sequence and learns to predict these masked tokens. For NSP, BERT is fed in 50% of cases with the actual next sentence B, in the other cases with a random sentence B from the corpus.

RoBERTa: RoBERTa, introduced by Liu et al. [11], retrains BERT with an improved methodology, much more data, larger batch size and longer training times. In RoBERTa the training strategy of BERT is modified by removing the NSP objective. Further, RoBERTa uses byte pair encoding (BPE) as a tokenization algorithm instead of WordPiece tokenization in BERT.

DistilBERT: We use a distilled version of BERT released by Sanh et al. [12]. DistilBERT provides a lighter and faster version of BERT, reducing the size of the model by 40% while retaining 97% of its capabilities on language understanding tasks [12]. The distillation process includes training a complete BERT model (the teacher) using the improved methodology proposed by Liu et al. [11], then DistilBERT (the student) is trained to reproduce the behaviour of the teacher by using cosine embedding loss.

XLNet: The previously discussed transformer-based models are limited to a fixed context length (such as 512 tokens), while legal documents are often long and exceed this context length limit. XLNet [13] includes segments recurrence, introduced in Transformer-XL [35], allowing it to digest longer documents. XLNet follows RoBERTa in removing the NSP objective, while introducing a novel permutation language model objective. In our work with XLNet, we fine-tune the classifier directly without LM fine-tuning (as LM fine-tuning of XLNet was computationally not possible on the hardware available for our experiments).

E. Dataset Splitting

Stratification of classification data aims at splitting the data in a way that in all dataset splits (training, validation, test) the target classes appear in similar proportions. In multi-label text classification *stratification* becomes harder, because the target is a combination of multiple labels. In *random splitting*, it is possible that most instances of a specific class end up either in the training or test split (esp. for low frequency classes), and therefore the split can be unrepresentative with respect to the original data set. Moreover, random splitting and different train/validation/test ratios create the problem that results from different approaches are hard to compare [15].

Depending on the dataset, other criteria can be used for dataset splitting, for example Azarbonyad et al. [36] split JRC-Acquis documents according to document's year, where older documents could be used in training, and newer in testing.

For splitting both JRC-Acquis and EURLEX57K, we use the iterative stratification algorithm proposed by Sechidis et al. [14], ie. its implementation provided by the scikit-multilearn library [37]. Applying this algorithm leads to a better document split with respect to the target labels, and in turn, helps with generalization of the results and allows for a fair comparison of different approaches. The reference splits of the dataset are available online [32].

In the experiments in Section V we use these dataset splits, but in addition for EURLEX57K also the dataset split of the dataset creators [6], in order to compare to their evaluation results.

F. Multilingual Training

JRC-Acquis is a collection of parallel texts in 22 languages – we make use of this property to train multilingual BERT [38] on an extended version of JRC-Acquis in 3 languages. Multilingual BERT provides support for 104 languages and it is useful for zero-shot learning tasks in which a model is trained using data from one language and then used to make inference on data in other languages.

We extend the English JRC-Acquis dataset with parallel data in German and French. The additional data has the same dataset split as in the English version, ie. if an English document is in the training set then the German and French versions will be in the same split as well.

V. Evaluation

This section first discusses evaluation setup (for example model hyperparameters) and then evaluation results for JRC-Acquis and EURLEX57K.

A. Evaluation Setup

Evaluation setup includes important aspects such as dataset splits, preprocessing, the specific model architectures and variants, and major hyperparameters used in training.

a) Dataset Splits:: The official JRC-Acquis dataset does not include a standard train-validation-test split, and as discussed in Section IV-E a random split exhibits unfavorable characteristics. We apply iterative splitting [14] to ensure that each split has the same label distribution as the original data. We split with an 80%/10%/10% ratio for training/validation/test sets. For the EURLEX57K the dataset creators already provide a split and a strong baseline evaluation. We run our models on the given split in order to compare results, and also create our own split with iterative splitting (dataset available in the mentioned GitHub repository [32]).

b) Text Preprocessing:: All described models have their own preprocessing included (e.g. WordPiece tokenization in BERT), we do not apply extra preprocessing to the text.

c) Neural Network Architectures:: For **AWD-LSTM**, we use the standard setup of the pretrained model included in FastAI, which has an input embedding layer with embedding size of 400, followed by three LSTM layers with hidden sizes of 1152 and weight dropout probability of 0.1.

TABLE III. ARCHITECTURE HYPERPARAMETERS OF TRANSFORMER MODELS

Model Name	# Layers	# Heads	Context Length	Is Cased	batch-size
BERT	12	12	512	False	4
Roberta	12	12	512	False	4
DistilBERT	6	12	512	False	4
XLNet	12	12	1024	True	2

For the transformer models, we start from pretrained models, the uncased BERT model [39], the RoBERTa model [40], DistilBERT [41], and the XLNET model [42].

In Table III, we see that many architectural details are similar for the different model types. The transformer models all have 12 network layers, except DistilBERT with 6 layers, and 12 attention heads. XLNet allows for longer input contexts, but for performance reasons we limited the context to 1024 tokens, and it was necessary to reduce the batch size to 2 to fit the model into GPU memory, and also we could not unfreeze the whole pretrained model (see below).

To create the text classifiers, we take the representation of the text generated by the transformer model or AWD-LSTM, and add two fully connected layers of size 1200 and 50, respectively, with a dropout probability of 0.2, and an output layer. We apply batch normalization on the fully connected layers.

d) Gradual Unfreezing:: Gradual unfreezing is one of the ULMFiT strategies discussed in Section IV-B, where the neural network layers are grouped, and trained starting with the last group, then incrementally unfrozen and trained further.

TABLE IV. GRADUAL UNFREEZING DETAILS: LEARNING RATES (LR), NUMBER OF EPOCHS (ITERS), AND LAYER GROUPS THAT ARE UNFROZEN.

Cycle	Max LR	# Iters	# Unfrozen Layers		
			BERT RoBERTa	DistilBERT	XLNet
1	2e-4	12	4	2	4
2	5e-5	12	8	4	6
3	5e-5	12	12	6	8
4	5e-5	36	12	6	8
5	5e-5	36	12	6	8

Except for DistilBERT, which has only 2 layers per layer group, all transformer models have 3 groups of 4 layers used in the unfreezing process. Table IV gives an overview of the training setup for the transformer models. We trained the classifier for 5 cycles, starting in cycle 1 with 4 layers and a $LR = 2e-4$, and 12 training epochs (Iters). The setup of the other cycles is shown in the table. Overall, we used the same setup for all transformer models with a goal of better comparison between models. (Remark: hand-picking LRs and training epochs might lead to slightly better results.)

Table V shows the main hyperparameters of AWD-LSTM training, we trained the model in 6 cycles, with LRs, epochs per cycle, and unfrozen layers as shown in the table.

TABLE V. GRADUAL UNFREEZING SETTINGS FOR AWD-LSTM

Cycle	# Max LR	# Unfrozen Layers	# Iterations
1	2e-1	1	2
2	1e-2	2	5
3	1e-3	3	5
4	5e-3	all	20
5	1e-4	all	32
6	1e-4	all	32

e) LM Fine-tuning:: For the transformer models we do LM fine-tuning for 5 iterations, with a batch size of 4 and LR of $5e-5$. Transformer fine-tuning is done with a script[1] provided by Hugging Face. For the AWD-LSTM model we first fine-tune the frozen LM for 2 epochs, and then in cycle two fine-tune the unfrozen model for another 5 epochs.

f) Hardware specifications: We trained the models on a single GPU device (NVIDIA GeForce GTX 1080 with 11 GB of GDDR5X memory). For inference, we use an Intel i7-8700K CPU @ 3.70GHz and 16GB RAM.

B. Evaluation Metrics

In the evaluations, in line with Chalkidis et al. [6], we apply the following evaluation metrics: *micro-averaged F1, R-Precision@K (RP@K)*, and *Normalized Discounted Cumulative Gain (nDCG@K). Precision@K (P@K)* and *Recall@K (R@K)* are popular measures in LTMC, too, but they unfairly penalize in situations where the number of gold labels is unequal to K, which is the typical situation in our datasets. This problem led to the introduction of more suitable metrics like RP@K and nDCG@K. In the following, we briefly discuss the metrics.

The $F1$-score is a common metric in information retrieval systems, and it is calculated as the harmonic mean between precision and recall. If we have a label L, Precision, Recall, and $F1$-score with respect to L are calculated as follows:

$$Precision_L = \frac{TruePositives_L}{TruePositives_L + FalsePositives_L}$$
$$Recall_L = \frac{TruePositives_L}{TruePositives_L + FalseNegatives_L}$$
$$F1_L = 2 * \frac{Precision * Recall}{Precision + Recall}$$

Micro-F1 is an extension of the $F1$-score for multi-label classification tasks, and it treats the entire set of predictions as one vector and then calculates the $F1$. We use grid search to pick the *threshold* on the output probabilities of the models that gives the best Micro-F1 score on the validation set. The threshold determines which labels we assign to the documents.

Propensity scores prioritize predicting a few relevant labels over the large number of irrelevant ones [43]. R-Precision@K ($RP@K$) calculates precision for the top K ranked labels, if the number of ground truth labels for a document is less than K, K is set to this number for this document.

$$RP@K = \frac{1}{N}\sum_{n=1}^{N}\sum_{k=1}^{K}\frac{Rel(n,k)}{min(K,R_n)}$$

Where N is the number of documents, $Rel(n,k)$ is set to 1 if the k-th retrieved label in the top-K labels of the n-th

[1]https://github.com/huggingface/transformers/blob/master /examples/language-modeling/run_language_modeling.py

document is correct, otherwise it is set to 0 . R_n is the number of ground truth labels for the n-th document.

Normalized Discounted Cumulative Gain *nDCG@k* for the list of top K ranked labels measures ranking quality. It is based on the assumption that highly relevant documents are more useful than moderately relevant documents.

$$nDCG@K = \frac{1}{N} \sum_{n=1}^{N} Z_{k_n} \sum_{k=1}^{K} \frac{2^{Rel(n,k)}-1}{log_2(1+k)}$$

N is the number of documents, $Rel(n, k)$ is set to 1 if the k-th retrieved label in the top-K labels of the n-th document is correct, otherwise it is set to 0. Z_{k_n} is a normalization factor to ensure $nDCG@K = 1$ for a perfect ranking.

C. *Evaluation Results*

The evaluation results are organized into three subsections, results for the JRC-Acquis dataset, results for the EURLEX57K dataset, and finally results from ablation studies.

1) JRC-Acquis: Table VI presents an overview of the results on the JRC-Acquis dataset for the transformer models and the AWD-LSTM baseline, and initial results from the multilingual model.

The observations here are as follows: Firstly, transformer-based models outperform the LSTM baseline by a large margin. Further, within the transformer models RoBERTa and BERT yield best results, the scores are almost the same. As expected, the distilled version of BERT is a bit lower in most metrics like Micro-F1, but the difference is small.

In this set of experiments, XLNet is behind DistilBERT, which we attribute to two main causes: (i) for computational reasons (given the available GPU hardware), we could *not* fine-tune the LM on XLNet, and in classifier training we could *not* unfreeze the full model. (ii) We used the same LR on all models; the choice of LR was influenced by a recommendation on BERT learning rates in Devlin et al. [10], and may not be optimal for XLNet. Overall, we could not properly test XLNet due to its high computational requirements, and did therefore not include it in the set of experiments on the EURLEX57K dataset.

The initial set of experiments with multilingual BERT (M-BERT) provides very promising results, on par with RoBERT and BERT. This is remarkable given the fact that we use the same amount of global training steps – which means, because our multilingual dataset is 3 times larger, that on individual documents we train only a 1/3 of the time. We expect even better results with more training epochs. LM fine-tuning of the M-BERT model was done on the text from all three languages (en, de, fr).

Regarding comparisons to existing baseline results, firstly because of the problem of different dataset splits (see Section IV-E) results are hard to compare. However, Steinberger et al. [16] report an F1-score of 0.48, Esuli et al. [44] report an F1 of 0.589 and Chang et al. [15] do not provide F1, but only P@5 (62.64) and R@5 (61.59).

For Table VII, we picked one transformer-based method, namely BERT, and analyzed its performance on the various JRC datasets resulting from *class reduction* described in Section III-A. By using inference on the EuroVoc hierarchy, we created, additionally to the default descriptors dataset, datasets for EuroVoc Top Terms (TT), Micro-Thesauri (MT), and EuroVoc Domains (DO). With the reduced number of classes, classification performance is clearly rising, for example from a Micro-F1 of 0.661 (descriptors) to 0.839 (EuroVoc domains). We argue that the results with the inferred labels show that our approach might be well-suitable for real-world applications in scenarios like automatic legal document classification or keyword/label suggestion – for example the RP@5 for domains (DO) is at 0.928, so the classification performance (depending on the use case requirements) may be sufficient.

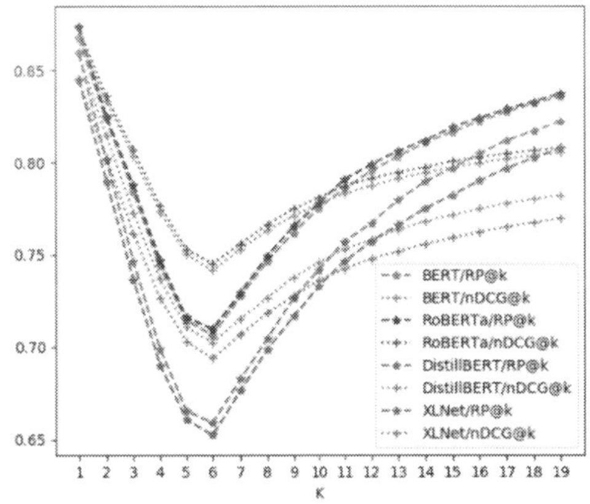

Figure 3. A visualization of RP@K and nDCG@K for all transformer models for JRC-Acquis.

Figure 3 contains a visual representation of RP@K and nDCG@K for the transformer models applied to the JRC-Acquis dataset. We can see how similar the performance of BERT and RoBERTa is for different values of K, and RoBERTa scores are consistently marginally better.

2) EURLEX57K: In this subsection we report the evaluation results on the new EURLEX57K dataset by Chalkidis et al. [6]. In order to compare to the results of the dataset creators, we ran the experiments on the dataset and dataset split (45K training, 6K validation, 6K testing) provided by Chalkidis et al. [6]. Below, we also show evaluation results on our dataset split (created with the iterative stratification approach). Table VIII gives an overview of results for our transformer models, and compares them to the strong baselines in existing work. Chalkidis et al. [6] evaluate various architectures, the results of the three best models presented here: BERT-BASE, BIGRU-LWAN-ELMO and BIGRU-LWAN-L2V. BERT-BASE is a BERT model with an extra classification layer on top, BIGRU-LWAN combines a BIGRU encoder with Label-Wise Attention Networks (LWAN), and uses either Elmo (ELMO) or word2vec (L2V) embeddings as inputs. Table VIII shows that our models outperform the previous baseline, the best results are delivered by RoBERTa and DistilBERT. The good performance of DistilBERT in these experiments is surprising (We need further future experiments to explain the results sufficiently. One intuition might be that the random weight initialization of the added layers was very suitable.).

Overall, the results are much better than for the smaller

TABLE VI. COMPARISON BETWEEN DIFFERENT TRANSFORMER MODELS, FINE-TUNED USING THE SAME NUMBER OF ITERATIONS ON JRC-ACQUIS.

	BERT	RoBERTa	XLNet	DistilBERT	AWD-LSTM	Multilingual BERT
Micro-F1	0.661	0.659	0.605	0.652	0.493	**0.663**
RP@1	0.867	0.873	0.845	**0.884**	0.762	0.873
RP@3	0.784	**0.788**	0.736	0.78	0.619	0.783
RP@5	0.715	0.716	0.661	0.711	0.548	**0.717**
RP@10	0.775	**0.778**	0.733	0.775	0.627	0.777
nDCG@1	0.867	0.873	0.845	**0.884**	0.762	0.873
nDCG@3	0.803	**0.807**	0.762	0.805	0.651	0.804
nDCG@5	0.750	**0.753**	0.703	0.75	0.594	0.752
nDCG@10	0.778	**0.781**	0.746	0.779	0.630	0.780

TABLE VII. BERT RESULTS FOR JRC-ACQUIS WITH *class reduction* METHODS APPLIED, WHICH LEAD TO 4 DATASETS: DE (DESCRIPTORS), TT (TOP-TERMS), MT (MICROTHESAURI, DO (DOMAINS)

	DE	TT	MT	DO
Micro-F1	0.661	0.745	0.778	0.839
RP@1	0.867	0.922	0.943	0.967
RP@3	0.784	0.838	0.871	0.905
RP@5	0.715	0.804	0.844	0.928
RP@10	0.775	0.857	0.908	0.974
nDCG@1	0.867	0.922	0.943	0.967
nDCG@3	0.803	0.858	0.888	0.919
nDCG@5	0.750	0.829	0.864	0.929
nDCG@10	0.778	0.852	0.896	0.952

JRC dataset, with the best Micro-F1 for JRC being 0.661 (BERT), while for EURLEX57K we reach 0.758 (RoBERTa).

Table IX presents the results for BERT on the additional datasets with Top Terms (TT), Micro-Thesauri (MT) and Domains (DO) labels inferred from the EuroVoc taxonomy (similar to Table VII, which presents the scores of JRC-Acquis). As expected from the general results on the EU-RLEX57 dataset, the values on the derived datasets are better than for JRC-Acquis, for example RP@5 is now at 0.956 for the domains (DO).

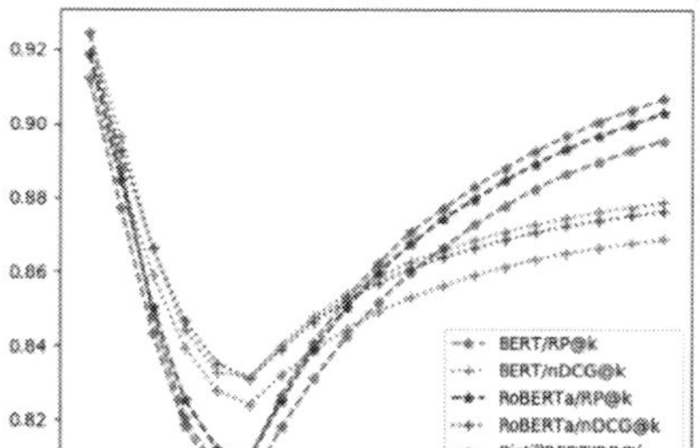

FIGURE 4. RP@K AND NDCG@K FOR THE TRANSFORMER MODELS TRAINED ON EURLEX57K.

Similar to Figure 3, Figure 4 shows RP@K and nDCG@K for BERT, RoBERTa and DistilBERT depending on the value of K. RoBERTa and DistilBERT are almost identical in their performance, BERT lags behind a little in this set of experiments.

Finally, in Table X, we trained a BERT model on our iterative split of the EURLEX57K dataset in order to provide a strong baseline for future work on a standardized and arguably improved version of the EURLEX57K dataset.

3) Ablation Studies: In this section, we want to study the contributions of various training process components – by excluding some of those components individually (or reducing the number of training epochs). We focus on three important aspects: (i) the use of Language Model (LM) fine-tuning, (ii) gradual unfreezing, (iii) and a reduction of the number of training cycles.

In Table XI, we compare the evaluation metrics when removing the LM fine-tuning (on the legal target corpus) step before classification model training to the original version including LM fine-tuning (in parenthesis). For all examined models, we can see a small but consistent improvement of results when using LM fine-tuning. The relative improvement in the metrics is in the range of 1%–3%. In conclusion, LM fine-tuning to the legal text corpus is a crucial step for reaching a high classification performance.

In Table XII, we examine the effect of two factors, the training epochs (Iter.) hyperparameter, and of the use of the gradual unfreezing technique. Regarding number of epochs, both models benefit from longer training, for BERT the difference is large (about 4% relative improvement in F1-score), while for the simpler DistilBERT model less training appears to be required, after 36 epochs it even provides better accuracy than BERT at this point, and finally only gains a 1.2% improvement from more training epochs. Secondly, we study the effect of Gradual Unfreezing (GU), which for BERT has a large impact, with a relative improvement in F1 of about 6%. In summary, longer training times benefit esp. more complex models like BERT, and gradual unfreezing is a very helpful strategy for optimizing performance.

VI. DISCUSSION

Much of the detailed discussion is already included in the *Evaluation Results* section (Section V-C), so here we will summarize and extend on some of the key findings.

In comparing model performance, starting with LSTM versus transformer architectures, the results show that the attention mechanism used in transformers is superior to LSTMs in finding aspects relevant for the classification task in long documents. Within the transformer models, firstly we did not

TABLE VIII. RESULTS FOR OUR TRANSFORMER-BASED MODELS ON EURLEX57K, AND STRONG BASELINES FROM CHALKIDIS ET AL.

	Ours			Chalkidis et al. [6]		
	BERT	RoBERTa	DistilBERT	BERT-BASE	BIGRU-LWAN-ELMO	BIGRU-LWAN-L2V
Micro-F1	0.751	**0.758**	0.754	0.732	0.719	0.709
RP@1	0.912	0.919	**0.925**	0.922	0.921	0.915
RP@3	0.843	**0.85**	0.848	-	-	-
RP@5	0.805	**0.812**	0.807	0.796	0.781	0.770
RP@10	0.852	0.860	**0.862**	0.856	0.845	0.836
nDCG@1	0.912	0.919	**0.925**	0.922	0.921	0.915
nDCG@3	0.859	**0.866**	**0.866**	-	-	-
nDCG@5	0.828	**0.835**	0.833	0.823	0.811	0.801
nDCG@10	0.849	0.857	**0.858**	0.851	0.841	0.832

TABLE IX. BERT RESULTS ON EURLEX57K WITH *class reduction* METHODS APPLIED, PLUS THE BASELINE RESULTS OF BERT-BASE (DE) FROM CHALKIDIS ET AL. [6].

	DE	TT	MT	DO	DE baseline
Micro-F1	0.751	0.825	0.84	0.883	0.732
RP@1	0.912	0.948	0.959	0.978	0.922
RP@3	0.843	0.896	0.915	0.939	-
RP@5	0.805	0.876	0.902	0.956	0.796
RP@10	0.852	0.909	0.943	0.986	0.856
nDCG@1	0.912	0.948	0.959	0.978	0.922
nDCG@3	0.859	0.907	0.924	0.947	-
nDCG@5	0.828	0.891	0.912	0.955	0.823
nDCG@10	0.849	0.904	0.931	0.97	0.851

TABLE X. BERT RESULTS ON EURLEX57K WITH THE NEW ITERATIVE STRATIFICATION DATASET SPLIT.

Micro-F1	RP@1	RP@5	nDCG@1	nDCG@5
0.760	0.914	0.809	0.914	0.833

TABLE XI. CLASSIFICATION METRICS FOR THE JRC-ACQUIS DATASET, WHEN *not* USING LM FINE-TUNING – IN PARENTHESES THE RESULTS *with* FINE-TUNING (FOR COMPARISON).

	BERT	RoBERTa	DistilBERT
Micro-F1	0.64 (0.66)	0.65 (0.66)	0.61 (0.62)
RP@1	0.86 (0.87)	0.87 (0.87)	0.86 (0.87)
RP@3	0.77 (0.78)	0.77 (0.79)	0.75 (0.76)
RP@5	0.70 (0.72)	0.70 (0.72)	0.67 (0.68)
RP@10	0.76 (0.78)	0.77 (0.78)	0.74 (0.75)
nDCG@1	0.86 (0.87)	0.87 (0.87)	0.86 (0.87)
nDCG@3	0.79 (0.80)	0.79 (0.81)	0.77 (0.78)
nDCG@5	0.74 (0.75)	0.74 (0.75)	0.71 (0.72)
nDCG@10	0.77 (0.72)	0.77 (0.78)	0.75 (0.76)

TABLE XII. ABLATION STUDY: BERT AND DISTILBERT PERFORMANCE ON JRC-ACQUIS REGARDING THE NUMBER OF TRAINING EPOCHS (ITER.) AND THE USE OF GRADUAL UNFREEZING (GU).

	# Iter.	Use GU	Prec.	Rec.	Mic.-F1
BERT	36	True	0.678	0.601	0.637
	108	False	0.674	0.575	0.621
	108	True	0.695	0.630	**0.661**
Distil-BERT	36	True	0.696	0.601	0.645
	108	False	0.663	0.583	0.620
	108	True	0.701	0.611	**0.653**

notice much difference between BERT and RoBERTa, which is not unexpected, as they are technically very similar. Overall, results were a bit better for RoBERTa. DistilBERT delivered surprisingly good results for the EURLEX57K dataset, and has the benefits of lower computational cost. Both for the JRC-Aquis and the EURLEX57K datasets, the results indicate that DistilBERT is better in retrieving the most probable label compared with RoBERTa and BERT. XLNet on the other hand, requires a lot of computational resources, and we were not able to properly train the model for that reason. Finally, the first set of experiments on multilingual training with M-BERT gave promising results, hence it will be further studied in future work.

The ablation studies showed the positive effects of the training (fine-tuning) strategies that we applied, both LM-finetuning on the target domain, as well as gradual unfreezing of the network layers (in groups) proved to be crucial in reaching state-of-the-art classification performance.

To compare the computational costs, we calculated inference times for each model on an Intel i7-8700K CPU @ 3.70GHz. DistilBERT provides the lowest run time at 12 ms/example. RoBERTa and BERT (which have an identical architecture) have very similar run times with 17.1 ms, and 17.3 ms/example, respectively. XLNet, the heaviest model, requires 77 ms/example.

For a fair comparison, we trained all transformer models with the same set of hyperparameters (such as learning rate and number of training epochs). With customized and hand-picked parameters for each training cycle we expect further improvements of scores, which will be studied in future work together with model ensemble approaches and text data augmentation.

VII. CONCLUSIONS

Natural Language Processing (In) this work we evaluate current transformer models for natural language processing in combination with training strategies like language model (LM) fine-tuning, slanted triangular learning rates and gradual unfreezing in the field of LMTC (large multi-label text classification) on legal text datasets with long-tail label distributions. The datasets contain around 20K documents (JRC-Acquis) and 57K documents (EUROLEX57K) and are labeled with EuroVoc descriptors from the 7K terms in the EuroVoc taxonomy. The use of an iterative stratification algorithm for dataset splitting (into training/validation/testing) allows to create standardized splits on the two datasets to enable comparison and reproducibility in future experiments. In the experiments, we provide new state-of-the-art results on both datasets, with a micro-F1 of 0.661 for JRC-Acquis and 0.754 for EUROLEX57K, and even higher scores for new datasets with reduced label sets inferred from the EuroVoc hierarchy (*top terms, microthesauri, and domains*).

The main contributions are: (i) new state-of-the-art LMTC classification results on both datasets for a problem type that is still largely unexplored [3], (ii) a comparison and interpretation of the performance of the applied models: AWD-LSTM, BERT, RoBERTa, DistilBERT and XLNet, (iii) the creation and provision (on GitHub) of new standardized versions of the two legal text datasets created with an iterative stratification algorithm, (iv) deriving new datasets with reduced label sets via the semantic structure within EuroVoc, and (v) ablation studies that quantify the contributions of individual training strategies and hyperparameters such as gradual unfreezing, number of training epochs and LM fine-tuning in this complex LMTC setting.

There are multiple angles for *future work*, including potentially deriving higher performance by using hand-picked learning rates and other hyperparameters for each model individually, and further experiments on using models such as multilingual BERT to profit from the availability of parallel corpora. Moreover, experiments with new architectures such as Graph Neural Networks [45] and various data augmentation techniques are candidates to improve classification performance.

ACKNOWLEDGEMENTS

This work was supported by the Government of the Russian Federation (Grant 074-U01) through the ITMO Fellowship and Professorship Program.

REFERENCES

[1] F. Sebastiani, "Machine learning in automated text categorization," ACM computing surveys (CSUR), vol. 34, no. 1, 2002, pp. 1–47.

[2] J. Mullenbach, S. Wiegreffe, J. Duke, J. Sun, and J. Eisenstein, "Explainable prediction of medical codes from clinical text," arXiv preprint arXiv:1802.05695, 2018.

[3] A. Rios and R. Kavuluru, "Few-shot and zero-shot multi-label learning for structured label spaces," in Proceedings of the Conference on Empirical Methods in Natural Language Processing. Conference on Empirical Methods in Natural Language Processing, vol. 2018. NIH Public Access, 2018, p. 3132.

[4] P. Ioannis et al., "Lshtc: A benchmark for large-scale text classification," arXiv preprint arXiv:1503.08581, 2015.

[5] E. Loza Mencía and J. Fürnkranz, Efficient Multilabel Classification Algorithms for Large-Scale Problems in the Legal Domain. Berlin, Heidelberg: Springer, 2010, pp. 192–215, retrieved: 09, 2020. [Online]. Available: https://doi.org/10.1007/978-3-642-12837-0_11

[6] I. Chalkidis, E. Fergadiotis, P. Malakasiotis, and I. Androutsopoulos, "Large-scale multi-label text classification on EU legislation," in Proc 57th Annual Meeting of the ACL. Florence, Italy: Association for Computational Linguistics, Jul. 2019, pp. 6314–6322, retrieved: 09, 2020. [Online]. Available: https://www.aclweb.org/anthology/P19-1636

[7] Eurepean Union Law Website. Retrieved: 09,2020. [Online]. Available: https://eur-lex.europa.eu

[8] S. Ruder, M. E. Peters, S. Swayamdipta, and T. Wolf, "Transfer learning in natural language processing," in 2019 NAACL: Tutorials, 2019, pp. 15–18.

[9] The European Union's multilingual and multidisciplinary thesaurus. Retrieved: 09,2020. [Online]. Available: https://eur-lex.europa.eu/browse/eurovoc.html

[10] J. Devlin, M.-W. Chang, K. Lee, and K. Toutanova, "BERT: Pre-training of deep bidirectional transformers for language understanding," in Proc. 2019 NAACL: Human Language Technologies, Volume 1 (Long and Short Papers). Minneapolis, Minnesota: ACL, Jun. 2019, pp. 4171–4186, retrieved: 09, 2020. [Online]. Available: https://www.aclweb.org/anthology/N19-1423

[11] Y. Liu, M. Ott, N. Goyal, J. Du, M. Joshi, D. Chen, O. Levy, M. Lewis, L. Zettlemoyer, and V. Stoyanov, "Roberta: A robustly optimized bert pretraining approach," arXiv preprint arXiv:1907.11692, 2019.

[12] V. Sanh, L. Debut, J. Chaumond, and T. Wolf, "Distilbert, a distilled version of bert: smaller, faster, cheaper and lighter," arXiv preprint arXiv:1910.01108, 2019.

[13] Z. Yang, Z. Dai, Y. Yang, J. Carbonell, R. R. Salakhutdinov, and Q. V. Le, "Xlnet: Generalized autoregressive pretraining for language understanding," in Advances in neural information processing systems, 2019, pp. 5754–5764.

[14] K. Sechidis, G. Tsoumakas, and I. Vlahavas, "On the stratification of multi-label data," in Joint European Conference on Machine Learning and Knowledge Discovery in Databases. Springer, 2011, pp. 145–158.

[15] W.-C. Chang, H.-F. Yu, K. Zhong, Y. Yang, and I. Dhillon, "X-bert: extreme multi-label text classification using bidirectional encoder representations from transformers," arXiv preprint arXiv:1905.02331, 2019.

[16] R. Steinberger, M. Ebrahim, and M. Turchi, "Jrc eurovoc indexer jex-a freely available multi-label categorisation tool," arXiv preprint arXiv:1309.5223, 2013.

[17] G. Boella et al., "Linking legal open data: breaking the accessibility and language barrier in european legislation and case law," in Proceedings of the 15th International Conference on Artificial Intelligence and Law, 2015, pp. 171–175.

[18] J. Liu, W.-C. Chang, Y. Wu, and Y. Yang, "Deep learning for extreme multi-label text classification," in Proceedings of the 40th International ACM SIGIR Conference on Research and Development in Information Retrieval, 2017, pp. 115–124.

[19] K. Bhatia, H. Jain, P. Kar, M. Varma, and P. Jain, "Sparse local embeddings for extreme multi-label classification," in Advances in neural information processing systems, 2015, pp. 730–738.

[20] J. Pennington, R. Socher, and C. D. Manning, "Glove: Global vectors for word representation," in Empirical Methods in Natural Language Processing (EMNLP), 2014, pp. 1532–1543. [Online]. Available: http://www.aclweb.org/anthology/D14-1162

[21] M. Peters, M. Neumann, M. Iyyer, M. Gardner, C. Clark, K. Lee, and L. Zettlemoyer, "Deep contextualized word representations," in Proc. 2018 NAACL: Human Language Technologies, Volume 1 (Long Papers). New Orleans, Louisiana: Association for Computational Linguistics, Jun. 2018, pp. 2227–2237, retrieved: 09, 2020. [Online]. Available: https://www.aclweb.org/anthology/N18-1202

[22] R. You, S. Dai, Z. Zhang, H. Mamitsuka, and S. Zhu, "Attentionxml: Extreme multi-label text classification with multi-label attention based recurrent neural networks," arXiv preprint arXiv:1811.01727, 2018.

[23] SKOS Simple Knowledge Organization System. Retrieved: 09,2020. [Online]. Available: https://www.w3.org/2004/02/skos/

[24] Resource Description Framework. Retrieved: 09,2020. [Online]. Available: https://eur-lex.europa.eu/browse/eurovoc.html

[25] RDF 1.1 Turtle. Retrieved: 09,2020. [Online]. Available: https://www.w3.org/TR/turtle

[26] E. Filtz, S. Kirrane, A. Polleres, and G. Wohlgenannt, "Exploiting eurovoc's hierarchical structure for classifying legal documents," in OTM Confederated International Conferences" On the Move to Meaningful Internet Systems". Springer, 2019, pp. 164–181.

[27] JRC-Acquis. Retrieved: 09,2020. [Online]. Available: https://ec.europa.eu/jrc/en/language-technologies/jrc-acquis

[28] EURLEX57K dataset. Retrieved: 09,2020. [Online]. Available: http://nlp.cs.aueb.gr/software_and_datasets/EURLEX57K/

[29] J. Howard and S. Ruder, "Universal language model fine-tuning for text classification," arXiv preprint arXiv:1801.06146, 2018.

[30] Fastai documentation. Retrieved: 09,2020. [Online]. Available: https://docs.fast.ai/

[31] Huggingface transformers. Retrieved: 09,2020. [Online]. Available: https://huggingface.co/transformers

[32] Legal Documents, Large Multi-Label Text Classification. Retrieved: 09,2020. [Online]. Available: https://github.com/zeinsh/Legal-Docs-Large-MLTC

[33] S. Merity, N. S. Keskar, and R. Socher, "Regularizing and optimizing lstm language models," arXiv preprint arXiv:1708.02182, 2017.

[34] A. Vaswani, N. Shazeer, N. Parmar, J. Uszkoreit, L. Jones, A. N. Gomez, Ł. Kaiser, and I. Polosukhin, "Attention is all you need," in Advances in neural information processing systems, 2017, pp. 5998–6008.

[35] Z. Dai, Z. Yang, Y. Yang, J. Carbonell, Q. V. Le, and R. Salakhutdinov, "Transformer-xl: Attentive language models beyond a fixed-length context," arXiv preprint arXiv:1901.02860, 2019.

[36] H. Azarbonyad and M. Marx, "How many labels? determining the number of labels in multi-label text classification," in International Conference of the Cross-Language Evaluation Forum for European Languages. Springer, 2019, pp. 156–163.

[37] Multi-label data stratification. Retrieved: 09,2020. [Online]. Available: http://scikit.ml/stratification.html#Multi-label-data-stratification

[38] BERT, Multi-Lingual Model. Retrieved: 09,2020. [Online]. Available: https://github.com/google-research/bert/blob/master/multilingual.md

[39] Huggingface BERT base uncased model. Retrieved: 09,2020. [Online]. Available: https://huggingface.co/bert-base-uncased

[40] Huggingface RoBERTa base model. Retrieved: 09,2020. [Online]. Available: https://huggingface.co/roberta-base

[41] Huggingface DistilBERT cased model. Retrieved: 09,2020. [Online]. Available: https://huggingface.co/distilbert-base-uncased

[42] Huggingface XLNET cased model. Retrieved: 09,2020. [Online]. Available: https://huggingface.co/xlnet-base-cased

[43] H. Jain, Y. Prabhu, and M. Varma, "Extreme multi-label loss functions for recommendation, tagging, ranking & other missing label applications," in Proceedings of the 22nd ACM SIGKDD International Conference on Knowledge Discovery and Data Mining, 2016, pp. 935–944.

[44] A. Esuli, A. Moreo, and F. Sebastiani, "Funnelling: A new ensemble method for heterogeneous transfer learning and its application to cross-lingual text classification," ACM Transactions on Information Systems (TOIS), vol. 37, no. 3, 2019, pp. 1–30.

[45] A. Pal, M. Selvakumar, and M. Sankarasubbu, "Magnet: Multi-label text classification using attention-based graph neural network," in Proc. 12th Int. Conf. on Agents and Artificial Intelligence - Volume 2: ICAART, INSTICC. SciTePress, 2020, pp. 494–505.

Towards Using Logical Reasoning for Assessing the Structure and State of a Human Debate

Helmut Horacek

German Research Center for Artificial Intelligence
Language Technology Division
Saarbruecken, Germany
Email: helmut.horacek@dfki.de

Abstract—**Supporting a human debate by logical reasoning facilities is a long-term research goal. Support comprises evidence about argumentative accuracy, detection of inconsistencies, and exposition of acceptable policy positions. This paper elaborates the role and embedding of argumentative utterances, through the use of linguistic tools, which address various aspects of the semantics of natural language. In addition, long-term issues, such as uncovering parts of the semantic content of arguments and its use for reasoning purposes are discussed.**

Keywords–Discourse parser; logical entailment; argumentation graph; argumentation framework.

I. Introduction

A major goal in the field of computational models for natural argument is to make logical reasoning capabilities accessible for discussions, ultimately in the course of incrementally developing human debates. This issue appears to be notoriously difficult, which is also reflected by some sort of a partition of the research area between natural language approaches and logical models of argumentation, based on non-monotonic reasoning [2], with extremely few connections.

An exception is the approach by Wyner and his colleagues [15], who attempt to interpret a human debate in terms of arguments in favor or disfavor of the issue at stake or some intermediate argument. This way, contributions to the debate can be converted into an *Argumentation Graph*, which is the basic logical structure for computing the state of sets of arguments. The functionality provided by logical reasoning can be exploited — prominently by exposing sets of acceptable, consistent arguments that represent reasonable policy positions of some party — this is an extremely valuable documentation of the state of a debate. Nevertheless, the mapping from natural language statements onto logical assertions is made on a rather superficial level: the proper natural language text is not analyzed below the level of arguments, and the method also relies on the assessment of the contributors to the debate — they have to state which previous argument their new one relates to, and whether it attacks or supports it. We examine a number of methods to expand and strengthen this approach, as an extension to our elaborations in [4].

This paper is organized as follows. In section 2, we analyze shortcomings of human assignments of arguments and resulting deficits. In section 3, we discuss potential examinations addressing these deficit, supported by linguistic tools. In section 4, we address the long-term issue of transferring portions of contents in the debate to the logical level. In section 5, we discuss future developments.

II. Sources for Support by Logical Reasoning

The method by [15] relies on rather accurate assessments of participants in a debate with regard to the role of arguments raised and their relation to the embedding debate. However, when a human debate evolves in a typical manner, people sometimes raise their arguments in a sloppy fashion. This is not surprising, since the majority of them are far from being well-trained attorneys. In contrast to the human perspective of communication, percolating the inaccuracy of arguments to the logical level is likely to limit the usefulness of a logical support system, which itself exhibits strong rigor. Hence, it is quite advisable to perceive arguments in the most accurate form. As already observed and discussed in [4], arguments may be inaccurate in at least the following ways:

1) A contribution to the debate may be not a proper argument, in the sense that this statement does not attack or support an argument raised before, but it may be associated with such an argument in another way, typically by expanding its description.
2) An argument may be indicated by a debater as attacker or supporter of some other argument, but this relation may be better conceived as an indirect one, since the argument directly attacks resp. supports another argument related to the one indicated.
3) Arguments may have logical flaws of various kind, ranging from logical inconsistencies (typically in the embedding context) to subtle domain-specific ones.

The first deficit may lead to multiple representations of what is essentially the same argument — this may lead to temporary inconsistencies and repeated attacks in the subsequent debate. A similar overhead in reasoning may result from the second deficit. Issues associated with the third deficit may be various. Therefore, it is important to obtain a representation of the debate as accurate as possible, to exploit the functionality of logical tools attached. To envision this goal, we aim at computing the role and relations of arguments automatically, which a participant in a debate can accept or overrule.

III. Use of Linguistic Tools to Support Assessing the Structure and State of a Human Debate

In order to address potential deficits of human assessment regarding position and role of an argument we envision a linguistic analysis of the arguments raised, resulting in evidence on the level of discourse. Two things are of interest:

1) the attachment point for a newly raised argument

1) Every householder should pay tax for the garbage which the householder throws away.
2) No householder should pay tax for the garbage which the householder throws away.
3) Paying tax for garbage increases recycling.
4) Recycling more is good.
5) Paying tax for garbage is unfair.
6) Every householder should be charged equally.
7) Every householder who takes benefits does not recycle.
8) Every householder who does not take benefits pays for every householder who does take benefits.
9) Professor Resicke says that recycling reduces the need for new garbage dumps.
10) A reduction of the need for new garbage dumps is good.
11) Professor Resicke is not objective.
12) Professor Resicke owns a recycling company.
13) A person who owns a recycling company earns money from recycling.
14) Supermarkets create garbage.
15) Supermarkets should pay tax.
16) Supermarkets pass the taxes for the garbage to the consumer.

Figure 1. Human debate as used by Wyner and his colleagues [15].

2) its argumentative role, *attack* or *support*, the fundamental links in an *Argumentation Framework*, or a further description of a previously raised argument.

Two linguistic tools can contribute to this purpose: (1) a discourse parser and (2) a textual entailment component. In both of these, analysis of semantics of natural language is incorporated to achieve the intended functionality.

A discourse parser can check for the rhetorical role of arguments and the relations between them, essentially operationalizing *Rhetorical Structure Theory* [5]. Thereby, the richness of the rhetorical relations in ordinary texts is not of primary interest for our purposes, in view of the limited set of argumentative relations, since only a few rhetorical relations give highly relevant indications. For instance, some semantically strong relations, such as *contrast* and *explanation*, typically cooccur with *attack* and *support*, respectively.

A textual entailment component can check for consistency or possible inconsistency. In particular, a high degree of consistency — assuming the component yields results associated with probabilities - is hardly compatible with an *attack* relation. The reverse direction — inferring textual entailment on the basis of argumentative relations — is possible in some cases. An *attack* relation implies contradiction, but only specific instances of a *support* relation constitute entailment. All these inferences, however, are defeasible on principled grounds: an argumentative relation may be challenged by an *undercutting defeater* [9], which attacks the argumentative relation itself rather than the argument attacking or supporting another one.

At the present state of the art, unfortunately, neither discourse parsers nor textual entailment components are very strong assistants, they give some indications only. Discourse parsers are generally reasonable on structural issues — stating direct or indirect relations between assertions, but they are less accurate on ontological grounds, that is, inferring rhetorical relations. This is mainly because statements raised in the course of a debate, unlike continuous text, are poor in terms of the use of discourse markers. Consequently, most relations are hypothesized as *elaborations*, while the stronger relations that in fact hold between the arguments are not recognized.

For analyzing the following examples, we refer to the web versions of the discourse parser developed at Nanyang Technological University [11] and of AllenNLP's textual entailment tool [12]. We refer to the running example Wyner and his colleagues often have used (see Figure 1).

The ultimate goal is to incrementally build an *Argumentation Graph*, starting from the point of debate — "Every householder should pay tax for the garbage which the householder throws away." and its opposite — 1) and 2) in Figure 1. We do not have a systematic procedure for this purpose yet; in particular, there are too many options for attachment points when the number of arguments grows. Instead, we illustrate contributions of the linguistic tools to the analysis of a few examples, including some controversial interpretations that have been discussed in previous work.

Recognizing the conflation of two statements — one elaborating the other — into a single argument can be supported by checking their rhetorical relation and the degree of entailment holding between them. For example, "Recycling more is good" 4) in Figure 1), indicated as a *support* for "Paying tax for garbage increases recycling" 3) is assessed as an *elaboration* by the discourse parser. Moreover, the textual entailment tool gives 66 percent entailment for this pair of statements, and only 1 percent contradiction, which are quite strong values.

Looking at another example, an *explanation* relation is predicted by the discourse parser, stating that "Every householder who takes benefits does not recycle" (7) in Figure 1) explains "Every householder who does not take benefits pays for every householder who does take benefits" 8); this is a strong indication that these arguments should be nested rather than in parallel, as assessed by the human in the debate [16].

Textual entailment gives a weak though rather consistent evidence about the polarity of an argument, whether it is an attack or a support — this may be helpful in case a user slips in the use of the interface. For example, according to the textual entailment tool, "Paying tax for garbage increases recycling." 3) (Figure 1) is entailed by "Every householder should pay tax for the garbage which the householder throws away" 1), at a 53 percent level, but it is assessed to be a contradiction at a 76 percent level to "No householder should pay tax ..." 2). By the way, the weaker assertion "Not every householder should pay tax for the garbage which the householder throws away" is rather undecided, it yields a contradiction at a 36 percent level, and entailment at a 26 percent level.

IV. Making Natural Language Content Accessible to Logical Reasoning

The proper natural language content of arguments is not transferred to the logical level, since arguments in an *Argumentation Graph* appear as atomic units. This abstraction prohibits reasoning about portions of natural language statements raised as an argument, within individual arguments, and across several ones. A more detailed logical model would enable testing whether a natural language statement is consistent in itself, and whether stating an *attack* or a *support* relation between two arguments is acceptable, that is, this does not imply a contradiction. A richer representation of arguments can also make more advanced versions of *Argumentation Frameworks* accessible — the basic version only deals with *attacks* — these may include structured arguments [8] and priorities [10] or different strengths [1] associated with arguments.

In order to make at least portions of natural language content accessible to logical reasoning, proper linguistic analysis has to be carried out, so that semantic issues have to be dealt with explicitly and not only within the scope of the discourse parser and the textual entailment tool. In [16] this task has elaborated for restricted English, but the results are not used for logical reasoning purposes.

In order to go beyond restricted English, the semantic representation needs to undergo some sort of a normative process, to cater for paraphrases and varieties of linguistic forms. An appropriate strategy appears to be breaking down representations into atomic relations, and mapping these relations onto the repertoire stored in a knowledge representation repository with a preferably large set of ontological definitions, the biggest one being OpenCyc [6], used as in [7]. Defining this uniformity-emphasizing mapping process constitutes a challenge involving semantic issues. In dependency of the argumentative statements in a specific debate, not all of them need to be broken down into atomic relations; some composite ones often reoccurring may be maintained.

A case for such composite relations can be made when recognition of *Argumentation Schemes* [13][14] within a debate is attempted, *Appeal to Expert Opinion* being such as a scheme. The arguments 11) to 13) in Figure 1 instantiate a part of this scheme, in terms of a *critical question* ("Professor Resicke is not objective.") 11), followed by the associated justification ("Professor Resicke owns a recycling company." 12) and "A person who owns a recycling company earns money from recycling." 13)). Treating "Owning a recycling company" as a single predicate is enough abstraction to recognize the presence of the *Argumentation Scheme*.

V. Conclusion and Future Work

In this paper, we have discussed methods for assessing the structure and state of a human debate. This is done by consulting linguistic tools to make structure and content of natural language arguments represented better and thus more accurately accessible to logical reasoning facilities.

First steps towards operationalizing the concepts exposed in the paper are installation of the tools we have referred to via their demo versions, in the hope of getting more accurate results - later versions are likely to better capture the semantics of rhetorical relations, by incorporating results of research, such as [3]. In addition, categorization of statements (such as, "... is good/bad") in combination of selected uses of linguistic tools can be defined to check/improve the argumentation structure incrementally built. Most importantly, a systematic procedure for building an *Argumentation Graph* needs to be developed. Thereby, focusing on suitable attachment points is important (a statement about supermarkets is likely to expand a previously raised argument about supermarkets), as well as a metric assessing the contextually obtained results of linguistic tools. Moreover, analyzing focused portions of the argumentative discourse may be suitable, taking into account the difference between a multi-party debate and a monological presentation, which is what discourse parsers expect.

A long term perspective lies in examining the natural language content of arguments, complementing the atomic perspective of logical reasoning about acceptability state of sets of arguments by internal structures that enable checking consistency - a first step towards addressing plausibility.

Limitations even in advanced versions of this approach will be reasoning functionality which requires world knowledge more detailed than what has been made accessible to logical reasoning, which virtually includes all background knowledge; limited elaborations for specific domains may be an exception. Moreover, irony is unlikely to be treated automatically in a useful manner; it has not been addressed in the argumentation context so far.

References

[1] T. J. M. Bench-Capon, "Persuasion in practical argument using value-based argumentation frameworks," Journal of Logic and Computation, vol. 13, no. 3, 2003, pp. 429—448, ISSN: 0955-792X.

[2] P. M. Dung, "On the acceptability of arguments and its fundamental role in nonmonotonic reasoning, logic programming and n-person games," Artificial Intelligence, vol. 77, 1995, pp. 321—358, ISSN: 0004-3702.

[3] N. Green and J. Crotts, "Towards automatic detection of antithesis," in Proceedings of the 20th Workshop on Computational Models of Natural Argument co-located with the 8th International Conference on Computational Models of Argument (COMMA 2020), Perugia, Italy, 2020, pp. 69—73.

[4] H. Horacek, "Towards bridging between natural language and logic-based representations of natural arguments," in CMNA 12, the 12th workshop on Computational Models of Natural Argument, Montpellier, France, 2012, pp. 21–25.

[5] B. Mann and S. Thompson, "Rhetorical Structure Theory: Toward a functional theory of text organization," Text, vol. 8, 1988, pp. 243—281, ISSN: 1327-9556.

[6] "OpenCyc," URL: https://github.com/asanchez75/opencyc/ [accessed: 2020-09-01].

[7] "OpenCyc," URL: https://www.qrg.northwestern.edu/OpenCyc/index_opencyc.html [accessed: 2020-09-01].

[8] H. Prakken, "An abstract framework for argumentation with structured arguments," Argument and Computation, vol. 1, no. 2, 2010, pp. 93—124, ISSN: 1946-2166.

[9] J. Pollock, "Defeasible reasoning," Cognitive Science, vol. 11, 1987, pp. 481—518, ISSN: 1551-6709.

[10] H. Prakken and G. Sartor, "Argument-based extended logic programming with defeasible priorities," Journal of Applied Non-Classical Logics, vol. 7, no. 1, 1997, pp. 25—75, ISSN: 1166-3081.

[11] "Rhetorical-Analysis-Demo," URL: http://alt.qcri.org/demos/Discourse_Parser_Demo/ [accessed: 2020-09-01].

[12] "Textual-Entailment-Demo," URL: https://demo.allennlp.org/textual-entailment/MjI2ODQ0OQ== [accessed: 2020-09-01]

[13] D. Walton, "Argumentation schemes for presumptive reasoning," Erlbaum, Mahwah, N.J., 1996, ISBN: 9780805820713.

[14] D. Walton, "Argumentation schemes," Cambridge University Press, 2008, ISBN: 978-0521723749.

[15] A. Wyner, T. van Engers, and K. Bahreini, "From policy-making statements to first-order logic," in EGOVIS, K. Normann Andersen, E. Francesconi, A. Gronlund, and T. M. van Engers (eds.), Springer Lecture Notes in Computer Science 6267, Springer Berlin Heidelberg New York, 2010, pp. 47—61, ISBN: 978-3-642-15171-2.

[16] A. Wyner, T. van Engers, and A. Hunter, "Working on the argument pipeline: Through flow issues between natural language argument, instantiated arguments, and argumentation frameworks," Argument & Computation, vol. 7, no. 1, 2016, pp. 69—89, ISSN: 1946-2166.

Employing Bert Embeddings for Customer Segmentation and Translation Matching

Tim vor der Brück

Lucerne School of Computer Science and Information Technology
Lucerne University of Applied Sciences and Arts
Rotkreuz, Switzerland
E-mail: tim.vorderbrueck@hslu.ch

Abstract—**In this work, we investigate the performance of Bert (Bidirectional Encoder Representations from Transformers) embeddings for two Natural Language Processing (NLP) scenarios based on semantic similarity and conduct a comparison with ordinary Word2Vec embeddings. The Bert embeddings are pre-trained on a multi-lingual dataset from Google consisting of several Wikipedias. The semantic similarity between two input texts is estimated in the usual way of applying the cosine measure on the two embeddings centroids. In case of Bert, these centroids are determined by two different approaches. In the first approach, we just average the embeddings of all the word vectors of the associated sentence. In the second approach, we only average the embeddings of a special sentence start token that contains the whole sentence representation. Surprisingly, the performance of ordinary Word2Vec embeddings turned out to be considerably superior in both scenarios and both calculation methods.**

Keywords–Bert embeddings; Targeted Marketing; Translation Matching.

I. Introduction

Word2Vec Word Embeddings [1] enjoy high popularity due to their ease of use and good performance for estimating semantic similarity between words, sentences, or entire texts. However, they do lack one important property: they cannot directly convey phenomena like homography or polysemy. Thus, the same word used in a completely different meaning (like *space* as universe and *space* as location) would still be assigned the same word vector. Thus, Bert and ELMo (Embeddings from Language Models) embeddings [2][3] were introduced to overcome this issue. These embeddings are completely context dependent and can therefore no longer be expressed by global lookup tables as it is the case for Word2Vec Embeddings. Instead, they are generated by a deep neural network applied to a given text segment. In this work, we compare the performance of Bert embeddings with ordinary Word2Vec embeddings on two different NLP application scenarios.

II. Scenario 1 - Customer Segmentation

Our business partner operates a commercial youth platform for the Swiss market, where registered members get access to third-party offers such as discounts and special events like concerts or castings [4]. Actually, several hundred online contests per year are launched over this platform sponsored by other firms, an increasing number of them require the members to write short free-text snippets. Depending on these text snippets, the members should be automatically mapped to the best fitting marketing target group (called youth milieus) to allow for more customer-focused and precise marketing campaigns. The 6 employed youth milieus are:

- progressive postmodern youth: people primarily interested in culture and arts
- young performers: people striving for a high salary with a strong affinity for luxury goods
- freestyle action sportsmen
- hedonists: rather poorly educated people who enjoy partying and disco music
- conservative youth: traditional people with a strong concern for security
- special groups: comprises all those who cannot be assigned to one of the upper five milieus.

In total, our business partner conducted three online contests, where the participants should

1) elaborate on a perfect holiday at a destination of their choice in case of a contest sponsored by a travel agency (Contest 1),
2) fantasize what they could do with a pair of new sneakers (Contest 2) and
3) how they would use one of several possible prizes (Contest 3).

To accomplish this matching, all marketing target groups are described by a set of keywords that conveys their typical characteristics. We then generate word embedding centroids for both the snippet and the keyword list. Afterward, we select that marketing target group for a certain text snippet, for which the cosine measure between both embedding centroids is maximal (see Figure 1). These selections are then compared with a gold standard annotation conducted independently by three different marketers.

III. Scenario 2 - Translation Matching

In this scenario, we investigate two independent translations of the same novel (*The purloined letter by Edgar Allen Poe*) into German. In particular, we aim to match each sentence of the first translation to the associated sentence of the second translation. The matching procedure is analogous to scenario 1, which means that we generate embedding vectors for all sentences and determine the sentence pairs with maximal cosine similarity between the associated embedding centroids.

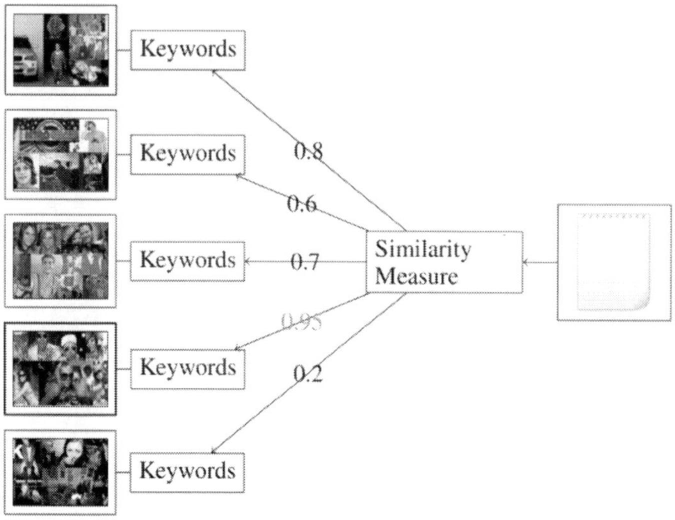

Figure 1. Procedure for mapping a text snippet to the best fitting target group.

TABLE I. CORPUS SIZES MEASURED BY NUMBER OF WORDS.

Corpus	# Words
German Wikipedia	651 880 623
Frankfurter Rundschau	34 325 073
News journal *20 Minutes*	8 629 955

TABLE II. OBTAINED ACCURACY OF EMBEDDING-BASED SIMILARITY ESTIMATION ON THREE ONLINE CONTESTS.

Method	Accuracy			
	Contest 1	Contest 2	Contest 3	Total
Word2Vec	0.347	0.328	0.227	0.330
Bert (AW)	0.046	0.223	0.061	0.118
Bert (ST)	0.109	0.149	0.136	0.07

IV. RESULTS

The Bert embeddings were trained on the multilingual data set comprising of several Wikipedias. The centroids of a text snippet were determined using two different approaches:

- average over All Words (AW)
- average only over the Start Tokens (ST) that represent the beginning of a sentence

For the first approach (AW), we used Gluon [5], an NLP library based on MXNet [6], while approach (ST) was based on a PyTorch implementation provided by *Hugging Face* [7].

Word2Vec was trained on the German Wikipedia, the German newspaper *Frankfurter Rundschau* and on the *20 minutes* journal (cf. [4]), which is freely available at various Swiss train stations. The sizes of the three corpora are given in Table I.

The obtained accuracy for the customer segmentation / translation matching is given in Table II / Table III.

V. DISCUSSION

Bert embeddings turned out to be rather unusable for the first task of target group matching. A possible reason is that all text snippets are compared with keyword lists, for which the word order is rather arbitrary and depends on the personal preferences of the marketers. The obtained accuracy values of Bert Embeddings for the second scenario of translation matching were indeed higher, however still considerably lagging behind the use of ordinary Word2Vec word embeddings. Furthermore, calculating the centroids from the Bert embeddings of the Start Token (ST) seems the superior approach to just averaging the individual word embeddings (AVG). A further reason for the rather poor performance of Bert embeddings in both scenarios is the fact that the data set used for training is multi-lingual. We expect the results to be superior in case of a monolingual model, since such a model reduces the number of different tokens possibly occurring in a given word context and, therefore, also the noise in the data.

TABLE III. EVALUATION ON TRANSLATION MATCHING.

Method	Accuracy
W2VC	0.726
Bert (ST)	0.423
Bert (AW)	0.279
Random	0.010

VI. CONCLUSION

We applied Bert embeddings to two different German NLP tasks, which are customer segmentation and translation matching. In both scenarios, we obtained a rather poor performance compared to ordinary Word2Vec embeddings. Possible future work comprises the use of monolingual training data for Bert as well as ELMo embeddings and other embedding methods.

ACKNOWLEDGMENT

Hereby, I want to thank all people that supported me with this work. Special thanks go to Marc Pouly who provided me with this dataset.

REFERENCES

[1] T. Mikolov, I. Sutskever, C. Ilya, G. Corrado, and J. Dean, "Distributed representations of words and phrases and their compositionality," in Proceedings of the Conference on Neural Information Processing Systems (NIPS), Lake Tahoe, Nevada, 2013, pp. 3111–3119.

[2] J. Devlin, M.-W. Chang, K. Lee, and K. Toutanova, "Bert: Pre-training of deep bidirectional transformers for language understanding," in Proceedings of NAACL, 2019, pp. 4171–4186.

[3] M. E. Peters, M. Neumann, M. Iyyer, M. Gardner, C. Clark, K. Lee, and L. Zettlemoyer, "Deep contextualized word representations," in Proceedings of NAACL, 2018, pp. 2227–2237.

[4] T. vor der Brück and M. Pouly, "Text similarity estimation based on word embeddings and matrix norms for targeted marketing," in Proceedings of NAACL, 2019, pp. 1827–1836.

[5] "GluonNLP," 2020, https://gluon-nlp.mxnet.io.

[6] T. Chen, M. Li, Y. Li, M. Lin, N. Wang, M. Wang, T. Xiao, B. Xu, C. Zhang, and Z. Zhang, "Mxnet: A flexible and efficient machine learning library for heterogeneous distributed systems," 2015.

[7] "Huggingface," 2020, https://huggingface.co.

Performance Analysis and Optimization of Semantic Queries

Philipp Hertweck

Fraunhofer IOSB
Karlsruhe, Germany
Email: philipp.hertweck@iosb.fraunhofer.de

Erik Kristiansen

Karlsruhe Institute of Technology
Karlsruhe, Germany
Email: erik@kristiansen.de

Tobias Hellmund

Fraunhofer IOSB
Karlsruhe, Germany
Email: tobias.hellmund@iosb.fraunhofer.de

Jürgen Moßgraber

Fraunhofer IOSB
Karlsruhe, Germany
Email: juergen.mossgraber@iosb.fraunhofer.de

Abstract—**Recently, the usage of triplestores has increased in complex computer systems. Traditionally, they are used for representing static knowledge. In the last years, systems started using semantic triplestores in highly dynamic scenarios, e.g., in the context of civil protection. In these use cases, performance characteristics are more and more important. There are various aspects influencing the query performance. We have noticed that already the query structure has a significant impact on the execution time. SPARQL Protocol And RDF Query Language (SPARQL) is a widely used standard for querying triplestores. In this work, we have developed SPARQL query patterns and evaluated their performance characteristics. For this, a literature review was done to select a suitable benchmark. As a result, we provide eight recommendations for formulating SPARQL queries. These can be easily used by everybody without a deeper knowledge about the implementation of the triplestore, which contains the desired data.**

Keywords–SPARQL Performance; Triplestore; Benchmark; Query optimization.

I. Introduction

The World Wide Web was originally designed to be used by humans; to foster machine understanding of the incomprehensible large amount of data in the web, the Semantic Web was envisioned. This vision focuses on the reuse, availability and interoperability of data. A milestone on the path to reach this vision is the Resource Description Framework (RDF [1]), which defines a data model that encompasses Unique Resource Identifiers (URIs) and requires data structured as triples. A triple is a statement about data that consists of *subject*, *predicate* and *object*. Since all three are identified by an URI, they can be uniquely recognized and linked by machines. For example, the Linked-data project [2] started to link and structure the semantic data available on the Internet.

A set of RDF triples forms a graph. These graphs are stored in so-called triplestores. To systematically retrieve data from such stores, the World Wide Web Consortium (W3C) standardized SPARQL [3], a declarative query language for RDF based data. There are other query languages for data represented in RDF, but as SPARQL is the de-facto standard query language for the Semantic Web, we do not consider other languages. Since the implementation of triplestores varies from product to product, the performance of each is different as well. Since a growing amount of (critical) information systems integrate data in form of triples, the performance of SPARQL queries is increasingly important. The following two examples show the wide range of usage of semantic technologies. Semantic integration [4] [5] can be applied in the context of crisis response to support decision support [6]. Another example shows the implementation of semantic data to protect cultural heritage [7].

There are several possibilities to optimize the execution of SPARQL queries. Either on the data (representation) itself, the triplestore's implementation (internal representation, query execution, query optimization, etc.) or on the usage of the triplestore. In this paper, we are focusing on the later. We examine: are there some easily applicable rules an end-user should follow while formulating SPARQL queries?

To approach this question, first a literature review of existing triplestore benchmarks was conducted (Section III). Different query patterns were developed (Section IV). Those were compared by executing them, with the help of the selected benchmark against a triplestore. Our evaluation (Section V) uses Apache Fuseki, since it is a commonly used, open source triplestore implementation. With this evaluation, the influencing factors within a SPARQL query were elaborated and eight recommendations (Section VI) for query formulations were derived.

The contributions of this paper are: 1) A literature review of existing SPARQL benchmarks and a selection, which can be used to evaluate the performance of different SPARQL query patterns. 2) Definition of multiple SPARQL query patterns, to determine the performance implications of different query characteristics. 3) Derivation of eight easily applicable recommendations for formulating SPARQL queries.

II. Related Work

Evaluating and optimizing the performance of SPARQL triplestores is not new. Inspired by numerous existing optimizations for relational databases (internal representation, query execution, query optimization, etc.), lots of work was done in improving triple store performance by optimizing the query execution. For example, Weiss et al. [8] propose a sextuple-indexing storage scheme to enhance query processing. Atre et al. [9] focus on a Bitmatrix to optimize Join-Operations in RDF data query processing. Having knowledge about the distribution of the triplestores contained data, heuristics can be used to reorder query patterns [10] to optimize the query execution.

All of these approaches focus on optimizing the triplestore implementation, either by applying automated query optimizations or by optimizing the storage or representation of the RDF triples. Usually this happens in the background without the need of any interaction of the user of the triplestore. In contrast, this work focuses on the user side. Daily work showed that performance characteristics of SPARQL query patterns are widely unknown for triplestore users. Rietveld et al. [11] showed in their evaluation that 72.66% of their analyzed user queries are formulated inefficiently. This is taken into account by the work of Loizou et al. [12]. The authors describe five heuristics for creating performant queries. Although their work is based on a formal evaluation of SPARQL queries, their results are five easily applicable heuristics, namely: 1) minimize optional graph patterns 2) use named graphs to localize SPARQL sub-graph patterns 3) reduce intermediate results 4) reduce the effects of cartesian products 5) specify alternative URIs.

In addition to these heuristics which should be considered, users should keep in mind that there might exist equivalent (or nearly equivalent) SPARQL queries wich are often exchangable in applications. An easy to use guideline, helping to choose the more performant variant is not available until now. To bridge this gap, we are taking a triplestore implementation and evaluate, which SPARQL query patterns are influencing the execution performance. We are aware that the triplestore implementation automatically optimizes the internal execution. Nevertheless, we still expect some aspects a user should be aware of, when formulating queries. These are taken into account for recommendations on formulating SPARQL queries.

III. SPARQL BENCHMARKS

A. Evaluation Criteria for the Review of SPARQL Benchmarks

To find a suitable SPARQL benchmark for our evaluation, we performed a literature review of existing benchmarks. In combination with the work of [13], we then developed a categorizing schema that helped identify a suitable benchmark for this work.

- **User defined ontology**: Is it possible for a user to use an arbitrary ontology in the benchmark?
- **Data generator**: Is there a generator available to generate new triples to easily scale the data set?
- **Query generator**: Is there a tool available, which can dynamically generate queries or is there a fixed set of queries? Are the performed queries statically or dynamically generated?
- **User defined queries**: Is it possible to run user defined queries?
- **Query execution**: Is a query execution driver (running the SPARQL queries on a triplestore) available? Does it return performance metrics?
- **Code availability**: Is the benchmarks source code publicly available?
- **Last update**: Date of last change in the benchmarks source code.
- **License**: Under which license is the source code published?

To make use of an existing benchmark in the context of this work, some of the just mentioned features are mandatory. First of all, the **code** must be available under an appropriate **license**. To scale the data set a **data generator** is needed. Since we want to compare different SPARQL queries, it must be possible to use **user defined queries**. To simplify the usage a **query execution** component is needed. The other features are beneficial though not mandatory.

B. SPARQL Benchmark Selection

To select a suitable benchmark, we started our literature review with the W3C list for RDF store benchmarking [14]. Those benchmarks were evaluated, using the just mentioned criteria. The results are presented in Table I.

For the sake of brevity, only a few benchmarks are introduced in the text. Further information can be found in the sources. The Lehigh University Benchmark (LUBM) [16] offers an ontology about universities. Data scaling is conducted by adding new universities, whereas newly added data has no interconnections with the previous data. The benchmark is highly quoted (1500 direct quotes). The Berlin SPARQL Benchmark [15] is built around an e-commerce system with different products, vendors and consumers and other common information, such has reviews. The benchmark dynamically creates queries during the runtime [29]. The introducing paper is quoted over 650 times. 'SP2Bench: A SPARQL Performance Benchmark' [21] models the behavior of people within a social network with actions such as 'Likes', group management, and befriending persons. The paper is cited nearly 500 times. 'DBpedia SPARQL Benchmark – PerformanceAssessment with Real Queries on Real Data' [30] created its queries from real-application queries distilled from the dbpedia-log [31] and performs these on the dbpedia data set. To this date, the benchmark nearly reached 300 cites. The Social Intelligence Benchmark (SIB) simulates the social media network of users and their interaction [22]. The project is not supported anymore. IGUANA [28] is the successor of this project. The paper was quoted 60 times to this date.

The *Berlin SPARQL Benchmark BSBM*, *Lehigh University Benchmark LUBM* as well as *LinkBench* fulfill our requirements. For this work, we decided to use the BSBM, since it is newer than the LUBM, but also widely used. Although the BSBM doesn't have a query generator, it implements a query templating engine, which allows to put placeholders in SPARQL queries, which again are substituted during query execution. This allows to generate different queries with the same structure.

IV. QUERY PATTERNS

After a benchmark was selected in the last section, the different SPARQL query patterns, used to derive the recommendations, need to be selected. Subsequently, we characterize and select the patterns for evaluation.

TABLE I. CONSIDERED BENCHMARKS

Name	User ontology	Data generator	User queries	Query generator	Executor	Code available	Last Update	License
Berlin SPARQL Benchmark BSBM [15]	No	Yes	Yes	No	Yes	✓	2012	Apache 2.0
Lehigh University Benchmark LUBM [16]	No	Yes	Yes	No	Yes	✓	2004	GPL 2.0
FedBench [17]	No	No	No	No	Yes	✓	2013	LGPL
Feasible [18]	No	No	Yes	Yes	No	✓	2018	AGPL
LargeRDFBench [19]	No	No	Yes	No	No	✓	2018	AGPL
University Ontology Benchmark UOBM [20]	No	Yes	No	No	No	✗	2005	GPL 2.0
SPARQL Performance Benchmark [21]	No	Yes	No	No	No	✓	2009	Berkeley License
Social Network Intelligence Benchmark [22]	No	Yes	No	No	Yes	✗	2015	GPL 3.0
Linked Data Integration Benchmark [23]	No	Yes	Yes	No	No	✓	2012	BSD
Linked Open Data Quality Assessment [24]	No	No	No	No	Yes	✓	2012	BSD
LinkBench [25]	Yes	Yes	Yes	No	Yes	✓	2015	Apache 2.0
Waterloo SPARQL Diversity Test Suite [26]	No	Yes	Yes	Yes	No	✓	2014	MIT
Semantic Publishing Benchmark [27]	No	Yes	No	No	Yes	✓	2019	Apache 2.0
IGUANA [28]	Yes	No	Yes	No	Yes	✓	2019	AGPL

A. *Identifying Query Patterns*

We studied the syntactical elements of SPARQL queries and developed variants of query patterns. Those query variants either make use of the SPARQL algebra equivalences or use specific elements of the SPARQL query language. In the first case we are expecting only small differences in performance, since triple store-internal optimizers already make use of semantic equivalences. The second case might show differences, due to the different query results. In some use-cases these different results matter, whereas there are use-cases where only the user's negligence or unawareness causes inperformant SPARQL queries. The results of this work should call the user's attention as well as provide easy usable guidelines for formulating performant queries.

To gather SPARQL patterns, queries used in various past projects were considered. In addition, informal interviews and discussions with users (colleagues, students, etc.) were conducted. This approach showed that the main focus while formulating SPARQL queries is on writing syntactically correct queries returning the right values. Performance impacts were rarely considered. As a result of the discussions, a list of query patterns causing uncertainty in their expected performance characteristic were developed. It is to be noted that the semantics of the compared query patterns might not be completely the same; yet, on the data set they are applied on, their result is expected to be the same.

To determine the influence of these patterns, we formulated two variants of each SPARQL query. Those pairs are used as query templates filled by the BSBM. With the concept of query templates, BSBM allows to use placeholders in a SPARQL query, which are replaced by random values before the query is executed. This allows to slightly change the content of the query, without changing its structure to avoid caching mechanisms in the triple store, which otherwise would tamper our results. Based on the execution times of those variants, we identified eight simple and applicable recommendations.

As an example: the first query variant of *Filter size* looks like this:

```
select ?review ?rating2 where {
    ?review bsbm:rating1 ?rating1.
    ?review bsbm:rating2 ?rating2
    filter (?rating1 >= %rating1% &&
            ?rating2 < %rating2%)
}
```

Listing 1. Variant 1 of *Filter size*

where *%rating1%* and *%rating2%* are placeholders, replaced by BSBM during execution. The performance of this variant is compared with the following one:

```
select ?review ?rating2 where {
    ?review bsbm:rating1 ?rating1.
    filter (?rating1 >= %rating1%)
    ?review bsbm:rating2 ?rating2.
    filter (?rating2 < %rating2%)
}
```

Listing 2. Variant 2 of *Filter size*

B. *Patterns for Evaluation*

We identified the following query patterns, with the described variants:

- **Number of results**: Querying instances with a large amount of instances (1) (Those numbers are used in Section V to identify the variants) or with a low number of instances (2).
- **Limiting results**: Getting all results (1) or limiting the number of results, using the *LIMIT* operator (2).
- **Projection**: Using a projection allows to specify the needed variables. Either selecting all *SELECT ** (1) or only one variable *SELECT ?var* (2), or only the number *SELECT(count(?var))* of results (3).

- **String functions**: Either filtering a variable based on a regular expression (1) or using one of the string functions, e.g., *STRSTARTS* (2).
- **Filter size**: Providing all expressions in one filter term, combined by the logical *AND* (1) or having multiple smaller filter expressions (2).
- **Filter position**: Since a SPARQL query contains a set of triple patterns, the position of the filter statement in this set can be changed: having the filter at the end (1) or at the beginning (2) of the query.
- **String filter**: Filtering for numerical (1) or text based values (2).
- **Inverse**: Specifying the triple forward *?r rev:reviewer ?p* (1) or inverse *?p ^rev:reviewer ?r* (2).
- **Variable types**: The *rdf:type* of subject and object are specified by the predicate's definition, meaning it is implicitly available (1). Therefore, adding this type of information explicitly to the query is worth investigating (2).
- **Optional**: Querying triple patterns usually requires matching all variables. Some of the variables might be optional. There are two possibilities querying optional variables: using the *OPTIONAL* statement (1) or *UNION* the triples with and without the variable (2).
- **Graph structure**: An object of a triple might be either an instance of another type or a primitive data value. By this, a query can filter for instances (querying the RDF graph structure) (1) or for a data value (2).
- **Triple order**: The order of triple patterns in a SPARQL query is arbitrary. In the first variant the first pattern matches a large amount of triples and the second pattern reduces the result (1). The second variant is the opposite; the first triple pattern already limits the result to a small amount (2).
- **Limit in subselect**: SPARQL supports splitting a query into multiple select statements. This enables the user to already *LIMIT* the result of the subselect. In this case we compare selecting products and labels, with limit 5 (1) and subselecting 5 products and then selecting the corresponding labels (2).
- **Distinct**: The *DISTINCT* keyword can be used to eliminate duplicates in the result (1). As a variant the weaker *REDUCED* can be used (which might remove duplicates, but there is no guarantee) (2).
- **Minus**: Using *not exists* allows to filter for triples that do not match (1):
  ?product rdfs:label ?label
  filter(not exists {?product bsbm:number ?n})
  As an alternative the *MINUS* operator allows to remove triple from the result that match a given triple (2):
  ?product rdfs:label ?label
  MINUS {?product bsbm:number ?n}
- **Path**: Querying a path can be either done by explicitly querying the relation (1) or by using a property path sequence, e.g., *^bsbm:reviewFor/rev:reviewer* (2).

Having a basic understanding of triple stores or relational databases in mind, it is clear that some of the variants are faster. This is especially the case when the final or intermediate data set is reduced. Although this is obviously clear, we decided to keep them in our list, on the one hand to quantify the difference and on the other hand to return this to the users mind.

As part of the query execution, a triple store has to parse the SPARQL query into an abstract representation. Usually this is done by an internal optimizer, which makes use of equivalences in the SPARQL algebra to change the queries to an equivalent representation. This is especially expected for the variants of *Filter size*, *Filter position* and *Triple order*. We validated our assumption by parsing our queries with the Apache Jena query parser [32], which is also part of the Fuseki triple store. This showed for *Filter size* that big filters are split into multiple single filters, therefore internally the two variants are processed the same way. Also a comparison of the *Filter position* variants showed that in the internal representation the filters are moved to the same place. However, the *triple order* was not changed. In addition, we noted that querying the *inverse* relation leads back to the forward relation.

V. Evaluation

In our evaluation, we compare the query execution time of the previously described query pattern variants. In the following, we briefly introduce our system set-up before giving the results of the performance analysis.

A. System Set-Up and Experimental Procedure

We executed the queries presented in the previous section using the Berlin SPARQL Benchmark and a Fuseki triple store hosting a BSBM data set. The benchmark as well as Fuseki were running on commodity hardware: Laptop with Intel i7 CPU and 16GB of RAM. As explained in section III, the Berlin SPARQL Benchmark offers the possibility to generate data sets of arbitrary size. In first tests 1.8 million triple showed useful for a smaller data set: not too big, but already showing effects. For a bigger data set, we decided to use 4 million triples, since this still allowed the execution on our hardware in a reasonable time.

First tests showed that the Heap-Space, available for the Fuseki triple store process, is an important factor: the combination of too many triples with a small Heap-Space results in exceptions thrown by the triplestore. 1.1 GB and 2.25 GB, respectively, turned out to be the minimum Heap-Space sizes for our data sets.

For our evaluation, we rely on the available features of the Berlin SPARQL Benchmark (BSBM): BSBM ontology, BSBM data generator and BSBM query execution. The BSBM query execution takes a set of SPARQL query templates. Parameters were replaced with a set of predefined values and sent to a SPARQL endpoint. As a result the individual execution times, together with number of Queries Per Second (QPS) are returned by the benchmark. Our evaluation is based on QPS as an average over multiple queries. In addition to the benchmark, small scripts were developed to ease the execution of the different query variants and to store the results in an ordered manner. To initialize the triplestore correctly (e.g., creating indices, caches, etc.) a warm up phase of 30 queries was introduced for each variant. For the test run, each query variant was executed 150 times.

TABLE II. EVALUATION OF QUERY VARIANTS

Query Pattern	4 million		1.8 million			
	7 GB	2.45 GB	7 GB	4 GB	1.11 GB	VI
Number of results	$\checkmark_2$	$\checkmark_2$	$\checkmark_2$	$\checkmark_2$	$\checkmark_2$	1
Limiting result	$\checkmark_2$	$\checkmark_2$	$\checkmark_2$	$\checkmark_2$	$\checkmark_2$	1
Projection	$\checkmark_3$	$\checkmark_2$	$\checkmark_3$	$\checkmark_3$	$\checkmark_3$	2
String functions	$\checkmark_2$	$\checkmark_2$	$\checkmark_2$	$\checkmark_2$	$\checkmark_2$	6
Filter size	✗	✗	✗	✗	✗	-
FilterPos	✗	$\checkmark_2$	✗	✗	✗	-
String filter	$\checkmark_1$	$\checkmark_2$	$\checkmark_1$	$\checkmark_1$	$\checkmark_2$	5
Inverse	✗	✗	✗	$\checkmark_1$	✗	-
Variables type	$\checkmark_1$	$\checkmark_1$	$\checkmark_1$	$\checkmark_1$	$\checkmark_1$	4
Optional	✗	✗	$\checkmark_1$	$\checkmark_1$	✗	-
Graph structure	$\checkmark_2$	$\checkmark_2$	✗	✗	✗	-
Triple order	$\checkmark_2$	$\checkmark_2$	$\checkmark_2$	$\checkmark_2$	$\checkmark_2$	3
Limit in subselect	$\checkmark_1$	$\checkmark_1$	✗	✗	✗	-
Distinct	✗	$\checkmark_2$	$\checkmark_2$	$\checkmark_2$	$\checkmark_2$	7
Minus	$\checkmark_2$	$\checkmark_2$	$\checkmark_2$	$\checkmark_2$	$\checkmark_2$	8
Paths	✗	✗	✗	✗	$\checkmark_2$	-

B. *Results*

Table II summarizes our evaluation results. Each column shows a configuration of the triplestore (available Heap-Space and number of inserted triples). If there was not a significant difference (10 %) in the execution time of the query variants it is marked with the ✗sign. A ✓indicates a difference, where the subscript points out, which of the variants had the better performance. The last column anticipates the recommendation, presented in the following Section VI.

Unsurprisingly, the basic rule of thumb - limiting the result set size - proved to be true. The query returning less data was faster for all variants: *Number of results*, *Limiting result* and *Projection*. Like described in the previous Section IV there was no difference for *Filter size*. Only one configuration for *FilterPos* showed a difference. These results were expected, due to the same internal representation. There are some patterns where a difference was noted only in one configuration (*FilterPos*, *Inverse*, *Paths*). So, those patterns generally do not have a significant impact on the queries' performance. The example of *FilterPos* (having the same internal representation, but performance difference in one configuration) shows, there are additional (not further analyzed) influencing factors.

There seems to be no big difference between *Optional* and *Union*. In two configurations the use of *Optional* was slightly faster than *Union*. Also filtering a *Graph structure* doesn't show a clear difference. For the larger data set of 4 million triples, filtering for a graph structure was a bit slower than filtering for data values.

As known from relational data bases, filtering for text based values (*String filter*) is slower (although it seems that this effect only appears for larger data sets). If searching in text is needed, then the functions provided by SPARQL should be preferred over generic regular expressions (*String functions*). It also showed that using specially provided functions (like *Reduced* instead of *Distinct* or *Minus* instead of *not exists*) can improve the query performance.

Surprisingly, it is to be noted that providing additional type information (*Variables type*) can slow down the query execution. It seems that adding this type information results in additional checks during the query execution and does not support the query optimization as one might expect.

Regarding the result of the query, the *triple order* is arbitrary. In any case, it is shown that this holds not valid for the performance: more selective triple patterns should be stated first. Unexpectedly, the triples were not automatically reordered during the execution by the triplestore based on heuristics of the contained data. Since reordering triples results in equivalent results and users often have knowledge (or at least some idea) about the selectivity of a triple pattern, they should be careful about the order. Reducing the intermediate result by *Limiting a subselect* does not provide any performance optimization in our tests. Surprisingly, a subselect without a *Limit* was faster in two configurations; we expected the performance impact of a limited result set to be higher, than that of a subselect.

VI. Recommendations

Based on the previously presented evaluation, the following recommendations should be kept in mind when writing SPARQL queries:

1) **Small result set**: If possible, limit the returned result. If the complete result is not processable by the client, make use of *LIMIT* and get the next chunk of data by using *OFFSET*.
2) **Use projections**: Clearly specify the variables of interest and do not select everything (*SELECT* *). If only the number of results is of interest, make use of *COUNT*.
3) **Reduce intermediate results**: If known, list the most selective triple query pattern first.
4) **Do not add additional types**: Do not add *rdf:type* triples if they aren't needed.
5) **Avoid filtering for text**: If possible prefer filtering for numbers instead of text.
6) **Use String-functions**: Prefer to use the SPARQL *STR-functions* instead of regular expressions.
7) **Use reduce**: If duplicates in the result are tolerable, use *REDUCE* instead of *DISTINCT*.
8) **Minus-Operator instead of Filter**: Express your filter expression in a *MINUS* and avoid *FILTER* in conjunction with *not exists*.

VII. Conclusion

The execution time of SPARQL queries often is crucial for applications relying on semantic data stores. Only a few, easily applicable guidelines are available for users writing performant SPARQL queries. In this work, we closed this gap by 1) selecting a SPARQL benchmark, to compare different variants of SPARQL queries 2) extracting common patterns in SPARQL queries and formulating variants to determine their impact on performance 3) providing eight easily applicable recommendations that can be considered while writing SPARQL queries.

In comparison with Loizou's work [12], we can confirm his findings 1) and 3) and expand the suggestions with our findings.

Besides the provided recommendations, the evaluation showed that the results vary from configuration to configuration. There are many factors that influence the execution time of SPARQL queries. Therefore, the presented recommendations can be used as hints and thumb rules to guide users through formulating SPARQL queries, without the need of any specialized knowledge. If the performance of specific queries is crucial for a system, dedicated benchmarking tests needs to be done with the given data set and triplestore implementation. Our extension to the BSBM and benchmark execution can be used to simplify further evaluations.

Future work can extend the evaluation to other triplestore implementations and data sets, as well as the comparison of different triplestores among each other. Notably, an analysis of different query patterns on different triplestores is interesting as well, to find out if our suggestions hold valid on different triplestore implementations. Some of the recommendations change the result of the SPARQL query, whereas it should be noted that some of the tips result in equivalent queries. In future work these recommendations can be implemented into the triplestore's optimizer to automatically transform into more efficient, but semantically equivalent queries.

REFERENCES

[1] World Wide Web Consortium (W3C), "Rdf 1.1 concepts and abstract syntax," 25.02.2014, retrieved 09. 2020. [Online]. Available: https://www.w3.org/TR/rdf11-concepts/

[2] "The Linked Open Data Cloud," retrieved 09. 2020. [Online]. Available: https://lod-cloud.net/

[3] World Wide Web Consortium (W3C) , "Sparql 1.1 overview," 21.03.2013, retrieved 09. 2020. [Online]. Available: https://www.w3.org/TR/sparql11-overview

[4] E. Kontopoulos et al., "Ontology-based representation of crisis management procedures for climate events," in 1st International Workshop on Intelligent Crisis Management Technologies for Climate Events (ICMT 2018), colocated with the 15th International Conference on Information Systems for Crisis Response and Management (ISCRAM 2018), 2018, pp. 1064–1073.

[5] T. Hellmund, M. Schenk, P. Hertweck, and J. Moßgraber, "Employing geospatial semantics and semantic web technologies in natural disaster management," SEMANTICS Posters and Demos, 2019.

[6] P. Hertweck et al., "The backbone of decision support systems: The sensor to decision chain," International Journal of Information Systems for Crisis Response and Management (IJISCRAM), vol. 10, no. 4, 2018, pp. 65–87.

[7] T. Hellmund et al., "Introducing the heracles ontology—semantics for cultural heritage management," Heritage, vol. 1, no. 2, 2018, pp. 377–391.

[8] C. Weiss, P. Karras, and A. Bernstein, "Hexastore: sextuple indexing for semantic web data management," Proceedings of the VLDB Endowment, vol. 1, no. 1, 2008, pp. 1008–1019.

[9] M. Atre, V. Chaoji, M. J. Zaki, and J. A. Hendler, "Matrix bit loaded: a scalable lightweight join query processor for rdf data," in Proceedings of the 19th international conference on World Wide Web, 2010, pp. 41–50.

[10] M. Stocker, A. Seaborne, A. Bernstein, C. Kiefer, and D. Reynolds, "Sparql basic graph pattern optimization using selectivity estimation," in Proceedings of the 17th international conference on World Wide Web, 2008, pp. 595–604.

[11] L. Rietveld and R. Hoekstra, "Yasgui: feeling the pulse of linked data," in International Conference on Knowledge Engineering and Knowledge Management, 2014, pp. 441–452.

[12] A. Loizou, R. Angles, and P. Groth, "On the formulation of performant sparql queries," Journal of Web Semantics, vol. 31, 2015, pp. 1–26.

[13] M. Saleem et al., "How representative is a sparql benchmark? an analysis of rdf triplestore benchmarks," in The World Wide Web Conference, ser. WWW '19. New York, NY, USA: Association for Computing Machinery, 2019, p. 1623–1633. [Online]. Available: https://doi.org/10.1145/3308558.3313556

[14] World Wide Web Consortium (W3C), "Rdf store benchmarking," 20.10.2018, retrieved 09. 2020. [Online]. Available: https://www.w3.org/wiki/RdfStoreBenchmarking

[15] C. Bizer and A. Schultz, "The berlin sparql benchmark," International Journal on Semantic Web and Information Systems (IJSWIS), vol. 5, no. 2, 2009, pp. 1–24.

[16] Y. Guo, Z. Pan, and J. Heflin, "Lubm: A benchmark for owl knowledge base systems," Journal of Web Semantics, vol. 3, no. 2-3, 2005, pp. 158–182.

[17] M. Schmidt et al., "Fedbench: A benchmark suite for federated semantic data query processing," in International Semantic Web Conference, 2011, pp. 585–600.

[18] M. Saleem, Q. Mehmood, and A.-C. N. Ngomo, "Feasible: A feature-based sparql benchmark generation framework," in International Semantic Web Conference, 2015, pp. 52–69.

[19] M. Saleem, A. Hasnain, and A.-C. N. Ngomo, "Largerdfbench: a billion triples benchmark for sparql endpoint federation," Journal of Web Semantics, vol. 48, 2018, pp. 85–125.

[20] L. Ma et al., "Towards a complete owl ontology benchmark," in European Semantic Web Conference, 2006, pp. 125–139.

[21] M. Schmidt, T. Hornung, G. Lausen, and C. Pinkel, "Sp^2bench: a sparql performance benchmark," in 2009 IEEE 25th International Conference on Data Engineering, 2009, pp. 222–233.

[22] M.-D. Pham, P. Boncz, and O. Erling, "S3g2: A scalable structure-correlated social graph generator," in Technology Conference on Performance Evaluation and Benchmarking, 2012, pp. 156–172.

[23] C. R. Rivero, A. Schultz, C. Bizer, and D. Ruiz Cortés, "Benchmarking the performance of linked data translation systems," in LDOW 2012: WWW2012 Workshop on Linked Data on the Web (2012), 2012.

[24] P. N. Mendes, H. Mühleisen, and C. Bizer, "Sieve: linked data quality assessment and fusion," in Proceedings of the 2012 Joint EDBT/ICDT Workshops, 2012, pp. 116–123.

[25] T. G. Armstrong, V. Ponnekanti, D. Borthakur, and M. Callaghan, "Linkbench: a database benchmark based on the facebook social graph," in Proceedings of the 2013 ACM SIGMOD International Conference on Management of Data, 2013, pp. 1185–1196.

[26] G. Aluç, O. Hartig, M. T. Özsu, and K. Daudjee, "Diversified stress testing of rdf data management systems," in International Semantic Web Conference, 2014, pp. 197–212.

[27] V. Kotsev et al., "Benchmarking rdf query engines: The ldbc semantic publishing benchmark," in BLINK@ ISWC, 2016, pp. 1–16.

[28] F. Conrads, J. Lehmann, M. Saleem, M. Morsey, and A.-C. N. Ngomo, "Iguana: a generic framework for benchmarking the read-write performance of triple stores," in International Semantic Web Conference, 2017, pp. 48–65.

[29] C. Bizer and A. Schultz, "Benchmarking the performance of storage systems that expose sparql endpoints," in Proc. 4 th International Workshop on Scalable Semantic Web Knowledge Base Systems (SSWS), 2008, p. 39.

[30] M. Morsey, J. Lehmann, S. Auer, and A.-C. N. Ngomo, "Dbpedia sparql benchmark–performance assessment with real queries on real data," in International semantic web conference, 2011, pp. 454–469.

[31] "DBpedia," retrieved 09. 2020. [Online]. Available: https://wiki.dbpedia.org/

[32] "Apache Jena," retrieved 09. 2020. [Online]. Available: https://jena.apache.org/documentation/query/index.html

Enabling System Artifacts Reuse Through the Semantic Representation of Engineering Models: a Case Study of Simulink Models

Roy Mendieta
The REUSE Company
Madrid, Spain
Email: roy.mendieta@reusecompany.com

Eduardo Cibrián
Computer Science and Engineering Department
Carlos III University of Madrid
Madrid, Spain
Email: ecibrian@inf.uc3m.es

Jose María Álvarez-Rodríguez
Computer Science and Engineering Department
Carlos III University of Madrid
Madrid, Spain
Email: joalvare@inf.uc3m.es

Juan Llorens
Computer Science and Engineering Department
Carlos III University of Madrid
Madrid, Spain
Email: llorens@inf.uc3m.es

***Abstract*—Currently, digital twins are being designed to provide a virtual version of complex physical systems. Modelling and simulation techniques and tools are used to design these engineering products embedding domain knowledge in many system artifacts available under different protocols, formats and meta-models. The cost of development of these virtual artifacts is usually very high implying the need of saving time and costs by means of increasing their reusability factor. A first step to ease the reuse relies on the ability of looking up a system artifact according to some input query. To do so, it is necessary to design a knowledge management strategy unifying the structure and representation of these artifacts and provide a search service that can exploit the indexed information. In this work, we propose a semantic model to represent system artifacts and demonstrate its application through a search service consuming simulation models (designed with the Matlab Simulink tool, a block diagram environment for multidomain simulation and Model-Based Design). Furthermore, an experiment has been conducted to show the precision and recall of this semantic search service.**

Keywords*–*information representation; physical system models; simulink; model reuse; knowledge reuse.

I. Introduction

Recently, we have seen the emergence of Model-based Systems Engineering (MBSE) as a complete methodology to address the challenge of unifying the techniques, methods and tools to support the whole specification process of a system (conceptual design, system requirements, design, analysis, verification or validation, etc.) around the application of models. In the context of the well-known Vee lifecycle model (a project management method focused on verification and validation activities early in the life cycle thereby enhancing the probability of building an error-free and good quality product [1]), it means that there is "formalized application of modeling" to support the left-hand side of this system life-cycle implying that any process, task or activity will generate different system artifacts, but all of them represented as models. This approach is considered a cornerstone for the improvement of the current practice in the Systems Engineering discipline since it is expected to cover multiple modeling domains, to provide better results in terms of quality and productivity, lower risks and, in general, to support the concept of continuous and collaborative engineering, easing the interaction and communication between people (engineers, project managers, quality managers, etc.).

Although MBSE represents a shifting paradigm for the development of critical systems, the plethora of engineering methods supported by different tools implies the need of not only easing the communication between people, but also considering its application to the universe of available tools. How could we do requirements management, simulation, diagramming, documenting, information retrieval or project management without the corresponding tools or Information Technologies (IT) systems? The more complex the problems are, the more complex computer tools must be delivered, and the main reason for that is, consequently, because those computer tools are demanded to be "smarter". Up to now, a computer tool is not human independent; it simply "acts" as smart according to its access to relevant data, information and knowledge. In order to enable a collaborative MBSE through IT systems, it is completely necessary to enable the possibility of communicating tools (interoperability) and reusing previous engineering designs saving costs and time.

In order to reuse the knowledge generated in Model-driven Engineering (MDE) methodologies, such as MBSE, it is necessary to understand the underlying concepts and relationships that allow us to make a semantic interpretation of the models. For example, in the automotive industry [2], modeling capabilities are applied to the whole engineering process, from the specification to the certification in a virtual twin environment. In the context of tool-chains for MDE, it is possible to find many suites, such as Matlab Simulink [3], that can be applied to different engineering activities: designing architectures (descriptive modeling), simulation (analytical modeling) or testing of digital systems.

However, no one size fits all, and engineering environments are usually integrating many different tools. This situation generates a good number of system artifacts that are part of a specific product or service. Reuse capabilities are therefore constrained by the possibility of linking every system artifact (traceability) and, then, being able to represent, search and customize those relevant system artifacts. In this manner, when a system artifact is selected for being reused (e.g., a component), it actually implies the necessity of bringing all connected system artifacts, such as requirements, test cases, logical models, etc. The reusability factor will depend on the capability of creating an underlying knowledge graph that can serve us to deliver services that require a holistic view of the system, such as change impact analysis, visualization or quality checking.

More specifically, in the context of model reuse, it is necessary to define a knowledge management strategy for reusing system artifacts. The use of semantics may help to improve the reusability factor of a system artifact by identifying similar artifacts through a comparison under a common and representation model. Model reuse still remains challenging due to the diversity of domains and information embedded in the models. Furthermore, engineering tools have not been designed to look up similar artifacts. The cost of reuse will mainly depend on the complexity of the entity to be reused [4] and, this implies, that an enriched representation may help to improve the first step to reuse: discoverability.

In order to build an underlying knowledge graph, there are works, such as Open Services for Lifecycle Collaboration (OSLC) Resource Shapes [5]–[7] or ISO Step meta-models, focusing on the description of artifact meta-data [8]. However, the representation of both artifact meta-data and contents is not fully addressed by a common representation model.

In this work, we aim to effectively reuse the knowledge embedded in Simulink models. The solution called Simulink2RSHP makes use of an ontology-based approach for indexing and retrieving information following a meta-model, Information Representation Model Based on Relationships (RSHP) [9]. Under this schema, both meta-data and contents are represented using a common domain vocabulary and taxonomy creating a property graph that can be exploited for system artifact discovery. To do so, a mapping between the Matlab Simulink meta-model [10] and the RSHP meta-model is defined to represent and serialize analytical models in a repository. Then, a retrieval process is implemented on top of this repository to allow users to perform text-based queries and look up similar artifacts. To validate the proposed solution, 38 Simulink models have been used and 20 real user queries have been designed to study the effectiveness, in terms or precision and recall, of the proposed solution [11] against the Matlab Simulink searching capabilities.

The paper is organized as follows: The related work is presented in Section II. Section III describes the background and defines the proposed solution for Simulink model reuse. Section IV describes the validation, while Section V summarizes the main conclusions and outlines some future research directions.

II. Related Work

Semantic representation of analytical models for retrieval purposes is the cornerstone of this work. In the case of models reuse, [12] presents a work to represent and retrieve Computer-Aided Design (CAD) by implementing a mapping function between the features of different CAD models. In [13], an ontology-based retrieval technique is introduced to perform a semantic similarity process between Unified Modeling Language (UML) class diagrams.

In the case of Simulink models, [14] describes a solution focused on design patterns to develop reusable model structures without considering semantic features. In [15], a tool for automatically identifying, classifying and formalizing submodel patterns in Simulink models is presented. This tool implements a retrieval process based on text-comparison.

Regarding RSHP applications for system artifact representation, some prior works can be found to reuse electric circuits designed in the Modelica language [16]. In [17], the authors also use a similar approach for SysML models where a mapping between the SysML meta-model and the RSHP meta-model is presented. Based on previous experiences, the RSHP meta-model fits to represent both meta-data and contents of different types of models. In the context of this work, Simulink models have been selected to test the feasibility of reusing analytical models applying the same principles of knowledge representation.

Unlike previous approaches, where reuse is based on specific features of the domain knowledge or where reuse is basically focused on text comparison, the proposed solution aims to improve the reuse of the embedded information in the Simulink models by providing: 1) A semantic representation of Simulink models using an existing meta-model like RSHP and 2) A retrieval process based on comparing the underlying graphs of a query against a repository of Simulink models.

III. Simulink2RSHP: Implementation of a tool for reuse Simulink models

A. *Background*

Since the first step to provide a reuse mechanism for Simulink models relies on the representation of information using the RSHP metamodel, the main building blocks of this framework are outlined here.

1) The RSHP metamodel: RSHP [9] is an information representation model based on defining concepts (artifacts) and relationships among them under specific semantics. It has been used for different types of information, such as textual, design models or source code using the same representation schema. The meta-model, as a class diagram, is presented in Figure 1 and it comprises the following elements:

- Artifact. An artifact is a knowledge container that can be represented through only Knowledge Elements or through other Artifacts.
- Knowledge Element. A Knowlege Element represents the occurrence of a Term. It is the smallest unit of knowledge.
- Term. A Term represents an element of the domain vocabulary (with some specific semantics, if defined).
- RSHP. An RSHP represents an n-array relationship between Artifacts.
- RSHP Semantics. It is the relationship type assigned to a relationship between two Artifacts.
- Meta-property. It is used to add meta-data to the Artifacts.

The RSHP meta-model has also been exposed as an OSLC Resource Shape. It can be serialized as Resource Description Framework (RDF) using the interface known as Open Services for Lifecycle Collaboration-Knowledge Manager (OSLC-KM) [5], which is a kind of flavor of OSLC as a result of the CRYSTAL European project [18].

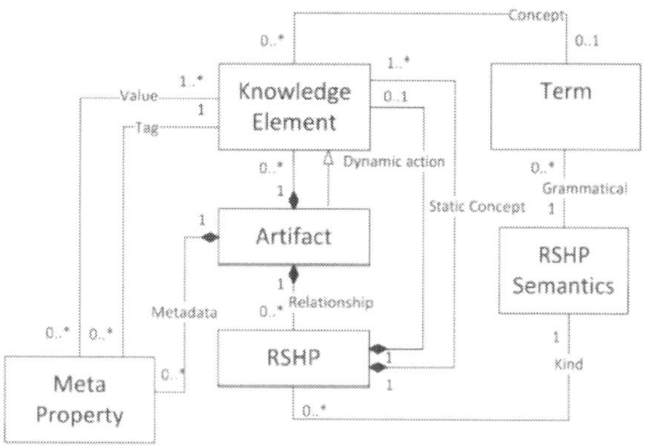

Figure 1. Metamodel of RSHP representation.

B. The RSHP reusability framework

The reuse semantic information needs to deal with a lot of factors that have to be considered in reuse techniques. Most frameworks are focused on specific types of information, such us software [19] restricting the knowledge manager capabilities.

One of the main objectives is to identify, classify, organize and represent Simulink models using semantics. To do so, the proposed solution applies a domain ontology to model such information and build a retrieval information process based not only on calculating the similarity of the underlying graphs between two artifacts.

The implementation of this approach makes use of a framework that supports semantic information indexing and retrieval, the CAKE API [20]. CAKE is an ontology-based framework that allows us to provide a technical solution exploiting a domain ontology to shift the representation of Simulink models from text-based (names of blocks, etc.) relationships to concept-based relationships. CAKE has a retrieve algorithm based on graph and pattern matching using two different levels: 1) Syntax/Structural; 2) Relationships/Semantic. In this manner, it is possible to enrich the domain language within the Simulink models to make a better interpretation of the embedded information. This mainly requires the mapping between the model and the domain ontology. CAKE uses the concept of ontology as a way to restrict concepts, which can be used to represent knowledge, as well as endow this vocabulary with syntactic, semantic and pragmatic information. Figure 2 shows how conceptual groupings are carried out in an aerospace domain, where the different models of aircraft (e.g., A350, A330) will be processed as a system. It is also shown an example of how knowledge is represented across the different layers within the CAKE-RSHP framework:

1) The controlled vocabulary layer refers to all terminology in a specific domain and it is the basis of the other layers.
2) Grouping terms by concepts allows us to add more semantics to the terminology and will be always restricted by the controlled vocabulary.
3) Thesaurus allows us to represent structure, for example a break down structure. Just as in previous stages thesaurus is restricted by the controlled vocabulary.

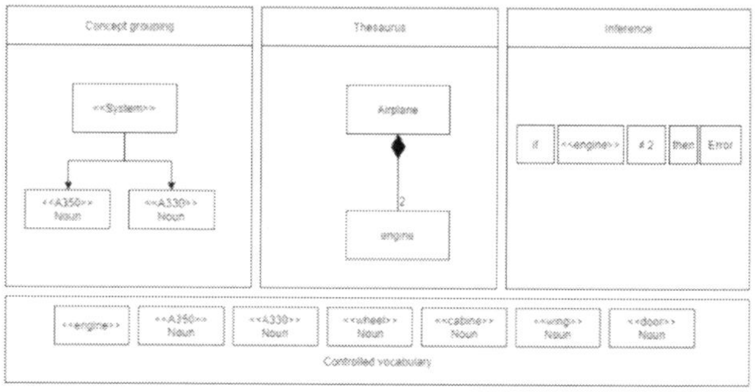

Figure 2. Example of the knowledge layers representation in RSHP.

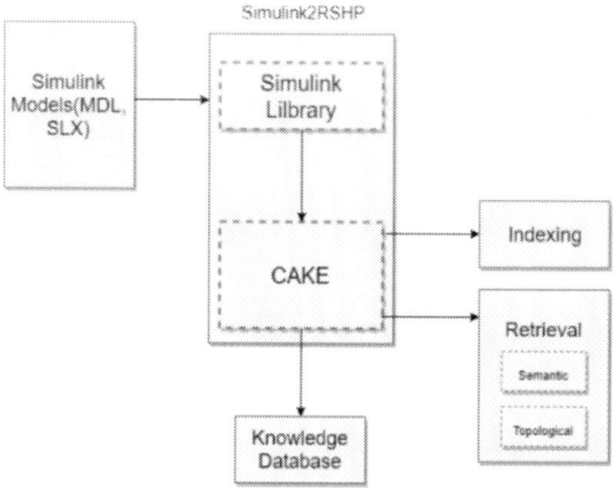

Figure 3. Conceptual architecture of the proposed solution (RSHP).

4) Inference layer allows to execute logic using terminology. This logic can be used to infer new knowledge, or to execute validation rules based on the domain knowledge. These rules can be also executed against any source of knowledge that is represented in RSHP using CAKE, for example logical models, physical models, even textual information.

C. Technological implementation

The proposed solution consists of an application developed in Visual Studio .Net 2019 with framework 4.8, which allows us to parse Simulink files using a Simulink software library for Java [21] and the integrated Keyboard/Video/Mouse (IKVM) to run Java code within the .NET framework, and to create a semantic representation of the Simulink models using the CAKE-RSHP model. As a consequence of using this framework, it is possible to use the built-in mechanisms already available for indexing and retrieving information. Figure 3 shows the architecture of the proposed solution, which consists of three main elements:

- Simulink2RSHP. This component groups Simulink Library and CAKE. Basically, it allows us to semi-automatically apply the mappings between the Simulink elements and the RSHP meta-model creating an underlying semantic graph based on the domain ontology, see Table I.
- Simulink Library. This component allows mapping the objects that are obtained from invoking the reading

TABLE I. EQUIVALENCE BETWEEN SIMULINK AND RSHP.

Simulink Element	RSHP Element
Model	Artifact
Block	Artifact
Block Type	Artifact Type
Block Name	Artifact Name, noun term
Block Properties	Metaproperties
Line	RSHP

processes of the Simulink library. Once the information is obtained from the files, it is represented using the CAKE API.

- CAKE. Once the information is represented in the RSHP language, it is possible to use the built-in capabilities for information retrieval and indexing. The CAKE API internally implements a pattern matching algorithm between graphs that returns a value of similarity.

A detailed explanation of the mapping between Simulink elements and the RSHP metamodel is provided in Table I.

- The global Simulink model is represented as a RSHP Artifact of type Simulink Model. This artifact contains meta-data, such as model image, creation date, modification date and any other additional description.
- Each block is represented as an Artifact and the properties of the blocks become RSHP Metaproperties of the artifact. It is important to mention that RSHP and Simulink are very compatible since Simulink blocks contain typology that is represented as the Artifact Type of each block artifact. There are cases where the blocks have names or descriptions. These are represented as the name and description attributes of the artifact.
- Simulink models, unlike SysML, have a single type of relation which is the line. This element is represented in RSPH as a relationship of type "Line".
- In cases where Simulink blocks have names, these names are represented as terms with a syntactic tag of type "Noun". This also adds more semantic information to the components.

Finally, CAKE also gives us the possibility of grouping the terminology in semantic clusters, which allow adding context to the representation language. In the case of experimentation (see Section IV), no groupings of terms were made.

IV. Case Study: Indexing and Retrieving Simulink Models

To illustrate the approach for reusing Simulink models, a case study of indexing and retrieving Simulink models has been conducted.

A. Research design

The experiment to evaluate the advantages of a semantic representation of Simulink models has been designed as follows:

1) Define a dataset of Simulink models from the public website repository of MathWorks [22]. General, automotive models and aerospace models have been downloaded to test different domains. This dataset comprises 38 physical models (21 general models, 9 automotive and 8 aerospace) that have been indexed.
2) Define a dataset of queries to evaluate the retrieval capabilities of the proposed solution. Each query has been designed with different common components of models to return a set of Simulink schemes [23]. These queries have also been indexed, see Table II.
3) Execute the experiment. For each query defined in the previous step, analyze the models retrieved by Simulink2RSHP taking into account all the semantic information represented into the dataset.
4) Analyze the results and validate them using the schema proposed in [24]. Extract measures of: 1) precision (fraction of retrieved information that is relevant); 2) recall (fraction of relevant information that is retrieved), and 3) a combination between the last two measures, the F1 score.

TABLE II. LIST OF QUERIES EXECUTED TO RETRIEVE SIMILAR MODELS.

Q	Query Description
Q_1	Signal connected to a memory and sum block
Q_2	Clock connected with logical operator
Q_3	Vertical channel
Q_4	Sensor
Q_5	Clock connected to an output
Q_6	Logical operator connected to other logical opperator
Q_7	Integrator connected to a Gain connected to a sum
Q_8	Integrator connected to a gravity component
Q_9	Gain connected to a product connected to another product
Q_{10}	Integrator connected to a signum block
Q_{11}	Clock connected to a relational operator connected to a constant
Q_{12}	Step
Q_{13}	Input connected to a Mux
Q_{14}	Input connected to a Function
Q_{15}	Costant connected to a switch
Q_{16}	Signum block connected to a transfer function
Q_{17}	Scope connected to an integrator connected to a Gain
Q_{18}	Signum connected to a product
Q_{19}	Ram
Q_{20}	Relay

B. Analysis of results

The analysis of results is based on the levels of "goodness" (see Table III) established in [25]. Table IV shows the metrics of precision, recall and F1 for each input query. It was found that 10% of queries are at an acceptable level of "goodness" for precision and 5% for recall. 10% of queries obtained a good level for precision metric and 5% for recall. In the same manner, 70% of the queries obtained an excellent level for both precision and recall metrics. Finally, just 10% of the queries obtained a value of precision below acceptable and, in the case of recall, just 20% of the queries, because the queries had components with incomplete semantic information (e.g., no name, no description).

TABLE III. GOODNESS LEVELS FOR PRECISION AND RECALL METRICS [25].

Level of "goodness"	Precision	Recall
Acceptable	≥20%	≥60%
Good	≥30%	≥70%
Excellent	≥50%	≥80%

TABLE IV. PRECISION, RECALL AND F1 METRICS FOR EACH QUERY.

	Precision	Recall	F1
Q_1	0.2857	0.6667	0.4000
Q_2	0.3333	1.0000	0.5000
Q_3	1.0000	1.0000	1.0000
Q_4	0.2000	0.3333	0.2500
Q_5	0.6250	0.8333	0.7143
Q_6	0.5000	0.5000	0.5000
Q_7	1.0000	1.0000	1.0000
Q_8	0.7500	0.8571	0.8000
Q_9	1.0000	0.9000	0.9474
Q_{10}	1.0000	0.9000	0.9474
Q_{11}	0.8000	1.0000	0.8888
Q_{12}	0.0000	0.0000	0.0000
Q_{13}	0.9412	0.9412	0.9412
Q_{14}	1.0000	1.0000	1.0000
Q_{15}	0.5000	1.0000	0.6667
Q_{16}	0.5000	1.0000	0.6667
Q_{17}	0.6667	1.0000	0.8000
Q_{18}	0.3333	0.7500	0.4615
Q_{19}	1.0000	1.0000	1.0000
Q_{20}	0.0000	0.0000	0.0000
Avg	**0.6218**	**0.7841**	**0.6742**

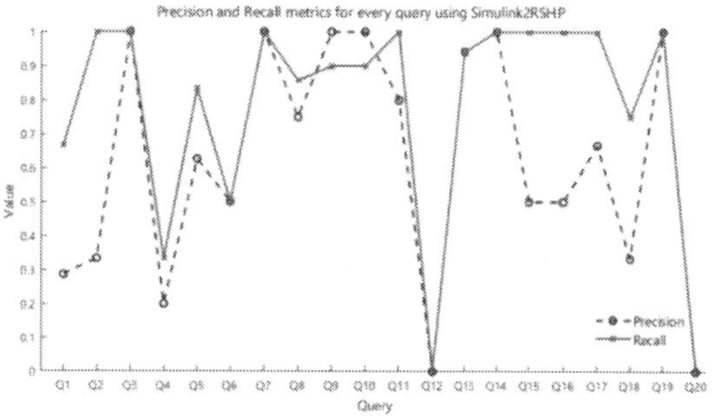

Figure 4. Precision and Recall metrics results obtained for the proposed solution.

The global average of the metrics was excellent for precision and good for recall, since they are above 60% and 70% respectively, as Figure 4 depicts. This is likely due to the fact that the degree of similarity between the input queries and the dataset of models was calculated using semantic and topological algorithms, since the more information available in the Simulink blocks, such as names and descriptions, the more accurate the results.

However, it was also determined the need to consider within the similarity algorithm more specific aspects of Simulink blocks. For example, in cases such as logical operator blocks, the algorithm assumes a similarity between these blocks regardless of the type of operator. In other words, for the algorithm there was a similarity between the logical operators AND and OR, regardless of whether they are semantically different.

This could be improved using semantic clusters and a controlled vocabulary, to differentiate this type of aspects, and consider more information when determining the similarity of the components. These capabilities are also available in the CAKE API, but in order to refine the algorithm it is necessary to spend more time populating the domain ontology. In general, it implies the creation of more specific terminology, thesaurus and semantic clusters for specific Simulink components.

C. Research limitations

One of the main limitations in the research lies in the size of the repository where the queries were made. To carry out more accurate test cases, it would be necessary to have a larger set of Simulink models. Furthermore, a more specific domain ontology for physical models would be necessary to take advantage of other CAKE API capabilities, adjusting the semantic representation to the matching algorithm.

Additionally, the creation of the queries was carried out by randomly selecting components presented in the sample models. A more robust experiment would require the study of each model and the behavior of users to create a more realistic dataset of queries.

V. CONCLUSIONS AND FUTURE WORK

Despite the importance of the reuse of physical models and the existing alternatives for reusing components and models, the existing MBD tools lack advanced retrieval mechanisms. Although these tools have not been designed for this purpose, the reuse mechanisms are a bit naive and, in most of the cases, a mere search query based on some keywords seems too simple to really exploit the information embedded in the models.

In this work, we have used a Simulink API to propose a process of semantic interpretation of models and have developed Simulink2RSHP which performs the mapping between elements of Simulink models and CAKE components. The Simulink2RSHP approach seems to be a promising alternative, considering that unlike many of the retrieval tools that perform text searches, it determines the similarity using a combination of semantic and topological algorithms. The results obtained in the experimentation demonstrate the feasibility of the approach. It is possible to build indexing and retrieval engines for physical models using a semantic representation.

As future work, improvements in the representation of system artifacts are planned, including terminology, thesaurus and semantic clusters. Other types of models will also be included in the experimentation, such as those supported in the Modelica language. In terms of experimentation, this small setting is representative to demonstrate the feasibility of the approach. However, larger settings including real user needs are completely required to provide a more significant and realistic validation.

ACKNOWLEDGMENT

The research leading to these results has received funding from the project H2020-ECSEL Arrowhead Tools under grant agreement n° 826452 and from specific national programs and/or funding authorities.

REFERENCES

[1] K. Forsberg, H. Mooz, and H. Cotterman, Visualizing project management: models and frameworks for mastering complex systems, J. Wiley and N. Y. Sons, Eds. John Wiley & Sons, 2005, ISBN: 0-978-0-471-64848-2.

[2] B. Schätz, S. Voss, and S. Zverlov, "Automating design-space exploration: Optimal deployment of automotive sw-components in an iso26262 context," in Proceedings of the 52nd Annual Design Automation Conference, ser. DAC '15. New York, NY, USA: Association for Computing Machinery, 2015, pp. 1–6. [Online]. Available: https://doi.org/10.1145/2744769.2747912

[3] Mathworks Inc. Simulink, "Homepage," URL: http://www.mathworks.com/products/simulink [Last accessed: 2020-09-03].

[4] G. Beydoun, A. Hoffmann, R. V. Garcia, J. Shen, and A. Gill, "Towards an assessment framework of reuse: a knowledge-level analysis approach," Complex & Intelligent Systems, vol. 6, no. 1, Apr. 2020, pp. 87–95. [Online]. Available: http://link.springer.com/10.1007/s40747-019-0116-1 [accessed: 2020-04-23]

[5] J. M. Álvarez Rodríguez, R. Mendieta, J. L. de la Vara, A. Fraga, and J. L. Morillo, "Enabling system artefact exchange and selection through a linked data layer," J. UCS, vol. 24, 2018, pp. 1536–1560.

[6] J. M. Álvarez Rodríguez, R. M. Zuñiga, and J. Llorens, "Elevating the meaning of data and operations within the development lifecycle through an interoperable toolchain," in INCOSE International Symposium, vol. 29, no. 1. Wiley Online Library, 2019, pp. 1053–1071.

[7] J. M. Álvarez Rodríguez, J. Llorens, M. Alejandres, and J. M. Fuentes, "Oslc-km: A knowledge management specification for oslc-based resources," in INCOSE International Symposium, vol. 25, no. 1. Wiley Online Library, 2015, pp. 16–34.

[8] P. Atzeni, L. Bellomarini, P. Papotti, and R. Torlone, "Meta-mappings for schema mapping reuse," Proc. VLDB Endow., vol. 12, no. 5, Jan. 2019, pp. 557–569. [Online]. Available: https://doi.org/10.14778/3303753.3303761

[9] J. Llorens, J. Morato, and G. Genova, RSHP: an information representation model based on relationships. Berlin, Heidelberg: Springer Berlin Heidelberg, 2004, pp. 221–253.

[10] Mathworks Inc. Simulink, "Documentation," URL: https://es.mathworks.com/help/simulink/ [Last accessed: 2020-09-05].

[11] W. B. Croft, D. Metzler, and T. Strohman, Search engines: Information retrieval in practice. Addison-Wesley Reading, 2010, vol. 520.

[12] B. Huang, S. Zhang, R. Huang, X. Li, and Y. Zhang, "An effective retrieval approach of 3d cad models for macro process reuse," The International Journal of Advanced Manufacturing Technology, vol. 102, no. 5, 2019, pp. 1067–1089.

[13] K. Robles, A. Fraga, J. Morato, and J. Llorens, "Towards an ontology-based retrieval of uml class diagrams," Information and Software Technology, vol. 54, no. 1, 2012, pp. 72–86.

[14] M. W. Whalen, A. Murugesan, S. Rayadurgam, and M. P. E. Heimdahl, "Structuring simulink models for verification and reuse," in Proceedings of the 6th International Workshop on Modeling in Software Engineering - MiSE 2014. Hyderabad, India: ACM Press, 2014, pp. 19–24. [Online]. Available: http://dl.acm.org/citation.cfm?doid=2593770.2593776

[15] J. Cordy, "Submodel pattern extraction for simulink models," ser. SPLC '13. ACM, 2013, pp. 7–10.

[16] E. Gallego, J. M. Álvarez Rodríguez, and J. Llorens, "Reuse of physical system models by means of semantic knowledge representation: A case study applied to modelica," Sep. 2015, pp. 747–757.

[17] R. Mendieta, J. L. de la Vara, J. L. Morillo, and J. M. Álvarez-Rodríguez, "Towards effective sysml model reuse," in MODELSWARD, 2017, pp. 536–541.

[18] n. . U. CRYSTAL, title = (Critical System Engineering Acceleration.

[19] T. Xin and L. Yang, "A framework of software reusing engineering management," in 2017 IEEE 15th International Conference on Software Engineering Research, Management and Applications (SERA), 2017, pp. 277–282.

[20] A. Rodrigues, "Tools Exhibits. In UML Modeling Languages and Applications," 2005, pp. 281–291.

[21] CQSE, "Simulink Library," URL: https://www.cqse.eu/en/products/simulink-library-for-java/overview/, [accessed: 2020-05-04].

[22] MathWorks, "Simulink - Examples," URL: https://es.mathworks.com/help/simulink/examples.html [accessed: 2020-09-04].

[23] Roymendieta, "SEMAPRO 2020 30010," URL: https://github.com/roymendieta/trc-research.github.io/tree/patch-1/SEMAPRO_2020_30010 [accessed: 2020-09-08].

[24] N. Juristo and A. M. Moreno, Basics of software engineering experimentation. Springer Science & Business Media, 2013.

[25] J. H. Hayes, A. Dekhtyar, and S. K. Sundaram, "Improving after-the-fact tracing and mapping: Supporting software quality predictions," IEEE software, vol. 22, no. 6, 2005, pp. 30–37.

Properties of Semantic Coherence Measures - Case of Topic Models

Pirkko Pietiläinen

University of Oulu
Oulu, Finland
Email: pirkkoptlnn@gmail.com

Abstract—**Measures of semantic relatedness and coherence are used in several Artificial Intelligence (AI) applications. Topic models is one of the fields where these measures have a role. In evaluating topic models, it is important to know well the properties of the used measure or measures. In this paper, it is first shown how 16 proposed coherence measures behave in finding the highest coherence in Latent Dirichlet Allocation (LDA) processing. With the collected exceptionally large corpus data from Wikipedia, it was then determined the correlations of the measures and the number of topics in LDA. From the average behavior of the measures, it is possible to conclude the range where the maximum values of coherence probably occur. Approximation of the size of a corpus giving statistically significant results in these respects is possible. Comparisons to human ratings are also included. The data and the R-codes for the calculations are made public. This paper explains many of the features affecting the use of coherence measures, including the roles of corpus/sample size, number of topics and the existence of local maxima of the measures. Differences of the measures and their correlations are also described.**

***Keywords*–Measuring Topic Coherence; LDA; Wikipedia; WordNet; Palmetto.**

I. Introduction

Topic models are used in a wide range of Natural Language Processing (NLP) applications. Examples of application fields where they have been found useful include information retrieval [1], classification [2], content analysis [3], data mining [4], sentiment analysis [1], social media analysis [5] and word sense induction [6].

The evaluation of the quality of topics and the quality of the whole model can be done using direct methods, e.g., coherence metrics, or indirect methods where the quality is observed after a task performed with produced topics, e.g., measuring classification accuracy variance when done with different topic models. Only the direct methods are examined here.

Coherence measures are based on the idea that the more relatedness there is in a topic, the more coherent the topic is. Relatedness can be, e.g., semantic or based on co-occurrences of the topic words in a reference corpus, or the measures can be combinations of different aspects of coherence quantification.

Aletras and Stevenson [7] investigate the correlation between several coherence measures and ratings given by human evaluators and find out that Normalized Point Mutual Information (NPMI) coherence measure gives the best correlation in a number of tasks. Lau et al. [8] conclude that especially cosine-measure as well as Jaccard and Dice-measures outperform the NPMI-measure, because they receive higher correlations with human ratings in several experiments. A coherence measure based on calculation of word statistics was proposed by Mimno et al. [9] and Wikipedia was used as the corpus in the studies by Newman et al. [10], where they found that measures using word co-occurrence statistics perform better than WordNet-based methods. Röder et al. [11] developed a set of coherence measures and tested them against human ratings.

Stevens et al. [12] studied topic coherence over many models and with large number of topics. They used coherence measures known as UCI and UMass measures to evaluate the models. Of the models studied, they concluded that each has its own strengths; LDA was one of the models studied.

Given these mixed results, the present study was designed to examine coherence measures more closely. The research question is: What can be learned from a large scale study of semantic topic coherence measures to guide their usage and explain the present mixed results? Recently developed new measures designed for exactly this purpose were included along with old ones, which has been widely used. So, altogether, 16 semantic coherence measures and their role in topic modeling were selected to be included to this study.

To produce the topics studied, a method among latest improved LDA model [13] [14] was selected. Because the number of topics is an important parameter in performance optimization of a topic model, the topics studied were produced with an exceptionally wide range of number of topics.The study consists of 16 coherence measures, most of which are widely used.

The main contribution of this paper is the description of the behavior of the selected coherence measures in an enhanced LDA topic learning. This is done using exceptionally large data from Wikipedia, where an approximation of the corpus size needed to perform statistically significant experiments can be given. In order to investigate the relation of the number of topics, k, to the coherence measurement results, our experiments cover a wide range of k-values. Average coherence curves of the measures are presented and the consequences discussed. In addition to the maximum coherence, the closest local maxima are examined as well. The same extensive data is also used to determine the correlations between all the measures and their correlation with the number of topics. Human ratings of the coherence measures are also presented. Finally, some recommendations to the users of topic models and coherence measures are made.

The structure of the paper is such that the topic model used is introduced in Section II, and then the ways to measure coherence are presented in Section III. Experiments are described in Section IV and after that the results of our experiments are listed in Section V. Correlations with human ratings are reported in Section VI, and in the final Section VII conclusions are drawn and what remains to be studied is discussed.

II. Latent Dirichlet Allocation

Unsupervised learning methods can be used to find latent topics from text corpora. One of the most used is LDA [15] and its many variants. The latest developments in topic models include incorporating to the models word vector representations trained on very large corpora. Instead of using only the words in the documents, the semantically related words from the corresponding word vectors are imported to the LDA process.

A topic model called Latent Feature LDA (LF-LDA) developed by Nguyen et al. [14] shows significant improvements on topic coherences when external word vectors are incorporated. Improvements can also be seen in classification and clustering tasks. For these reasons, the LF-LDA model by Nguyen et al. [14] is used in the present study.

Our preliminary experiments showed that in terms of coherence it is more feasible to use similar corpora as both training and actual corpus. For example, using word vectors trained on Google News [16] with Wikipedia corpus produces topics having lower coherences than when Wikipedia has been used as the training corpus as well. So, throughout the experiments of this paper, GloVe (Global Vectors) [17] word representations, which are pre-trained on Wikipedia, were chosen to be used.

III. Measuring coherence

Topic coherence measures can be divided to two groups according to whether they are planned specially for measuring topic coherence, or adapting to this purpose measures developed for other purposes. The first type of measures are the set of coherence measures recently proposed by Röder et al. [11]. They are described in the Subsection B called Palmetto-measures.

The more a topic word set contains words, that are semantically related with each other, the more interpretable and coherent the topic is. With this in mind, measures of semantic relatedness available in WordNet [18], are used here as well and the expression (1) is applied.

Topic coherence is usually defined as the average similarity of each word pair in a set of top-n most probable words produced by the topic model in use. Coherence C is usually calculated with the expression, see, e.g., [7]

$$C = \frac{\sum_{i=1}^{n-1} \sum_{j=i+1}^{n} f(w_i, w_j)}{\binom{n}{2}} \tag{1}$$

Here $\{w_1, w_2, ...w_n\}$ are the topic words, and f are measures of semantic relatedness, like measures in Section III-A.

In this paper, the value of the number of topics k, for which the average coherence between topic words is highest, is called the optimal or best number of topics.

A. *WordNet-based relatedness measures*

Topics are considered coherent when their most probable words are semantically related. For this reason, the measures of semantic relatedness have also been used as coherence measures. WordNet [18] is a central resource in lexical semantics. By using WordNet it is possible to measure semantic similarity and relatedness between two concepts [19]. Ten measures have been developed, which use WordNet as their central resource, and therefore they are called WordNet-based measures. Six of these measure similarity and four of them measure the more general relatedness.

Similarity measures in WordNet are based on the hierarchy of concepts, and half of them quantify the similarity of two concepts using the most specific common ancestor of the pair of concepts, namely Jiang and Conrath (JCn) [20], Lin [21], and Resnik [22]. The rest of the similarity measures are based on the lengths of the paths between two concepts. They have been developed by Wu and Palmer (WuP) [23], Rada et al. (Path) [24], and Leacock and Chodorow (LCh) [25].

The four measures of relatedness are: Hirst and StOnge (HsO) [26], Lesk [27], and two vector measures [19]. The first one, Hirst and StOnge, makes use of the path direction and length between the concepts. The vector measures and Lesk measure calculate the relatedness using the definition texts of the concepts.

All ten WordNet-measures were used in this study, namely measures of HsO, LCh, Lesk, WuP, Resnik, JCn, Lin, Path, vec_p and vec. The first eight were obtained using the WS4J-package (WordNet Similarity for Java) [28] version 1.0.1 . Measures vec and vec_p [29] were from WordNet::Similarity [19].

B. *Palmetto-measures*

Unlike the Wordnet-based measures, a set of new measures was developed especially for topic coherence purposes by Röder et al. [11]. They first studied all the ways how to quantify coherence. Out of these quantifications they made a large number of combinations, and then investigated which ones correlated best with human ratings.

The ways of quantifications were: a) how to evaluate permutations of the top probable topic words. b) ways of computing probabilities of single words as well as joint probabilities of word pairs in an external reference corpus, and the size of sliding window was one parameter here, c) probabilistic confirmation measurement applied to quantifications a) and b), and finally, d) a huge number of combinations resulting from the former phases are combined to one single coherence measure. These measures were tested against several human rating data sets, and the best measure is called C_V and the second best is called C_P.

Measure C_V combines the indirect cosine measure with NPMI and with a sliding window size of 110 words. The second best, C_P combines Fitelson's [30] confirmation measure with a sliding window of 70 words. Four other previously proposed coherence measures were described and tested against human ratings in the same framework as the new ones. They are in the order of human test results: C_{NPMI}, C_A both proposed by Aletras [8], C_{UCI} proposed by Newman [10] and C_{UMass} was proposed by Mimno [9]. C_{NPMI} uses a window size of 5 words and C_{UCI} has window size of 10 words. As an external reference corpus, the English Wikipedia is always used.

Röder et al. [11] have made available both Java software and web-service possibilities to calculate six Palmetto-measures and all of these six measures are used in this study.

IV. Experiments

To discover latent topics from corpora, LF-LDA [14] latent model is used. It differs from ordinary latent models in that it is improved by incorporating word vector representations or embeddings [17] to the model. The LDA [15] model has two hyper parameters, which are kept constant in all of these experiments: $\alpha = 50/k$ where k is the number of topics, and $\beta = 0.01$ following, e.g., Fang [31]. The mixture weight λ was set to 1.0, because it is one of the values often used in this type of connections - $\lambda = 0.6$ is also frequently used. The number of the most probable topical words was always 10. The number of topics k varied from 4 to 200, and sparse points between 250 and 600. Note, that in all of these experiments, LF-LDA is the only part with randomness in addition to random selection of Wikipedia samples.

As pre-trained vector representations, the 50-dimensional `vectors.6B.50d.txt` from the GloVe-project trained on 6 billion token corpus containing a Wikipedia 2014 dump with 1.6 billion tokens and Gigaword5 repository [17] were used. More details, e.g., information on available versions, can be found on the GloVe-project's web site [17].

Four consecutive, equal-sized samples from a 2010 Wikipedia corpus [32] were extracted. This corpus contains the raw text of the articles in the English part of the Wikipedia, only shorter than 2000 character long documents, links and navigation texts and other irrelevant material removed. Note that the vocabulary of a 2010 Wikipedia is a subset of the vocabulary of a 2014 Wikipedia, not the other way around. Stop-words and the words that were not included in the used GloVe-vectors (on the average 6.5 % of the remaining words) were removed. No lemmatization was performed, so that the corpus remained closer to the natural language. The starting point of the first sample was randomly selected. Then, 20% and 10% samples from those four original samples were extracted in order to get information on the effect of sample size. The properties of the twelve samples are given in Table I. To

TABLE I. PROPERTIES OF THE TWELVE CORPORA EXTRACTED FROM WIKIPEDIA.

sample size	documents	words	vocabulary size	names of the corpora
	$4 * 10^4$	10^7	$1.7 * 10^5$	**A,B,C,D**
20%	$8 * 10^3$	$2 * 10^6$	$8 * 10^4$	**A20,B20,C20,D20**
10%	$4 * 10^3$	10^6	$6 * 10^4$	**A10,B10,C10,D10**

demonstrate that topics of neighboring k-values, here $k = 6$ and $k = 7$, can be very similar, they are presented in Figures 1 and 2. This feature has consequences on the results, as can be seen later.

Topic0: son century father ancient god king great family name daughter
Topic1: album band song music series film released video featured movie
Topic2: education university law national state public government elected council college
Topic3: system type engine systems can using use used standard structure
Topic4: war army forces force navy naval british troops military fleet
Topic5: park located road area league county south city railway club

Figure 1. An example set of six topics. The words of each topic are permuted pairwise and 16 measures are obtained for each pair.

The words of each topic are permuted pairwise and 16 measures are obtained for each pair. The topic group averages for these 16 measures are calculated. The example set of six topics of corpus **A**, $k = 6$, in Figure 1 is present also on the first, second and third row of Table IV, meaning that this set has the highest coherence when the measures Lin and C_{UMass} are applied, the second highest when measured by Resnik and the third highest value when measures Wup and JCn are applied.

Topic0: education university law research school social college students national based
Topic1: album band music song film released series songs featured video
Topic2: located area railway park river town county city north near
Topic3: war army force military forces british united states december union
Topic4: season league championship games team cup championships football champion game
Topic5: son father god king daughter her emperor mother his lord
Topic6: engine type system using can systems used use surface design

Figure 2. A set of seven topics, $k = 7$, corpus **A**, has also one of the highest coherences.

Because the topics are almost the same in Figures 1 and 2, the example set of Figure 2 can also be found in Table IV. It has the highest coherence when the measures JCn and C_V are applied, the second highest with WuP and Lin, and the third highest with Resnik. White areas of Table IV indicate that k-values co-occur within a corpus. The underlined k-values occur in both groups of measures: WordNet-based (on the left) and Palmetto-measures (on the right), and colored areas have no co-occurrences.

V. Results

At first, it is important to look at examples of the semantic coherence measures considered here. Normalization to one is used with all the measures so that it is possible to make comparisons between them, because this type of normalization preserves the proportional relationships of the data. It is done by dividing each data value by the sum of the data values of the same object. As an example, for k=[4,600] the values of the measure LCh ranges from 1.3345959 to 1.5078795 and those of Path from 0.109415 to 0.14231707. When they are normalized by dividing all LCh values by the sum of all values between k=[4,600], which is 296.99, and doing the same to the Path measure respectively with the sum of Path values 26.79, the ranges take the values from 0.0044936978 to 0.0050771585 (LCh) and from 0.0040834493 to 0.005311379 (Path).

The normalized values of measures LCh and Path, when k=[4,600], are presented in Figure 3. It can be seen that both measures have many local maxima close to the maximum coherence value. This means that there are several almost as optimal number of topics, whose coherence values differ only a little. This property is repeated in all of the studied semantic coherence measures, both WordNet- (Figure 3) and Palmetto-measures (Figure 4).

The example of LCh and Path in Figure 3 is important in another aspect, too. They can be seen to find their maxima at the same k-values. That happens because LCh and Path have very similar functional shape in the areas in question. So, the two measures, for which the theoretically predicted behavior is similar, really exhibit similar behavior in our experiments. That is an indication of reliability of the present approach, meaning that the predicted behavior is not disturbed by any part of our data processing. Because of the existence of

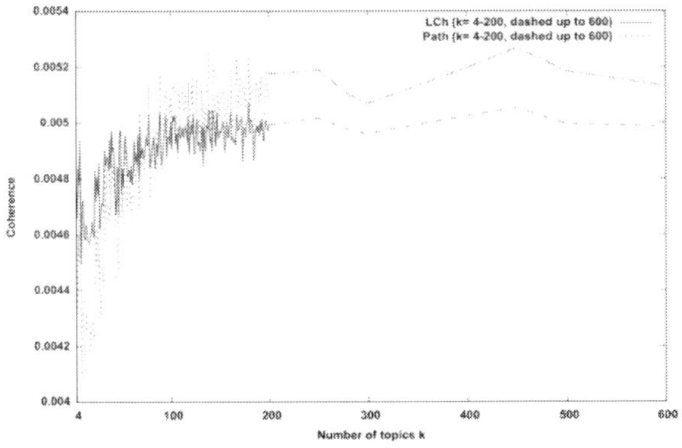

Figure 3. LCh and Path, both normalized to one, and as a function of Number of topics k in corpus **A.**

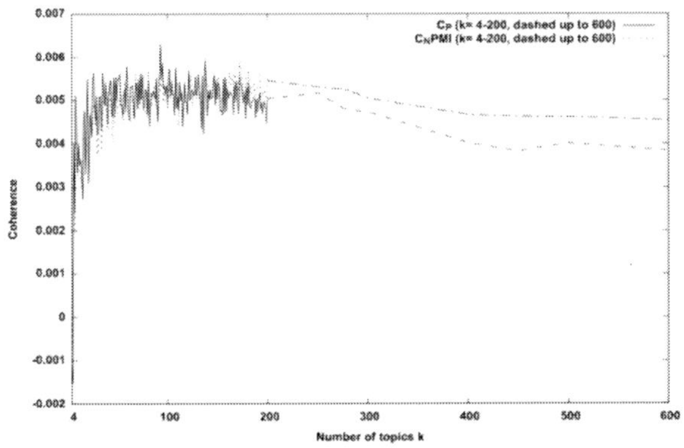

Figure 4. C_{P} and C_{NPMI}, both normalized to one, and as a function of Number of topics k in corpus **A.**

the many close local maxima in Table IV (see last page of this document) not only the maximum found by each measure but three highest coherence values of each measure are considered. Good examples supporting this decision are rows A10 columns C_{NPMI} and C_{UCI} in Table IV, where the three highest coherences are located at k = 51, 88, and 120 in this order for C_{NPMI}, but only the order differs from C_{UCI}. Six measures having most white areas in Table IV are listed in

TABLE II. SIX HIGHEST PERCENTAGES OF CO-OCCURRING NUMBER OF TOPICS k ON THREE TOPMOST COHERENCE VALUES IN TABLE IV.

C_{NPMI}	Lch	Path	Resnik	Lin	C_{UCI}
94%	92%	89%	89%	86%	81 %

Table II. These figures tell us that, e.g., 94% of top-3 k-values of measure C_{NPMI} occur also in some other measure's set of top-3 k-values.

A. Averages

First, the properties of the average behavior of the measures are presented.

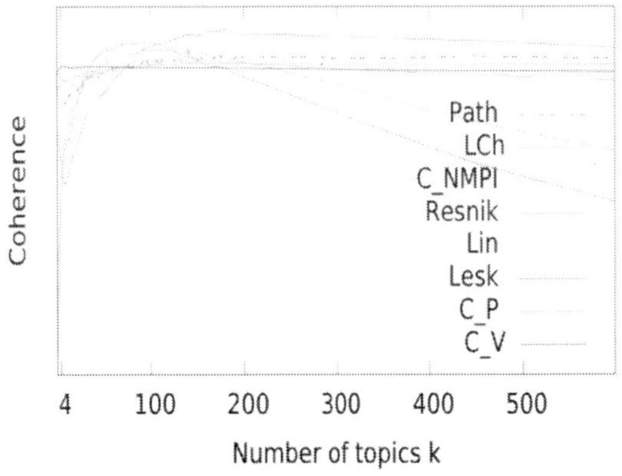

Figure 5. Averages over all twelve corpora of normalized C_{NPMI}, LCh, Path, Resnik, Lin, Lesk, C_{V} and C_{P} -measures.

Many typical properties of the semantic coherence measures are depicted in Figure 5. First, it can be noted that while there are similarities, there are big differences in the way they behave in the very low part in the k-axis. After about k=10, the curves show same type of behavior until after about k=100 their ways apart. Some seem to decrease, the others do not. The measures selected to Figure 5 are due to their appearance in Table II and Figure 6. In the light of this study, it is possible that the optimal number of topics can be found in the area of k = several hundreds.

B. Correlations

A good way of finding differences and similarities between the coherence measures is to examine their correlations with each other. A histogram of all statistically significant correlations between the semantic coherence measures is depicted in Figure 6. Note that the data is of general nature and includes an exceptionally large sample of word pairs. The data consists of N compared word pairs

$$N = \binom{10}{2} \sum_{k=4}^{K} k = 1\ 045\ 080, \qquad (2)$$

where $K = [200, 250, 280, 300, 400, 450, 500, 600]$. There are over one million measurements of similarity of word pairs for each corpus **A** – **D20**. To our knowledge, there is no other so large data collection used in finding the correlations of the semantic similarity measures.

The highest correlations, 0.97, occur between Path and LCh and between C_{NPMI} and C_{UCI}. These four measures are present also in Table II. The second best correlation 0.90 is found between C_{NPMI} and C_{P}. C_{P} does not appear in Table II, but is the third in Palmetto group with 61% of co-occurrences, or white areas in Table IV. Path is again participating with Lesk in the next highest correlation 0.86.

All correlation calculations with the tests of statistical significance are included in the additional material [33]. Both original data and the R-code for producing information in Figure 6 are included.

C. The effect of corpus size

The most surprising result was that there is so little statistically significant differences between variables in 100% corpus size and the smaller 20% or 10% sized, see Table I, corpora. The following properties against the corpus size were tested:

- **correlations between the sixteen measures**
  There is no significant difference of means of correlations between the groups of 100%, 20% and 10%.
- **average of three optimal number of topics in Table IV.**
  The biggest corpus has the highest average of the optimal number of topics 91.9 not differing from the next 20% sample significantly ($p = 0.07388$), where the average was 79.5. The smallest sample had the average 71.3, which does not differ significantly from the 20% but differs significantly ($p = 0.00263$) from the 100% group.
- **average co-occurrences of three optimal number of topics in Table IV.**
  The mean co-occurrence percentages were 60.9, 68.3 and 64.5, respectively, in the 100%, 20% and 10% groups, and there is no statistically significant difference between the groups.
- **WordNet- and Palmetto-measures as two separate groups.**
  The results are included in the next Section V-D.

D. Differences between WordNet- and Palmetto-measures

Co-occurrences in Table IV between WordNet- and Palmetto-measures do not have statistically significant differences, as WordNet-measures have on the average 67% co-occurences of the best three number of topics, and Palmetto-measures 60%, respectively. On the contrary, the means of three best number of topics of WordNet- and Palmetto- groups differ highly significantly ($p << 0.0001$).

There is only one highly significant correlation between any WordNet- and Palmetto-measures, namely between HsO and C_{UCI} with 0.57 correlation, as can be seen in Figure 6. That is also the highest correlation between WordNet- and Palmetto-measures. The correlations within each group are much higher. It is also noteworthy in Figure 6 that none of the Palmetto-measures have any correlation with the number of topics, whereas some of the WordNet-measures have relatively high correlations with the number of topics k. The effect of corpus size is also different in these groups. On the whole, when both types of measures are evaluated together, there is no difference of correlations between corpus sizes. The same is true with Palmetto-measures, but not with WordNet-measures, where correlations of 100% and 20% sized groups differ significantly ($p = 0.03$).

VI. CORRELATIONS WITH HUMAN RATINGS

Because coherence is measured using relatedness scores of word pairs, examples of data sets, which compare human judgements of the relations of two words are presented here.

Similarly as earlier in this study, the relatedness of word pairs of four well known human ratings data sets were measured. MC (Miller an Charles) [34] is the smallest one, consisting of only 28 word pairs, and there were 38 human annotators. RG (Rubenstein and Goodenough) [35] has 65 pairs and 51 annotators. Both data sets are available on the web [36]. Lau [37] collected coherence judgements for 600 topics using Amazon Mechanical Turk with a developed quality control of the annotations. Only the top-5 topic words data set was used here. Hill [38] collected human ratings of similarity of word pairs, and they had 500 annotators. These Simlex-datasets are also available on SemR-11 pages cited above. In our comparisons, Simlex subset of nouns, which consists of 666 noun pairs, was used.

There is the list of correlations between each coherence measure and human ratings in terms of MC, RG, Lau and Simlex in Table V. Pearson and Spearman correlations between human ratings RG, MC, Simlex nouns, and LAU data and ten WordNet-measures (HsO − vec) and six Palmetto-measures ($C_{\text{A}} - C_{\text{UMass}}$) using the same measurement methods as earlier in this study. Statistical significance of the correlations are included in Table V.

Four examples indicate that the correlations tend to be lower with the bigger data sets, and the bigger the data set the more statistical significance is reached. Also there is no clear one measure with the highest human ratings. In addition it can be concluded that the behavior of WordNet- and Palmetto-measures differ with respect to human ratings data sets. For example Palmetto measures reach higher ratings with Lau data set, whereas WordNet-measures do the same with Simlex data set.

The average correlations of the data sets in Table V (at the end of the text of this document) were calculated in the same way as in Figure 6. Now, it is possible to compare the correlations in Figure 6, where the data consists of millions of word pairs, see Section V-B, to the statistically significant correlations of the measures in Table V, where the data is limited at most to 666 word pairs. Out of 16 measures five: Lesk, Lin, C_{P}, C_{NPMI} and C_{UCI}, have exact match with the results of Figure 6, when comparing the two highest correlation co-measure. For example, Lesk has the highest correlation with Path, and the second highest with HsO, just like in Figure 6, and the same is happening with the average correlations of the measures in Table V, and in the same order. As example of the consistency of the measures is WuP; it has the highest correlation with Resnik in both calculations, 0.84 in the Topic Model calculations, and 0.83 in the case of human ratings.

TABLE III. AVERAGE PEARSON CORRELATIONS OF WUP IN CASES OF WIKIPEDIA DATA OF FIGURE 6 AND HUMAN RATINGS DATA SETS OF TABLE V.

WuP :	Resnik	Lin	LCh	HsO	Path
Figure 6	0.84	0.72	0.61	0.58	0.54
Table V	0.83	0.79	0.84	0.59	0.69

Seven of the measures have partial match, including different order of the highest and the second highest: HsO, LCh, WuP. Resnik, Path, C_A and C_{UMass}. Two of the rest of cases, vec_p and C_A did not reach statistical significance in results of Figure 6, and that's why they could not be compared. With JCn, only one co-measure reached statistical significance in Section V-B. The average correlation of measure vec is the highest with vec_p, and the second highest with Resnik. These results can be considered, for their part, to describe the consistency of the methods used in this study.

VII. Conclusion and Future Work

The paper analyzes the effect of different semantic coherence measures when determining a topic model. Of the other variables in topic modeling, this study addresses the variable corpus by calculating the results for twelve randomly chosen samples from Wikipedia, the variable of number of topics by using a wide range of number of topics (k= between 4 and 600). Word embeddings used, LDA parameters, average document length in corpora and other variables need to be taken into account in further studies.

The average coherence values of sets of ten topmost topic words show no clear maximum, as can be seen in Figure 3. Instead, there are many local maxima, which have very small differences in their coherence values. For these reasons, not only the number of topics corresponding to the maximum coherence, but also similarly k- values of the two second highest coherences, were listed in Table IV. It can be seen that many measures find the three highest coherence values, but not necessarily in the same order. This behavior supports methods that do not rely one the highest coherence value but use methods like coherence @n [31]. On average, these maxima appear mainly after $k \approx 100$, see Figure 5. So, conclusions made from studies using only smaller k-values might suffer from a lack of generality.

From our result in Section V-C, it can be concluded that increasing the sample size after a limit of 8000 documents with two million words, see Table I, does not have any effect on most of the results. So, an approximation for the minimum corpus size capable to produce general results in this respect can be given. For determining correlations and co-occurrences, this study shows that even a smaller corpus of 4000 documents is enough.

Although the used measure sets, Palmetto and WordNet, include similar elements, the results indicate, that there are differences as well, see Section V-D. The most notable difference is that correlations between these groups are substantially lower than correlations within each group. It is interesting that the measure reaching the highest correlation with human ratings in the study of Röder et al. [11], see Section III-B, does not correlate with any of the other 15 measures studied here, see Figure 6.

Users of the coherence measures studied here should also take into account the relatively high correlation between the number of topics k and some of the measures, as seen in Figure 6.

Different data sets of human ratings do not give similar results for the coherence measures studied here, see Table V. This leads us to think that further research with human ratings data sets is needed.

Appreciated is a comment pointing out that a more detailed discussion on why the measures studied show similarities and differences would be needed here. That is an excellent topic for a further investigation of the current topic.

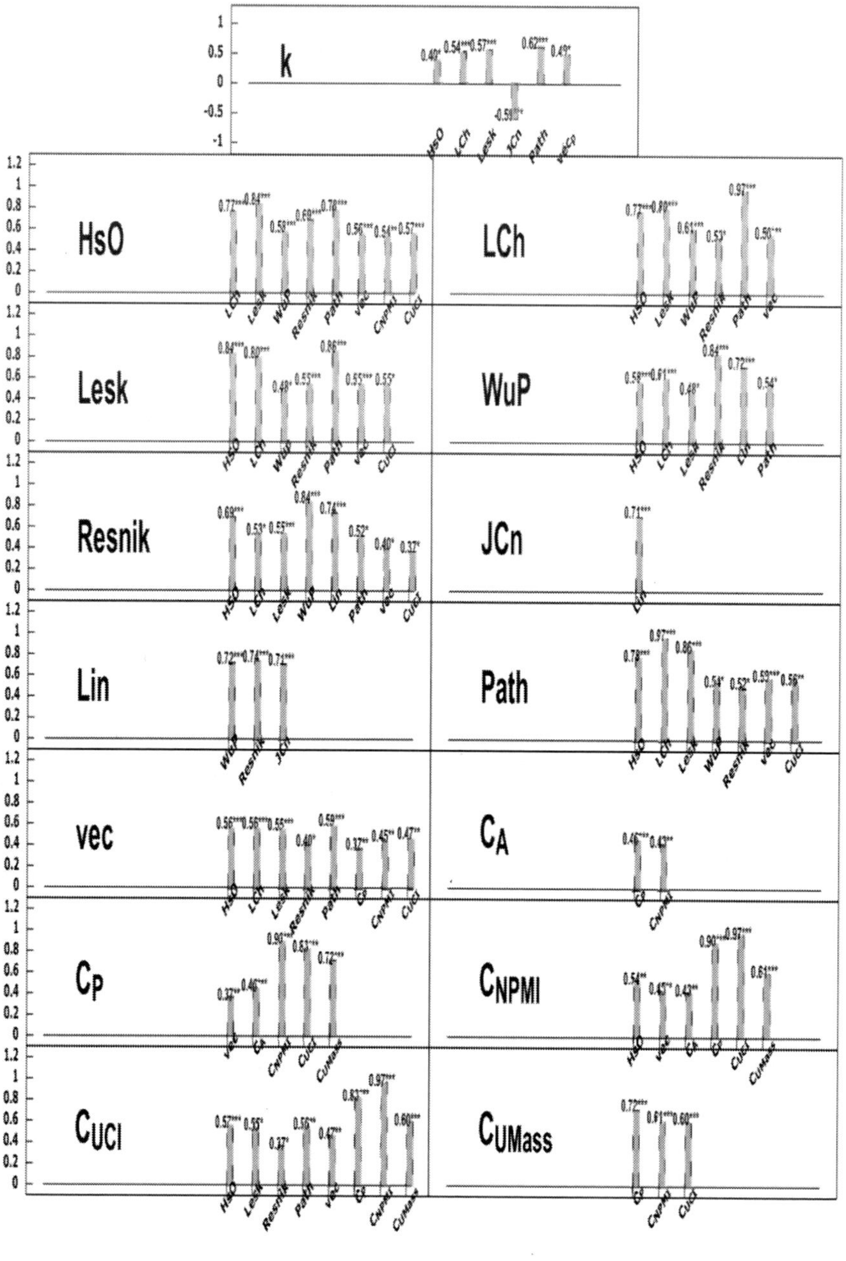

Figure 6. Average correlations of all 12 corpora between the coherence measures with each other and also with the number of topics k . *** means statistically highly significant with $p<0.001$, ** : $p<0.01$, and * : $p<0.05$.

TABLE IV. k-VALUES OF THREE HIGHEST COHERENCE VALUES FOR 12 CORPORA (A - D10) GIVEN BY 16 COHERENCE MEASURES (HsO – C_{UMass}).

	HsO	LCh	Lesk	WuP	Resnik	JCn	Lin	Path	vec_p	vec	C_A	C_P	C_V	C_{NPMI}	C_{UCI}	C_{UMass}
A	95	179	112	23	23	7	6	179	116	116	14	93	7	172	172	6
	112	450	115	7	6	23	7	450	178	102	9	138	9	95	181	25
	102	139	174	6	7	6	23	139	144	108	12	95	21	181	162	23
A20	164	146	143	7	7	6	7	143	124	36	12	99	4	95	95	77
	19	143	164	8	6	59	6	146	144	87	10	64	16	99	77	64
	90	132	173	10	12	7	93	144	146	60	7	151	24	59	183	62
A10	175	187	93	37	37	8	37	187	129	4	20	51	6	51	120	32
	93	145	164	93	93	93	8	145	163	6	51	102	76	88	51	52
	37	175	137	175	112	4	93	175	4	129	24	114	80	120	88	61
B	150	198	198	108	62	58	90	198	250	85	69	69	5	69	69	11
	196	147	164	89	90	54	62	147	92	89	7	11	6	81	158	10
	117	161	196	109	89	52	89	161	280	135	6	46	22	158	11	26
B20	170	143	129	33	33	33	33	149	5	67	10	101	5	66	101	10
	171	149	149	8	109	25	109	143	153	60	4	66	12	101	102	9
	190	187	171	5	63	48	5	170	181	142	14	10	6	95	95	25
B10	73	127	127	73	73	116	31	127	4	4	73	11	14	80	80	10
	146	146	181	64	105	31	73	147	5	135	23	80	7	88	68	11
	175	175	164	105	175	21	105	146	135	6	48	10	20	68	88	12
C	140	7	140	7	140	32	70	7	144	133	9	68	5	107	107	26
	155	8	193	70	113	104	98	5	143	106	17	107	11	140	140	41
	113	5	192	140	70	80	140	8	160	132	12	40	28	126	126	35
C20	50	153	188	11	11	11	11	133	132	111	8	140	5	157	157	33
	157	133	180	50	48	50	50	166	86	67	13	67	9	140	96	8
	144	166	144	48	50	10	48	153	133	152	14	81	7	96	140	14
C10	66	164	66	6	12	121	6	157	64	37	21	42	4	21	21	29
	69	189	103	17	140	4	12	189	117	48	9	9	8	16	22	19
	90	145	185	152	16	28	89	164	25	99	8	112	5	19	69	74
D	100	166	188	6	6	6	6	166	135	83	113	103	12	92	92	17
	149	7	191	7	10	183	7	143	185	146	9	113	113	113	189	19
	188	6	100	9	7	54	8	188	198	167	8	32	103	162	196	24
D20	97	116	107	48	48	4	48	144	7	72	12	78	41	109	109	14
	118	144	144	73	73	48	73	116	29	106	4	73	39	73	73	7
	107	169	184	20	91	91	46	169	197	91	16	55	40	100	100	16
D10	90	69	77	22	77	32	36	69	26	15	12	69	7	57	58	5
	79	141	79	36	90	36	12	280	39	45	6	57	8	58	57	64
	93	67	69	12	67	29	22	141	41	57	18	58	47	69	20	67

TABLE V. PEARSON AND SPEARMAN CORRELATIONS BETWEEN FOUR HUMAN RATINGS (MC - SIMLEX NOUNS) AND 16 COHERENCE MEASURES (HsO – C_{UMass}). NOTE: HERE VALUES **without any** ASTERISKS ARE STATISTICALLY HIGHLY SIGNIFICANT WITH $p<0.001$. AND ** : $p<0.01$, AND * : $p<0.05$, – : $p>0.05$ AND N.D. MEANS NO DATA.

	HsO	LCh	Lesk	WuP	Resnik	JCn	Lin	Path	vec_p	vec	C_A	C_P	C_V	C_{NPMI}	C_{UCI}	C_{UMass}
MC(P)	–	0.57*	–	0.55*	0.59	–	0.53*	–	0.60	**0.88**	–	0.79	–	0.77	0.67	–
MC(S)	–	0.58*	0.60	0.55*	0.68	–	0.56*	0.56*	0.70	**0.90**	–	0.81	0.65	0.82	–	–
RG(P)	0.54	0.60	0.44	0.53	0.61	–	0.54	0.54	n.d.	n.d.	–	0.75	–	**0.77**	0.71	–
RG(S)	0.49	0.56	0.55	0.51	0.55	–	0.46	0.54	n.d.	n.d.	–	**0.85**	0.50	0.84	0.83	0.45
Lau(P)	0.19	–	0.15	0.18	0.25	0.33	0.29	–	n.d.	n.d	0.38	**0.61**	0.31	0.55	0.51	0.28
Lau(S)	0.25	–	0.19	0.20	0.31	0.39	0.37	–	n.d.	n.d.	0.39	**0.52**	0.33	0.49	0.46	0.26
Simlex n.(P)	0.35	**0.52**	0.25	0.45	0.41	0.35	0.51	0.51	0.28	0.35	–	0.24	0.13	0.17	0.18	–
Simlex n.(S)	0.36	0.49	0.31	0.47	0.41	**0.51**	**0.51**	0.48	0.22	0.33	–	0.22	0.21	0.16	0.18	–

REFERENCES

[1] J. L. Boyd-Graber, Y. Hu, and D. Mimno, Applications of topic models. now Publishers Incorporated, 2017, vol. 11.

[2] T. N. Rubin, A. Chambers, P. Smyth, and M. Steyvers, "Statistical topic models for multi-label document classification," Machine learning, vol. 88, no. 1-2, 2012, pp. 157–208.

[3] J. Chuang et al., "Computer-assisted content analysis: Topic models for exploring multiple subjective interpretations," in Advances in Neural Information Processing Systems workshop on human-propelled machine learning, 2014, pp. 1–9.

[4] R. Alghamdi and K. Alfalqi, "A survey of topic modeling in text mining," Int. J. Adv. Comput. Sci. Appl.(IJACSA), vol. 6, no. 1, 2015.

[5] J. W. Mohr and P. Bogdanov, "Introduction—topic models: What they are and why they matter," 2013.

[6] L. Li, B. Roth, and C. Sporleder, "Topic models for word sense disambiguation and token-based idiom detection," in Proceedings of the 48th Annual Meeting of the Association for Computational Linguistics, 2010, pp. 1138–1147.

[7] J. H. Lau, D. Newman, and T. Baldwin, "Machine reading tea leaves: Automatically evaluating topic coherence and topic model quality." in EACL, 2014, pp. 530–539.

[8] N. Aletras and M. Stevenson, "Evaluating topic coherence using distributional semantics," in Proceedings of the 10th International Conference on Computational Semantics (IWCS 2013)–Long Papers, 2013, pp. 13–22.

[9] D. Mimno, H. M. Wallach, E. Talley, M. Leenders, and A. McCallum, "Optimizing semantic coherence in topic models," in Proceedings of the Conference on Empirical Methods in Natural Language Processing. Association for Computational Linguistics, 2011, pp. 262–272.

[10] D. Newman, J. H. Lau, K. Grieser, and T. Baldwin, "Automatic evaluation of topic coherence," in Human Language Technologies: The 2010 Annual Conference of the North American Chapter of the Association for Computational Linguistics. Association for Computational Linguistics, 2010, pp. 100–108.

[11] M. Röder, A. Both, and A. Hinneburg, "Exploring the space of topic coherence measures," in Proceedings of the Eighth ACM International Conference on Web Search and Data Mining. ACM, 2015, pp. 399–408, https://github.com/AKSW/Palmetto/wiki/How-Palmetto-can-be-used, accessed: 2020-09.

[12] K. Stevens, P. Kegelmeyer, D. Andrzejewski, and D. Buttler, "Exploring topic coherence over many models and many topics," in Proceedings of the 2012 Joint Conference on Empirical Methods in Natural Language Processing and Computational Natural Language Learning. Association for Computational Linguistics, 2012, pp. 952–961.

[13] H. Jelodar et al., "Latent dirichlet allocation (lda) and topic modeling: models, applications, a survey," Multimedia Tools and Applications, vol. 78, no. 11, 2019, pp. 15 169–15 211.

[14] D. Q. Nguyen, R. Billingsley, L. Du, and M. Johnson, "Improving topic models with latent feature word representations," Transactions of the Association for Computational Linguistics, vol. 3, 2015, pp. 299–313, https://github.com/datquocnguyen/LFTM, accessed: 2020-09.

[15] D. M. Blei, A. Y. Ng, and M. I. Jordan, "Latent Dirichlet allocation," the Journal of machine Learning research, vol. 3, 2003, pp. 993–1022.

[16] T. Mikolov, I. Sutskever, K. Chen, G. S. Corrado, and J. Dean, "Distributed representations of words and phrases and their compositionality," Advances in neural information processing systems, 2013, pp. 3111–3119, https://code.google.com/archive/p/word2vec/, accessed: 2020-09.

[17] J. Pennington, R. Socher, and C. D. Manning, "GloVe: Global vectors for word representation," Proceedings of the Empiricial Methods in Natural Language Processing (EMNLP 2014), vol. 12, 2014, pp. 1532–1543, http://nlp.stanford.edu/projects/glove/, accessed: 2020-09.

[18] Princeton University, ""About WordNet. WordNet Princeton University." 2010, http://wordnet.princeton.edu, accesed: 2020-09.

[19] T. Pedersen, S. Patwardhan, and J. Michelizzi, "WordNet:: Similarity: measuring the relatedness of concepts," in Demonstration Papers at HLT-NAACL 2004. Association for Computational Linguistics, 2004, pp. 38–41.

[20] J. J. Jiang and D. W. Conrath, "Semantic similarity based on corpus statistics and lexical taxonomy," in Proc of 10th International Conference on Research in Computational Linguistics, ROCLING97, 1997, pp. 19–33.

[21] D. Lin, "An information-theoretic definition of similarity." in Proc. of the 15th International Conference on MachineLearning, vol. 98, 1998, pp. 296–304.

[22] P. Resnik, "Using information content to evaluate semantic similarity in a taxonomy," in Proceedings of the 14th International Joint Conference on Artificial Intelligence, 1995, pp. 448–453.

[23] Z. Wu and M. Palmer, "Verbs semantics and lexical selection," in Proceedings of the 32nd annual meeting on Association for Computational Linguistics. Association for Computational Linguistics, 1994, pp. 133–138.

[24] R. Rada, H. Mili, E. Bicknell, and M. Blettner, "Development and application of a metric on semantic nets," Systems, Man and Cybernetics, IEEE Transactions on, vol. 19, no. 1, 1989, pp. 17–30.

[25] C. Leacock and M. Chodorow, "Combining local context and wordnet similarity for word sense identification," WordNet: An electronic lexical database, vol. 49, no. 2, 1998, pp. 265–283.

[26] G. Hirst and D. St-Onge, "Lexical chains as representations of context for the detection and correction of malapropisms," WordNet: An electronic lexical database, vol. 305, 1998, pp. 305–332.

[27] S. Banerjee and T. Pedersen, "Extended gloss overlaps as a measure of semantic relatedness," in Proceedings of the 18th international joint conference on Artificial intelligence, vol. 3, 2003, pp. 805–810.

[28] H. Shima, "WS4J-package (WordNet Similarity for Java)," 2014, https://code.google.com/p/ws4j/, accessed: 2020-09.

[29] S. Patwardhan, "Incorporating dictionary and corpus information into a context vector measure of semantic relatedness," Ph.D. dissertation, University of Minnesota, Duluth, 2003.

[30] B. Fitelson, "A probabilistic theory of coherence," Analysis, vol. 63, no. 3, 2003, pp. 194–199.

[31] A. Fang, C. Macdonald, I. Ounis, and P. Habel, "Examining the coherence of the top ranked tweet topics," in Proceedings of the 39th International ACM SIGIR conference on Research and Development in Information Retrieval, 2016, pp. 825–828.

[32] C. Shaoul and C. Westbury, "The Westbury Lab Wikipedia Corpus," Edmonton, AB: University of Alberta, 2010, psych.ualberta.ca/~westburylab/downloads/westburylab.wikicorp.download.html, accessed: 2020-09.

[33] P. Pietilänen, "Data and r-code, additional material to this article," 2020, https://pp.ouluresearch.fi, accessed: 2020-10.

[34] G. A. Miller and W. G. Charles, "Contextual correlates of semantic similarity," Language and Cognitive Processes, vol. 6, no. 1, 1991, pp. 1–28, https://doi.org/10.1080/01690969108406936, accessed: 2020-09.

[35] H. Rubenstein and J. B. Goodenough, "Contextual correlates of synonymy," Communications of the ACM, vol. 8, no. 10, 1965, pp. 627–633.

[36] S. Barzegar, B. Davis, M. Zarrouk, S. Handschuh, and A. Freitas, "Semr-11: A multi-lingual gold-standard for semantic similarity and relatedness for eleven languages," in Proceedings of the Eleventh International Conference on Language Resources and Evaluation (LREC 2018), May 2018, https://tinyurl.com/yyz7jvem, accessed: 2020-09.

[37] J. H. Lau and T. Baldwin, "The sensitivity of topic coherence evaluation to topic cardinality," in Proceedings of the 2016 Conference of the North American Chapter of the Association for Computational Linguistics: Human Language Technologies, 2016, pp. 483–487, https://github.com/jhlau/topic-coherence-sensitivity, accessed: 2020-09.

[38] F. Hill, R. Reichart, and A. Korhonen, "Simlex-999: Evaluating semantic models with (genuine) similarity estimation," Computational Linguistics, vol. 41, no. 4, 2015, pp. 665–695.

Pynsett: A Programmable Relation Extractor

Alberto Cetoli
QBE Europe
London, UK
Email: alberto.cetoli@uk.qbe.com

Abstract—**This paper proposes a programmable relation extraction method for the English language by parsing texts into semantic graphs. A person can define rules in plain English that act as matching patterns onto the graph representation. These rules are designed to capture the semantic content of the documents, allowing for flexibility and ad-hoc entities. Relation extraction is a complex task that typically requires sizable training corpora. The method proposed here is ideal for extracting specialized ontologies in a limited collection of documents.**

Keywords–Relation Extraction; Semantic Graphs.

I. Introduction

The goal of relation extraction is to identify relations among entities in the text. It is an integral part of knowledge base population [1], question answering [2], and spoken user interfaces [3]. Precise relation extraction is still a challenging task [4], [5], [6], with most existing solutions relying on training data that contains a limited set of relations.

In many useful cases, the relations need to be customized to a specific ontology relevant only in a small collection of documents, making it difficult to acquire enough examples. This challenge occurs frequently in an industrial context, where a common solution is string-matching or regular expressions. Zero-shot learning has been used to overcome this limit: for example, one can understand relation extraction as a question answering problem [7]. This approach can be quite successful, leveraging on recent reading comprehension progress: it trains a system on extracting semantic content first, then applies the learned generalization to create flexible rules for relation extraction.

While impressive, question answering does not completely solve the challenge of relation extraction, the major problem being generalizing the query to all the possible variations in which it can be formulated. Moreover, while using a question answering approach improves the recall of the extractor, it can also lower the precision of the matches due to mistaken reading comprehension. Representing relations using questions as surface forms does not achieve the same level of precision of rule-based syntactic matches. For relations of this type, the generalization needed is limited.

Linguistic theories allow to generate a semantic representation that offers a useful generalization of the sentence content, while at the same time providing a framework for precise rule matching. By using *Discourse Representation Theory* [8] or Neo-Davidsonian semantics [9], it is possible to describe a collection of sentences as a set of predicates. In these frameworks, the relation extraction rules become a pattern matching exercise over graphs. The works of *Reddy et al.* [10], [11] as well as *Tiktinsky et al.* [12] are an inspiration for this paper.

Further flexibility comes from representing words using word embeddings [13]. In this paper, each lemma is associated to an entry in the *Glove* dataset [14]. In addition, specialized entities are written as a list of embeddings.

Writing a discourse as a collection of predicates is isomorphic to a graph representation of the text. The main idea of this paper is to discover relations in the discourse by matching specific sub-graphs. Each pattern match is effectively a graph query where the data is the discourse. The main contribution of this work is two-fold. First, it suggests a way to semantically encode sentences. Second, it defines a method for creating a set of flexible rules for low-resource relation extraction where relations are represented using their surface forms. The paper is organized as follows: Section II describes how the system is implemented. Subsequently, Section III discusses some preliminary results, while Section IV summarizes prior works on the subject. Finally, the paper wraps up in Section V. This paper's code can be found at [15].

II. Implementation

A. *Semantic representation*

Sentences are transformed into graphs following a similar method to [11]. We start with a dependency parser [16] and apply a series of transformations to obtain a neo-Davidsonian form of the sentence, where active and passive tenses are represented with the same expression, all words are lemmatized, and co-reference is added to the representation. For example, the text *Jane is working at ACME Inc as a woodworker. She is quite taller than the average* becomes in a predicate form

```
Jane(r1), work(e1), ACME_Inc(r2), woodworker(r3),
AGENT(e1, r1), at(e1, r2), as(e1, r3),
Jane(r4), be(e2), tall(r5), average(r6), quite(r7),
AGENT(e2, r4), ADJECTIVE(e2, r5), than(r5, r6),
ADVERB(r5, r7), REFERS_TO(r1, r4), REFERS_TO(r4, r1)
```

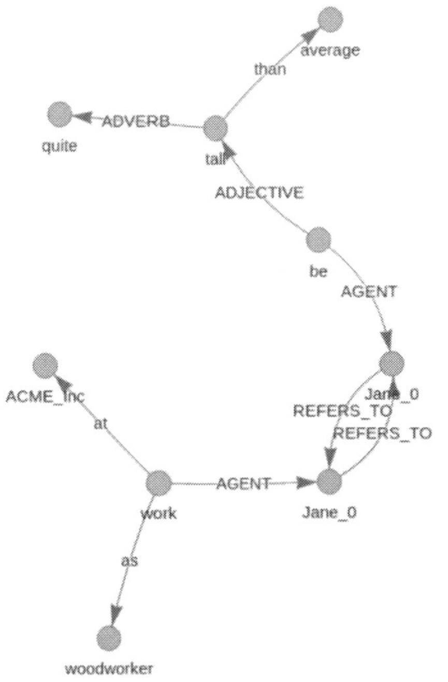

Figure 1. The text in Section II-A becomes a semantic graph with co-reference links.

In this representation, the text is a graph (Figure 1), where the nodes are nouns, verbs, adverbs, and adjectives, and the edges are the semantic relations among them. The representation used in this work aims to be optimized for the task of extracting relations and for speed.

B. Types of edges

The main semantic relations employed by the system are explained in the following:

AGENT, PATIENT: the subject and object of the sentence are converted to agent and patient edges coherently with the verb's voice. In addition, these relations are propagated to relevant subordinates.

ADJECTIVE, ADVERB: adjectives and adverbs are connected to the relevant node through an edge. The only exceptions are negation adverbs, which become part of the node's attributes to facilitate the matching procedure, as explained in Section II-E.

OWNS: possessive pronouns are translated into a relation induced by the pronoun's semantics.

PREPOSITIONS: all the prepositions become edges (Figure 1). Ideally - in a future work - a further semantic layer should be added to classify the preposition's meaning in context.

SUBORDINATES: the subordinate clauses are linked to the main one through the SUBORDINATE edge. One additional type is the ADVOCATIVE_CLAUSE, marking a conditional relation among sentences. This is a placeholder for future versions of the system where ideally rules can be extracted from the text.

C. Conjunctions

In order to facilitate graph matching, the conjunction list is flattened and linked to the head node whenever possible. For example, the sentence *Jane is smart and wise* becomes, in predicate form

```
Jane(r1), be(e1), smart(r2), wise(r3),
AGENT(e1, r1), ADJECTIVE(e1, r2), ADJECTIVE(e1, r3)
```

Effectively, 'AND' and 'OR' disappear from the graph. This is a crude approximation that facilitates the relation extraction at the expense of semantic correctness.

D. Co-reference

An additional level of semantics is added by linking together two nouns that co-refer, using the REFERS_TO edge. Currently, the system uses the pre-trained AllenNLP co-reference algorithm [17]. The system - while performing well on the Ontonotes 5 dataset - can increase the noise in the graph by introducing spurious connections. In order to increase the precision of the model, only pronouns and named entities can match.

E. Matching of words

Words are represented using the Glove word embeddings of their lemma and a few different tags:

- Negated: a *True/False* value that indicates whether a word is associated with a negation: if a verb is negated, the adverb does not appear as a new node, rather the verb is flagged using this tag. In this way, *work* can never match *does not work*.
- Named Entity Type: a label indicating the entity type of the node, as per *Ontonotes* 5.0 notation [18].
- Node type: indicates whether it is a verb, a noun, an adjective, or an adverb.

For example, the noun Jane is represented internally as

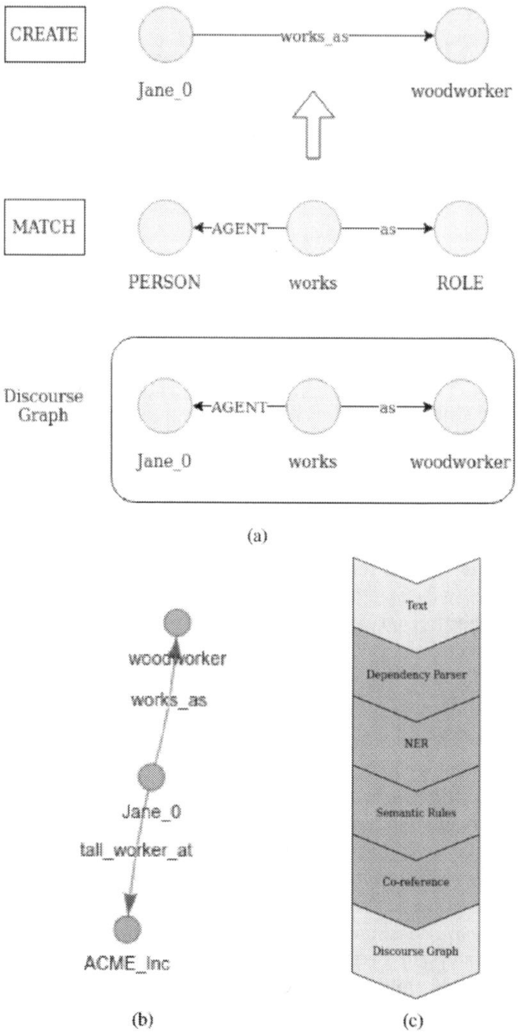

Figure 2. (a) The *MATCH* clause defines the sentence/graph that triggers the rule. The rule then creates an edge between the entities. (b) The resulting relations graph from the two rules in Section II-F. (c) The implementation pipeline transforms an input text onto the discourse graph.

```
{
    vector: EMBEDDING[Jane]
    lemma: "Jane",
    negated: False,
    entity_type: PERSON,
    node_type: noun
}
```

Two words match if the dot product between their lemmas' embeddings is greater than a specific threshold, and all the other tags coincide. For example, the words *carpenter* and *woodworker* match. This solution can in principle be augmented with an external ontology, where synonyms and hypernyms would trigger a match as well. In addition, the system allows to cluster a set of words under the same definition.

```
DEFINE TEAM AS [team, group, club];
DEFINE UNIVERSITY AS [university, academy, polytechnic];
DEFINE LITERATURE AS [book, story, article, series];
```

All words within the threshold distance would trigger a match. For example, the word *tome* would match the word *book*, thus falling into the *LITERATURE* category.

F. Matching of sentences

At the end of the processing pipeline, the input text becomes a union of connected graphs, the *discourse graph*. The current framework defines rules that act on the discourse graph by declaring two components: a *MATCH* clause, which defines the trigger for the rule, and a *CREATE* clause, which creates the relation edge. Relations must connect two entities marked by the symbol #. For example, the sentence *Jane#1 works at Acme#2* tags *Jane* and *Acme* for an edge to connect them. The matching sentence can contain Named Entities (PERSON, ORG, DATE, etc) as well as an internally-defined entity (Section II-E). An example is as follows

```
DEFINE ROLE AS [carpenter, painter];

MATCH "PERSON#1 works as a ROLE#2."
CREATE (works_as 1 2);

MATCH "PERSON#1 works at ORG#2 as a ROLE. PERSON is tall."
CREATE (tall_worker_at 1 2);
```

Please note that a *MATCH* clause is written as a sentence, but it is internally parsed into a graph. A rule is triggered if this semantic representation is a sub-graph of the *discourse graph*. Two nodes are considered equal if they match according to the method in Section II-E. The rules are represented as simple pattern matching rules, as in Figure 2 (a). Also, notice that, for the second rule in the above example, more than one sentence is specified. This is because the *MATCH* clause can be a text as complex and free-flowing as the documents that are being parsed. The trigger sentences also solve co-reference: in the second rule, the person that works is the same person that is tall. This second clause expresses the compositional potential of the rules. In future versions of the framework, one could add more complex mangling of the sentences where simple logical constraints are added (and/or), or information is extracted from mathematical formulas.

Each rule behaves according to the method defined above. When a graph triggers a rule, an edge is created in the *relations graph*, as show in Figure 2 (b). In this final representation, the knowledge is condensed into the pre-defined relations.

G. Implementation details

Every text in the system is processed according to the pipeline in Figure 2 (c), and eventually transformed into a *discourse graph*. The dependency parser is Spacy [16], which also enriches the discourse graph with Named Entities. Co-reference uses the AllenNLP system, as described in [17]. The semantic transformation rules - available in the open source code [19] - are implemented through a purpose-made in-memory graph database [20]. Sentences of arbitrary complexity can be parsed by the current system, compatibly with the accuracy of the dependency parser. This is true both for the input text and the matching rules.

A rule matcher algorithm goes through the list of rules, performs the matching and creates the relations graph according to the method described in Section II-F. The computational cost of rule-matching is $O(N)$, where N is the number of rules. Further improvements should include a rule retriever algorithm, which pre-filters the rules according to the discourse graph. Due to speed optimization, the rules are applied only once: the reasoning induced by the rules is only one step deep. Ideally, in a future version, the rules should be applied with a Prolog-like resolution tree[21].

III. Preliminary Results

The current version of the system can be tested against the test set of the TACRED corpus [22]. Let us consider only two relations: *date_of_birth* and *date_of_death* defined as follows

```
DEFINE PERSON AS {PERSON};
DEFINE DAY AS {DATE};
DEFINE YEAR AS {DATE};
DEFINE AT_TIME AS {DATE};
DEFINE AT_MOMENT AS [Monday, Tuesday
     , Wednesday, Thursday, Friday, Saturday, Sunday];

MATCH "PERSON#1 is born AT_TIME#2"
CREATE (DATE_OF_BIRTH 1 2);

MATCH "PERSON#1 is born on DAY#2"
CREATE (DATE_OF_BIRTH 1 2);

MATCH "PERSON#1 is born in YEAR#2"
CREATE (DATE_OF_BIRTH 1 2);

MATCH "PERSON#1 dies AT_MOMENT#2"
CREATE (DATE_OF_DEATH 1 2);

MATCH "PERSON#1 dies on DAY#2"
CREATE (DATE_OF_DEATH 1 2);

MATCH "PERSON#1 dies in YEAR#2"
CREATE (DATE_OF_DEATH 1 2);
```

For both relations, there are no false positives (precision is 100%) while the recall is less competitive: the date of birth relation has 33% recall, whereas the date of death scores 3.6%. This result compares unfavourably with the state of the art on TACRED (F1 71.2% [23]), however, a direct comparison is beyond the scope of this work. The system presented here is not a machine learning model and only aims to create a flexible rule-based framework for precise relation extraction.

IV. Related Works

A corpus of works is dedicated to map the output of grammatical parsers onto semantic structures: an early work can be found in the CCGBank manual [24], where a set of heuristic rules guide the translation from a constituency parse to a CCG (Categorial Combinatorial Grammar) structure. Further works [11] apply transformation rules over dependency trees with the goal of achieving logical forms for semantic parsing. Abstract Meaning Representation [25] is also used to generate graphs from sentences.

A more recent approach [12] is tailored to produce enhanced UD Trees (Universal Dependencies Trees) - suited for information extraction tasks - from dependency structures. The task of extracting relations by using their surface form has been addressed in the influential OpenIE framework [26]. Similarly, prior work on zero-shot relation extraction [7] attempts to represent relations by using questions. Hearst patterns [27], [28] can be used to extract hierarchical relationships from a text, without using semantic representations of documents. Finally a recent work by *Shlain et al.* [29] is closely related to the current paper, where they leverage a syntactic representation of the documents to implement flexible search queries.

V. Conclusions and Future Work

This paper presents a flexible rule-based relation extractor for limited resource sets. Flexible rules can be created, thus allowing for a quick relation extractor using specialized ontologies. The main advantage of this approach is control over the rules and precision in the extracted content. An extension of the system should allow customized ontologies to be used for word matching. Moreover, more Named Entities should be included, possibly allowing for specialized extractors within the internal pipeline. This work uses word embeddings imported from the Glove vectors. A more modern approach could employ pre-trained language models to create the relevant embeddings. As a final limitation, the system does not assign a temporal dimension to events yet. This information should be extracted from verb tenses and added to the discourse graph.

ACKNOWLEDGEMENTS

The author is grateful to Stefano Bragaglia for insightful discussions.

REFERENCES

[1] H. Ji and R. Grishman, "Knowledge base population: Successful approaches and challenges," in Proceedings of the 49th Annual Meeting of the Association for Computational Linguistics: Human Language Technologies - vol. 1, ser. HLT '11. Stroudsburg, PA, USA: Association for Computational Linguistics, 2011, pp. 1148–1158. [Online]. Available: http://dl.acm.org/citation.cfm?id=2002472.2002618

[2] K. Xu, S. Reddy, Y. Feng, S. Huang, and D. Zhao, "Question answering on freebase via relation extraction and textual evidence." Proceedings of the 54th Annual Meeting of the Association for Computational Linguistics (vol. 1: Long Papers), 2016, pp. 2326–2336.

[3] K. Yoshino, S. Mori, and T. Kawahara, "Spoken dialogue system based on information extraction using similarity of predicate argument structures," in Proceedings of the SIGDIAL 2011 Conference, ser. SIGDIAL '11. Stroudsburg, PA, USA: Association for Computational Linguistics, 2011, pp. 59–66. [Online]. Available: http://dl.acm.org/citation.cfm?id=2132890.2132898

[4] R. Bunescu and R. Mooney, "A shortest path dependency kernel for relation extraction," in Proceedings of Human Language Technology Conference and Conference on Empirical Methods in Natural Language Processing. Vancouver, British Columbia, Canada: Association for Computational Linguistics, 2005, pp. 724–731. [Online]. Available: https://www.aclweb.org/anthology/H05-1091

[5] Z. Guo, Y. Zhang, and W. Lu, "Attention guided graph convolutional networks for relation extraction," in ACL, 2019, p. 241–251.

[6] Y. Luan, L. He, M. Ostendorf, and H. Hajishirzi, "Multi-task identification of entities, relations, and coreference for scientific knowledge graph construction," in Proceedings of the 2018 Conference on Empirical Methods in Natural Language Processing. Brussels, Belgium: Association for Computational Linguistics, 2018, pp. 3219–3232. [Online]. Available: https://www.aclweb.org/anthology/D18-1360

[7] O. Levy, M. Seo, E. Choi, and L. S. Zettlemoyer, "Zero-shot relation extraction via reading comprehension," in CoNLL. Proceedings of the 21st Conference on Computational Natural Language Learning (CoNLL 2017), 2017, pp. 333–342.

[8] H. Kamp and U. Reyle, From Discourse to Logic - Introduction to Modeltheoretic Semantics of Natural Language, Formal Logic and Discourse Representation Theory. Springer, 1993.

[9] T. Parsons, Events in the Semantics of English. MIT Press, 1990.

[10] S. Reddy, M. Lapata, and M. Steedman, "Large-scale semantic parsing without question-answer pairs," Transactions of the Association for Computational Linguistics, vol. 2, 2014, pp. 377–392.

[11] S. Reddy, O. Tackstrom, M. Collins, T. Kwiatkowski, D. Das, M. Steedman, and M. Lapata, "Transforming dependency structures to logical forms for semantic parsing," Transactions of the Association for Computational Linguistics, vol. 4, 2016, pp. 127–140.

[12] A. Tiktinsky, Y. Goldberg, and R. Tsarfaty, "pybart: Evidence-based syntactic transformations for IE," in Proceedings of the 58th Annual Meeting of the Association for Computational Linguistics: System Demonstrations, ACL 2020, Online, July 5-10, 2020, A. Çelikyilmaz and T. Wen, Eds. Association for Computational Linguistics, 2020, pp. 47–55. [Online]. Available: https://www.aclweb.org/anthology/2020.acl-demos.7/

[13] T. Mikolov, I. Sutskever, K. Chen, G. Corrado, and J. Dean, "Distributed representations of words and phrases and their compositionality," CoRR, vol. abs/1310.4546, 2013. [Online]. Available: http://arxiv.org/abs/1310.4546

[14] J. Pennington, R. Socher, and C. D. Manning, "Glove: Global vectors for word representation," in Empirical Methods in Natural Language Processing (EMNLP), 2014, pp. 1532–1543. [Online]. Available: http://www.aclweb.org/anthology/D14-1162

[15] "Pynsett source code," 2020. [Online]. Available: https://github.com/fractalego/pynsett/tree/semapro2020

[16] M. Honnibal and I. Montani, "spaCy 2: Natural language understanding with Bloom embeddings, convolutional neural networks and incremental parsing," ExplosionAI, 2017.

[17] K. Lee, L. He, M. Lewis, and L. Zettlemoyer, "End-to-end neural coreference resolution," in EMNLP, 2017, pp. 188–197.

[18] E. Hovy, M. Marcus, M. Palmer, L. Ramshaw, and R. Weischedel, "Ontonotes: The 90the NAACL, Companion Volume: Short Papers, ser. NAACL-Short '06. Stroudsburg, PA, USA: Association for Computational Linguistics, 2006, pp. 57–60. [Online]. Available: http://dl.acm.org/citation.cfm?id=1614049.1614064

[19] "List of transformation rules," 2020. [Online]. Available: https://github.com/fractalego/pynsett/tree/semapro2020/pynsett/rules/parsing

[20] "In-memory graph database," 2020. [Online]. Available: https://github.com/fractalego/parvusdb

[21] R. Kowalski, "Predicate logic as programming language," vol. 74. IFIP Congr., 1974, pp. 569–574.

[22] Y. Zhang, V. Zhong, D. Chen, G. Angeli, and C. D. Manning, "Position-aware attention and supervised data improve slot filling," in Proceedings of the 2017 Conference on Empirical Methods in Natural Language Processing (EMNLP 2017), 2017, pp. 35–45. [Online]. Available: https://nlp.stanford.edu/pubs/zhang2017tacred.pdf

[23] L. Baldini Soares, N. FitzGerald, J. Ling, and T. Kwiatkowski, "Matching the blanks: Distributional similarity for relation learning." Proceedings of the 57th Annual Meeting of the Association for Computational Linguistics, 2019, pp. 2895–2905.

[24] J. Hockenmaier and M. Steedman, "Ccgbank: User's manual," 2005. [Online]. Available: https://catalog.ldc.upenn.edu/docs/LDC2005T13/CCGbankManual.pdf

[25] L. Banarescu et al., "Abstract Meaning Representation for sembanking," in Proceedings of the 7th Linguistic Annotation Workshop and Interoperability with Discourse. Sofia, Bulgaria: Association for Computational Linguistics, 2013, pp. 178–186. [Online]. Available: https://www.aclweb.org/anthology/W13-2322

[26] J. Christensen, Mausam, S. Soderland, and O. Etzioni, "An analysis of open information extraction based on semantic role labeling," in Proceedings of the Sixth International Conference on Knowledge Capture, ser. K-CAP '11. New York, NY, USA: Association for Computing Machinery, 2011, p. 113–120. [Online]. Available: https://doi.org/10.1145/1999676.1999697

[27] M. A. Hearst, "Automatic acquisition of hyponyms from large text corpora," in COLING 1992 vol. 2: The 15th International Conference on Computational Linguistics, 1992. [Online]. Available: https://www.aclweb.org/anthology/C92-2082

[28] S. Roller, D. Kiela, and M. Nickel, "Hearst patterns revisited: Automatic hypernym detection from large text corpora," in Proceedings of the 56th Annual Meeting of the Association for Computational Linguistics (vol 2: Short Papers). Melbourne, Australia: Association for Computational Linguistics, 2018, pp. 358–363. [Online]. Available: https://www.aclweb.org/anthology/P18-2057

[29] M. Shlain, H. Taub-Tabib, S. Sadde, and Y. Goldberg, "Syntactic search by example," 2020. [Online]. Available: https://arxiv.org/abs/2006.03010

Querying the Semantic Web for Concept Identifiers to Annotate Research Datasets

André Langer, Christoph Göpfert and Martin Gaedke

Distributed and Self-organizing Systems Group
Chemnitz University of Technology
Chemnitz, Germany
Email: {andre.langer,christoph.goepfert.martin.gaedke}@informatik.tu-chemnitz.de

Abstract—**Researchers are encouraged to describe and publish research datasets so that others can find and reuse it. Following a semantic approach, well-known concept identifiers are necessary that can be used as values for meta-data properties to describe relevant characteristics of such a research artifact. Multiple research disciplines, communities or initiatives have already created and published standardized terms as taxonomies or ontologies for that. However, these developments are distributed on the Web. As a consequence, it can be difficult for researchers to become aware of already recommended structured terminologies. Thus, they will further rely on ambiguous, literal annotations. In this paper, we investigate existing data sources in the Semantic Web that contain relevant terms to describe a research dataset in a structured, content-oriented and fine-grained way and how to integrate it in corresponding applications. We therefore analyze both Linked Data services and traditional terminology services on how to retrieve and filter terms for particular research-relevant characteristics. It is shown that a variety of well-structured community-specific terminologies with relevant concepts already exist, but that community-overspanning building blocks are nevertheless missing. Furthermore, filtering and mapping particular concepts is still a challenge to improve interdisciplinary publishing.**

Keywords–Linked Data; Research Data Management; Data Publishing; FAIR; NFDI.

I. Introduction

The publication of research datasets is increasingly recognized as an essential part of scientific research [1]. Publishing research data in the World Wide Web has various advantages for both the creator and the consumer of the data [2]. It facilitates the reproducibility of research results, raises awareness and allows to discover, reuse and repurpose existing datasets [3]. However, the publication of scientific artifacts also poses challenges, in particular regarding the description and provisioning of a research dataset. In contrast to other types of publications, which can traditionally be classified by librarians, research datasets have to be annotated by the originating researcher or at least domain experts as they are normally not self-descriptive. The *FAIR Guiding Principles for scientific data management and stewardship* [4] address this challenge by defining requirements for publishing research datasets. These principles are intended to make data discoverable to humans and machines. Since their original publication in 2016, the *FAIR Principles* have received broad support, particularly from research journal publishers, including *Springer Nature*, *GigaScience*, or *Gates Open Research*.

Based on these principles, additional information about the dataset should be provided, such as administrative metadata on the creator, the involved institution and publication license, technical metadata on the media type, extent, recording software or device, and also further domain-specific descriptive metadata. Focusing on predicates, a set of established ontologies already exists that can be used to provide a basic metadata description for research datasets, including properties from initiatives, such as the *DataCite [5], Dublin Core Metadata Element Set (DCMES) [6], DCMI Terms [7], DCAT-AP [8], MARC [9], MODS [10], PREMIS [11]*, or projects like *schema.org* [12]. However, approaches on providing structured content and domain related object values are apparently still vague.

Nowadays, the provision of structured descriptive meta information on the content of the research dataset seems often neglected or only done in natural language in the abstract or a separate *ReadMe* description of the dataset [13]. Persistent Digital Object Identifiers (DOIs) are commonly provided to reference the dataset resource itself, but other concepts that describe characteristics of the dataset are provided as a free-text string in many research disciplines, although controlled vocabularies or established identifiers for common concepts would be possible to use as well that also allow semantic linking operations. This hinders the discovery and selective filtering possibilities in established data repository directories and crawling services, especially in an interdisciplinary context.

This situation can be improved, if the meta description of a research dataset does not only rely on predefined, well-understood properties provided by established ontologies, but also makes heavier use of unambiguous identifiers for object values in a Resource Description Framework (RDF) statement. A Linked Data-based approach allows to define type restrictions for the range of these object values and enables inference operations to discover even taxonomically similar concepts with different terms in the description.

Relying on single controlled vocabularies can only partially solve this issue. Ontologies already include a set of predefined persistent identifiers for concepts but they are limited in their expressiveness and focus only on a small scope of characteristics that can be described. In contrary to that, a comprehensive, atomic description of content characteristics requires many more necessary identifiers that have to be provided in a simple fashion. Sometimes, existing identifiers from general-purpose services in the Web, such as *DBpedia* [14], *Wikidata* [15] or *ConceptNet* [16], can be additionally used, but research dataset related concepts are likely to be too specialized in order to be listed there.

Even within the same research area, there can be vastly different types of research data characteristics. National and international research initiatives, such as the *National Research Data Infrastructure (NFDI)* in Germany, have started to work on harmonizing these terminologies into taxonomies, but we nevertheless face a distributed scenario where to query and retrieve existing relevant concept identifiers from.

Within this paper, we will discuss possibilities and challenges in querying concept identifiers from multiple existing sources in the application domain of research dataset meta descriptions. Our results can be used to build semantic-aware Web applications in the future that can provide structured explicit Linked Data research dataset meta descriptions with an improved user experience. The paper is part of the *PIROL* [17] PhD project about Publishing Interdisciplinary Research over Linked Data and has the following contributions:

1) We systematize existing data sources for concepts relevant for research dataset meta descriptions.
2) We describe a concept on how to query and filter these decentralized knowledge bases for relevant identifiers.
3) We run performance measurements on how to retrieve these identifiers in a Web application for research dataset management

The rest of the paper is structured in the following way: Section II describes the problem domain in detail and defines requirements. Section III provides a systematic mapping of existing knowledge sources for domain-specific research dataset concepts. Section IV discusses a proof-of-concept and different query strategies on how to incorporate these data sources into an application, which is then evaluated in Section V. Section VI contrasts our work to other existing approaches and Section VII summarizes our results and gives an outlook to future work.

II. Interdisciplinary Research Dataset Description

When publishing a research dataset, additional meta information has to be provided that can be used later so that other researchers are able to discover it based on their particular needs. Therefore, the corresponding meta information has to satisfy the following five aspects:

A1 The provided information has to be correct
A2 The provided information has to be machine-readable
A3 The provided information has to be sufficiently extensive
A4 The provided information has to be comprehensive
A5 The provided information has to be usable across multiple user groups

A1 is a necessity, as the provided meta information will be the foundation to discover a particular research dataset.

A2 is given, when a separate digital metadata description file is provided. However, this can either be done as a quite unstructured natural-language text, in a semi-structured way with key-value pairs, where the values can again contain descriptive continuous text, or highly structured where both the keys and values contain unambiguous identifiers.

A3 is commonly a trade-off between what can be stated about the data set and what is relevant information to actually discover it. An extensive number of statements can be made to describe the research dataset, but it should focus on filter criteria important for the consumer.

A4 asks for a certain understandability of the provided information, both for humans and machines. The provided terms have to represent a commonly known concept in this knowledge domain.

A5 is important especially in an interdisciplinary context when research data is not only relevant for a particular community but across multiple disciplines. It should therefore be possible to identify and link related or similar concepts.

Discovery operations nowadays commonly apply a keyword-based or fuzzy search on existing metadata descriptions in combination with some kind of natural language processing and named entity recognition. The metadata description itself concentrates on administrative meta information, whereas the description of the dataset content is either based on plain descriptive text or literal keywords. Figure 1 illustrates a scenario, where a research associate publishes, e.g., a research dataset that contains a set of recorded videos of elderly men walking.

Figure 1. Example metadata description for a video dataset in JSON-LD.

To improve the discovery and reuse of existing research dataset meta descriptions, such a Linked Data based approach can be valuable. The exemplary description satisfies aspect A1-A4, but we still face challenges when we want to find this research dataset among multiple disciplines based on certain filter criteria. Therefore, it is necessary on one hand to provide structured RDF statements on a research dataset subject, and on the other hand to make use of well-known unambiguous identifiers from controlled vocabularies for predicates and values in these statements. In this research activity, we particularly put focus on Uniform Resource Identifiers (URIs) that are provided as object values in these descriptions to express a concrete concept in an unambiguous way. We follow the hypothesis that this is an important requirement to improve the interdisciplinary discoverability of research data among multiple disciplines with the means of terminology mapping and linking and Linked Data inference capabilities for related concepts and sub-concepts.

In order to identify concept groups of major relevance, our pre-analysis consisted out of three steps:

Examine established vocabularies for attribute groups The *DataCite / OpenAIRE* metadata schema specification and schema.org/Dataset were reviewed for common attributes and yielded the following reoccuring concept domains: *topic, resource type, (file) format/media type, rights/license, discipline, measurement technique/device, material, audience*.

Examine UI of established research dataset repositories We carefully analyzed the input interface for research dataset meta description of *Zenodo* [18], *Open Science Framework (OSF)* [19] and *Mendeley* 20 and identified similar terminology groups as in the previous step.

Examine meta descriptions of existing research datasets We verified the results through the result list of the *Google Dataset Search*. Apart from the already identified groups, it was obvious that additional relevant knowledge-domain specific concepts are often mentioned in the content description field text such as *demographic characteristics, examined objects, research and evaluation methods, metrics, measurement characteristics, models* or other applied paradigms.

In the following, we assume the existence of reusable terminologies as several communities have already worked on a standardization of such vocabularies throughout the last decades to represent particular research-related concepts. However, this knowledge is scattered along the entire Web in a decentralized way and can be found in different types of data sources. This complicates the reuse of existing terminology. In the following, we are, therefore, interested in existing data sources that fulfill the following requirements:

REQ1 DOMAIN The data source provides research-relevant terminologies of a specific domain that can be used as object values in the meta description of a research dataset

REQ2 SCHEME The data source provides the information in a semantic data serialization format with a clearly defined meta scheme to group and access similar concepts

REQ3 LABELING The data source provides labeled entities and persistent URIs for each concept

REQ4 API The data source offers a mechanism to access and filter these concepts remotely

REQ5 EXTENT The data source is actively maintained and has a complete or at least sufficient extent of entries

III. Sources for Research Data Concept Identifiers

Resource URIs from *DBpedia*, *Wikidata* or *ConceptNet* are commonly used in the Linked Open Data Cloud (LODC) to provide links to nameable entities. However, they focus on general-purpose data whereas scientific descriptions might need a domain-specialized vocabulary that is not part of *Wikipedia* or similar services. Additionally, the information there might be incomplete or of intermediate data quality.

We therefore conducted a systematic search for alternative sources for research dataset related concepts and mapped them to 4 groups as mentioned in the following sections. Deprecated or unavailable services were excluded from the mapping. We also excluded entity related groups for which appropriate authority services already exist, such as for identifying individual persons (Open Researcher and Contributor ID (ORCID)) [21], organizations (GRID [22], GND [23], LCCN [24], VIAF [25]), geographical information, such as countries and cities, or publications

A. *Ontology catalogs*

Ontology catalogs are a directory or collection of proposed vocabularies with a certain focus. Within these ontology catalogs, "1) metadata should be stored and handled based on a well defined syntax and semantics, i.e., a documented schema, 2) the catalog software must offer both a user interface and a widely accepted API for access by other software like applications and data portals" [26], as shown in Table I. The focus is set on providing standardized schemes and established ontologies with well-known properties, but these vocabularies might also contain (sub-)class definition or instances with a unique identifier that is appropriate to describe and filter certain meta-data value specific concepts.

TABLE I. COMPARISON OF ONTOLOGY CATALOGUES

Name	DOMAIN	SCHEME	LABELING	API	EXTENT (2019)
NCBO BioPortal	+ (biomed)	+	+	+	+ (792 vocabs)
LOV	+ (various)	+	+	+	+ (682 vocabs)
AberOWL	+ (various)	+	+	+	+ (522 vocabs)
ORR	+ (marine)	+	+	+	+ (499 vocabs)
OLS	+ (biomed)	+	+	o	+ (233 vocabs)
Ontobee	+ (biomed)	+	+	+	+ (201 vocabs)
IBC AgroPortal	+ (agro)	+	+	+	+ (106 vocabs)
Smart City OC	+ (smart city)	+	o	-	+ (70 vocabs)
RDA	+ (various)	-	+	-	+ (60 vocabs)
finto	+ (various)	+	+	o	+ (47 vocabs)
DCC	+ (various)	-	+	-	+ (40 vocabs)
HeTOP	+ (biomed)	+	+	-	+ (36 vocabs)
LinkedData.es	+ (various)	+	+	-	+ (35 vocabs)
Biblioportal	+ (biblio)	+	+	o	+ (31 vocabs)
SIFR BioPortal	+ (biomed)	+	+	+	+ (30 vocabs)
gfbio	+ (biomed)	+	+	o	+ (29 vocabs)
ONS Geography	+ (geography)	+	+	+	o (7 vocabs)

B. *Authority services*

Several terminology, thesauri and taxonomy services already exist for general or specific application domains, commonly built with the Simple Knowledge Organization System (SKOS) vocabulary as exemplary shown in Table II. Although they are often provided as a searchable Web page or data dump download without any API, they commonly also provide uniform resource identifiers and a hierarchical concept classification.

TABLE II. COMPARISON OF A SELECTED SUBSET OF AUTHORITY SERVICES BASED ON [27]

Name	DOMAIN	SCHEME	LABELING	API	EXTENT (2019)
EU NALs/Eurovoc	+ (general)	-	+	+	+ (150 groups)
Library of Congress	+ (general)	-	+	-	+ (70 groups)
UNESCO	+ (general)	-	+	o	+ (7 groups)

C. *Instance datasets*

This category basically contains all services from the Linked Open Data Cloud that provide structured meta information on a particular entity. Beside many less relevant concepts for research activities, they are also eligible to describe a research object related concept and provide established resource URIs. Table III focuses on aggregators of instance data sets and most prominent instance data providers.

TABLE III. COMPARISON OF INSTANCE DATASET PROVIDERS

Name	DOMAIN	SCHEME	LABELING	API	EXTENT (2019)
LOD Cache	o (general)	-	o	+	+ (50b stmts.)
LOD-a-lot	o (general)	o	o	-	+ (28b stmts.)
DBpedia	o (general)	+	o	+	+ (9.5b stmts.)
Wikidata	o (general)	+	+	+	+ (7.9b stmts.)
BTC	o (general)	+	o	-	+ (2b stmts.)
YAGO	o (general)	+	+	+	+ (1.4b stmts.)

D. Other concept sources

Beside these ontology, terminology and instance data collections and services, a variety of other data sources exist that might be relevant to retrieve concept identifiers. They are typically provided on separate websites in static text files by services like DataHub [28]. Examples are specifications, such as *CERIF* [29] or *KDSF* [30], use case-related developments, such as from data.gov.uk, or individual recommendations, such as vocabularies for representing data licenses, geographical information or file specific aspects. If these concepts are relevant for research dataset annotation processes or tool development, they can be downloaded and stored as a local data source and are therefore not further considered here.

Dedicated encyclopedic dictionary services exist, such as WordNet [31] and related projects like ConceptNet [16] or BabelNet [32], Wiktionary [33] or OmegaWiki [34]. Applications to annotate research datasets can also benefit from these service as they can also provide APIs, but were not in the particular focus of this research.

We also examined the usage of semantic search engines for concept discovery and retrieval purposes. However, at the point of writing, none of the existing Linked Data search services from the past was publicly available and functional, such as *Swoogle [35], Sindice [36], Falcons, SWSE, LOTUS or IBM Watson*.

E. Discussion

We manually reviewed the mentioned data sources against the relevant concept that we identified in Section II. It became obvious that no data source contained all relevant concepts. The list below shows exemplary data sources:

demographics BioPortal
device AberOWL, OLS, OntoBee
discipline UNESCO and other Authoritative Services
file format Static vocabularies
license Static vocabularies
measurements NCBO BioPortal
research methods LOV

Instead, we face a scattered scenario, where available terminologies and ontologies are provided only by some established aggregation services, or not at all (such as for certain *devices, materials, methods, metrics, models etc.*). In other cases, a researcher needs explicit knowledge on where to find terms for a particular knowledge domain in a decentralized landscape. It may even be misleading, that portals related to biomedical aspects might also identify interdisciplinary relevant concepts.

Characteristics of a research dataset meta description, such as the *topic* or *examined object*, are challenging to systematize at all. In these cases, the usage of established Linked Data entity description services, such as *DBpedia, Wikidata* or *ConceptNet*, is considerable to make use of persistent identifiers for a distinguishable concept.

Beside that, the interdisciplinary reuse of existing terms is hindered by the variety of representation formats for the hierarchical grouping of related concepts. Using rdf:type or a categorization is an approach commonly used by instance data sets to state that a concept is an instance of a specific type. Other concepts are represented as subclasses in the Web Ontology Language (OWL) or as a terminological hierarchy in SKOS. Hybrid approaches relying on SKOS and certain RDF Schema (RDFS) and OWL properties do also exist.

IV. Ad-hoc Terminology Querying

In practice, frontend Web applications to describe research datasets contain input interfaces where users have to enter or select a particular concept with a certain domain focus. Text input of literals is still dominating. Auto-suggestion elements can be applied in combination with Linked Data sources [37] so that a user can select the correct concept out of a list of existing concepts which can be solely based on the input literal or restricted to a certain concept type. In order to bridge the gap between existing terminology and ontology services and frontend user interaction, we focus on concept queries that can retrieve RDF statements (description, URI, etc.) for a given concept label/URI or which can retrieve a list of concepts based on a given type or super class via the SPARQL Protocol and RDF Query Language.

When relevant databases, such as listed in Section III, exist and the requirements from Section II are satisfied, it is possible to query concepts of a particular characteristic, as shown in Figure 2, by either

- importing relevant terminologies in a centralized data base
- running follow-up queries along relevant data sources
- using federated query approaches along multiple endpoints.

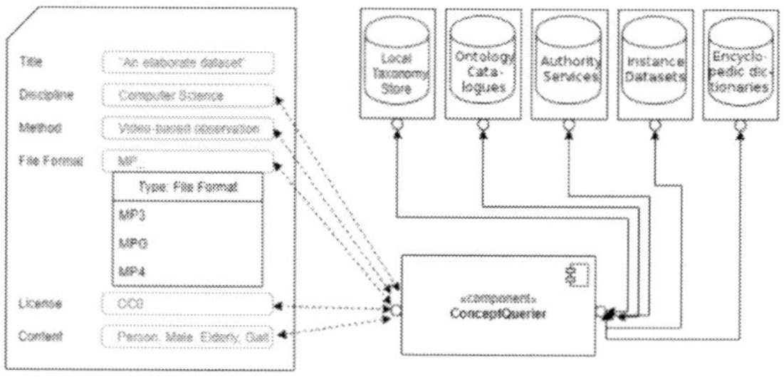

Figure 2. Conceptual architecture of a Concept Query Component.

The *ConceptQuerier* component provides a WebAPI that accepts requests with parameters stating the data the user has already entered in a text input field together with optional filters that describe the scope of the concepts that shall be retrieved. Such a component might analyze these parameters in advance and then query a set of appropriate services for existing concepts. This can either be done until the first Web service is able to satisfy the scope and returns corresponding concept data or in a parallel fashion, where the *ConceptQuerier* aggregates the results of multiple Web service responses.

Querying a remote service for a label or entity URI is considered as an already-understood trivial task. However, restricting existing resources based on filters requiring a particular class is more challenging as the type and hierarchy of an entity has to be identified additionally and the name of this type can either be filtered based on a keyword or based on a qualified identifier as conceptually shown in Figure 3.

```
SELECT DISTINCT ?concepturi ?conceptlabel
WHERE {
    ?concepturi rdfs:label ?conceptlabel .
    ?concepturi rdf:type ?type .
    ?type rdfs:label ?typelabel .
    FILTER(CONTAINS(lcase(str(?typelabel)),lcase(str(?query)))).
    # ... - other additional concept scope filter patterns -
}
```

Figure 3. Conceptual SPARQL query for concepts of a particular type, where ?query contains the type restriction of the Web application text input field.

V. EVALUATION

We have implemented a software prototype [38] as a proof of concept of such a *ConceptQuerier* in a *NodeJS* based Web application. It offers a simple Web form with multiple text input fields which have an auto-suggest extension that provides concepts of a corresponding scope. After entering a keyword in such a text field, an AJAX request is created and sent to local a */suggest* REST API endpoint of our demo application, containing the entered literal string and a list of filter expressions defined in advance by a developer based on the domain scope of the input field in a JSON string. The *ConceptQuerier* implements a simple query strategy to SPARQL endpoints investigated in this paper to the Wikidata and DBpedia SPARQL endpoint. It first retrieves a list of matching concept URIs and then executes a DESCRIBE on each entity URI to get additional meta information for each of these concepts.

We used this application to measure a selection of indicators for service quality and data quality metrics of the identified concept data sources in order to assess to which extent they are appropriate in practice to retrieve Linked Data identifiers for concepts of a particular knowledge domain. We therefore focused on a PopulationCompletenessMetric, RelevanceMetric and LatencyMetric calculated on the *extent* (Table IV) and *processing time* (Table V) for the retrieved result list for four exemplary concept groups: *gender* (for a structural interdisciplinary demographic characteristic), *license* (for a data-related, interdisciplinary aspect), *file format*(for a computer domain-specific characteristic) and *research method* (for a research-concept oriented characteristic).

Querying via a SPARQL endpoint concrete concept labels or concept URIs was a trivial task. Retrieving concepts which are an instance or sub concept of a certain class was also straight-forward and yielded results in less than *1.0* second as long as caching strategies were established (**) or the entity URI of the super concept is known. However, this is typically not the case and includes a tedious manual lookup activity. And these URIs differ in practice between multiple data sources as long as no linking/inference operation is executed in the background. We therefore focused on a keyword-based search for appropriate super classes and retrieved a list of concepts based on these classes. This aspect and the measured latency times make these concept queries inappropriate for federated SPARQL approaches.

We evaluated at least one appropriate representative for each of the identified data source groups. For ontology catalogs, candidates were the *BioPortal* and *LOV*. Querying the *BioPortal* Ontology Catalog had to be done over the REST API and included the manual retrieval of subclasses from identified ontologies (*), as the provided SPARQL interface was only in beta status and limited to ontology meta information. For authoritative terminology services, we focused on *EuroVoc* and additionally provided *EU Named Authority Lists*. For instance data collections, we selected *Wikidata* and the *LODCache*. But the SPARQL endpoint of *LODCache* always ended with a timeout without text search index optimizations. Instead, we therefore considered *DBpedia*.

TABLE IV. RETRIEVED INSTANCES PER REQUESTED CLASS LABEL

Concept Group	LOV	BioPortal	EuroVoc	Wikidata	DBpedia
Gender	27	37*	4	34	28
License	11	42*	41	435	108
File Format	128	51*	172	4201	432
Research Method	16	149*	0	16	5

We used existing fulltext index query extensions of the services, where possible. Retrieving concepts based on a keyword search in associated class labels had the advantage that also concepts from different but similar groups could be retrieved (e.g., a query via *Wikidata* for instances containing the string *"license"* also returned *435* relevant concepts from groups, such as *"software license"*, *"free license"* or *"data copyright license"*, in comparison to a URI based constraint *wd:Q207621* with only *47* results). However, this also resulted in extended processing times which were ten times higher in our experiment than in the explicit case, and might also lead to false-positive results (the search for concepts related to *"gender"* in *Wikidata*, e.g., returned *546* results, where the majority instantiated the group *"tennis tournament edition by gender"*). Additionally, the terms used for describing a certain concept class differed between the services (*"License"* vs. *"Licence"*, *"Media Type"* vs. *"File Format"*, or *"Research Method"* vs. *"Scientific Method"*).

TABLE V. PROCESSING TIME PER REQUESTED CONCEPT LABEL IN SECONDS

Concept Group	LOV	BioPortal	EuroVoc	Wikidata	DBpedia
Gender	1.5s	1.5s*	1.0s	2.7s	0.2s**
License	1.5s	1.5s	1.4s	5.3s	0.2s**
Media Type	1.8s	2.9s	1.0s	5.8s	0.5s**
Research Method	1.5s	3.9s	1.0s	13.2s	0.2s**

False-positive results also originated from the data basis of the data provider itself. Queries for *"File Format"*, e.g., in *Wikidata* and *DBpedia* returned many concepts with multiple literal duplicates representing the same concept with additional appendices in the label, or no *file format* at all. Despite the high number of results from instance data providers for this use case, a high-quality population completeness was not given as some concepts were still missing. But using this kind of data sources for retrieving other specialized concept groups (such as research objects, devices, material) was still a valid strategy in comparison to approaches based on general taxonomies or ontology catalogs, where none of these concepts might be provided in a controlled fashion at all.

Searching for other, research-specific entities, such as a *research method*, revealed actual weaknesses of the tested data sources. Surprisingly, 3 out of 4 tested data sources returned some results for such a concept class. However, the obtained concept results were limited and also contained inappropriate concepts, e.g., from *DBpedia*. Services providing research-oriented, domain specific taxonomies or ontologies are a better choice in such a case as they commonly provide controlled terms and vocabularies.

From a technical point of view, it is demonstrated that a *ConceptQuerier* with a homogeneous interface to query multiple Linked Data concept sources was feasible to implement. However, separate queries had to be carefully designed for each data provider as the underlying data model differed on how concepts are classified into groups, based on rdf:type, rdfs:Class/subClass relationships, skos:broader or even skos:inScheme.

VI. Related Work

Using standardized identifiers to classify publications is already common for decades in a librarian environment [39–41]. Authoritative services exist there to represent entities, such as *authors*, *disciplines*, *keywords*, *publications* and *publishers* [42]. In this context, the usage of Linked Data in a librarian environment was discussed and applied multiple times [43]. However, this topic also became increasingly important for the description and discovery of other scientific publication artifacts. Especially the publication of research datasets requires expert insights where only the originating researcher can precisely provide a meta description of the provided content. Embedded librarians [44] might help to reuse existing classification systems, but interdisciplinary data exchange requires atomic research concepts [45] from established terminologies to support Quality-Driven Information Filtering among different disciplines [46]. The Semantic Web community has already presented concepts on federated SPARQL engines [47], and how to execute SPARQL queries over the Web of Data [48] and how to establish links between similar concepts from multiple ontologies [49]. Beyond that, science put emphasis on the development of ontologies, such as *DataCite*, *SWAP*, *LinkedScience*, *SciData* or *ModSci]*, for modelling relationships between scientific branches and scientific entities with a focus on established predicates. Querying and proxying decentralized data sources, such as NCBO, was discussed for single examples, such as the *BioPortal* [50] or *ONKI* [51]. Beside that, general-purpose encyclopedia and thesaurus-based terminology-providing services exist [52, 53]. Dedicated semantic terminology services providing concrete interdisciplinary concepts are still rare and limited to discipline-specific approaches, such as [54]. In both cases, relying on a single API to query for particular concepts will fail if these terminologies are very specific and not present in the knowledge base of the addressed service. Research dataset related concepts might be such an example, where an approach to query specific data sources as presented in this paper can provide better results.

VII. Conclusion

In this paper, we presented an analysis of data sources that provide labels and persistent identifiers for concepts that can be used as values in meta descriptions of research datasets and other interdisciplinary relevant scientific publications. We have identified four groups of potentially relevant services (ontology catalogs, authoritative services, instance dataset collections, static independent vocabularies). We provided an implementation of a Web-based prototype that is capable of querying these remote concept sources based on a particular concept scope represented by a concrete type or class label. In an evaluation, we showed a varying service and data quality of existing data sources. Response times, especially for a keyword-based class search, are still too high to consider remote services for ad-hoc queries in real-time user interaction. Apart from that, different underlying data models require adapted query patterns for each data service which make federated query approaches difficult in practice. From a content-perspective, we still face a scattered distributed scenario, as none of the data sources provided a set of discipline-overspanning, research-focusing, interdisciplinary-usable concepts in a single point of access. To improve the interdisciplinary discovery and reuse of research datasets, additional research in the future is needed.

Acknowledgment

This work was funded by the Deutsche Forschungsgemeinschaft (DFG, German Research Foundation) – Project-ID 416228727 – SFB 1410

References

[1] C. C. Austin *et al.*, "Research data repositories: Review of current features, gap analysis, and recommendations for minimum requirements," *IASSIST Quarterly*, vol. 39, no. 4, p. 24, Jun. 2016.

[2] C. Steinhof, "Success criteria of research data repositories and their relevance for different stakeholder groups," masterthesis, Fachhochschule Potsdam, 2018.

[3] D. S. Sayogo and T. A. Pardo, "Exploring the determinants of scientific data sharing: Understanding the motivation to publish research data," *Gov. Inf. Q.*, vol. 30, pp. 19–31, 2013.

[4] M. D. Wilkinson *et al.*, "The FAIR Guiding Principles for scientific data management and stewardship," *Scientific Data*, vol. 3, no. 1, 2016.

[5] Datacite. Accessed: 2020-07-10. [Online]. Available: https://schema.datacite.org/

[6] Dublin core metadata element set (dcmes). Accessed: 2020-07-10. [Online]. Available: https://www.dublincore.org/specifications/dublin-core/dces/

[7] Dcmi terms. Accessed: 2020-07-10. [Online]. Available: https://www.dublincore.org/specifications/dublin-core/dcmi-terms/

[8] Dcat-ap. Accessed: 2020-07-10. [Online]. Available: https://www.dcat-ap.de/

[9] Marc. Accessed: 2020-07-10. [Online]. Available: http://www.loc.gov/marc/

[10] Mods. Accessed: 2020-07-10. [Online]. Available: https://rd-alliance.github.io/metadata-directory/standards/mods.html

[11] Premis. Accessed: 2020-07-10. [Online]. Available: https://www.loc.gov/standards/premis/

[12] schema.org. Accessed: 2020-07-10. [Online]. Available: https://schema.org/docs/documents.html

[13] M. Assante, L. Candela, D. Castelli, and A. Tani, "Are Scientific Data Repositories Coping with Research Data Publishing?" *Data Science Journal*, no. 15, 2016.

[14] Dbpedia. Accessed: 2020-07-10. [Online]. Available: https://wiki.dbpedia.org/

[15] Wikidata. Accessed: 2020-07-10. [Online]. Available: https://www.wikidata.org/wiki/Wikidata:Main_Page

[16] Conceptnet. Accessed: 2020-07-10. [Online]. Available: https://conceptnet.io/

[17] A. Langer, "PIROL : Cross-domain Research Data Publishing with Linked Data technologies," in *Proceedings of the Doctoral Consortium Papers Presented at the 31st CAiSE 2019*, M. La Rosa, P. Plebani, and M. Reichert, Eds. Rome: CEUR, 2019, pp. 43–51.

[18] Zenodo. Accessed: 2020-07-10. [Online]. Available: https://zenodo.org/

[19] Osf. Accessed: 2020-07-10. [Online]. Available: https://osf.io/

[20] Mendeley. Accessed: 2020-07-10. [Online]. Available: https://data.mendeley.com/

[21] Orcid. Accessed: 2020-07-10. [Online]. Available: https://orcid.org/

[22] Grid. Accessed: 2020-07-10. [Online]. Available: https://www.grid.ac/

[23] Gnd. Accessed: 2020-07-10. [Online]. Available: https://www.dnb.de/DE/Professionell/Standardisierung/GND/gnd_node.html

[24] Lccn. Accessed: 2020-07-10. [Online]. Available: https://www.loc.gov/marc/lccn_structure.html

[25] Viaf. Accessed: 2020-07-10. [Online]. Available: https://www.viaf.org/

[26] E. Lapi, N. Tcholtchev, L. Bassbouss, F. Marienfeld, and I. Schieferdecker, "Identification and utilization of components for a linked open data platform," in *2012 IEEE 36th Annual Computer Software and Applications Conference Workshops*, 2012, pp. 112–115.

[27] Skos datasets. Accessed: 2020-07-10. [Online]. Available: https://www.w3.org/2001/sw/wiki/SKOS/Datasets

[28] Datahub. Accessed: 2020-07-10. [Online]. Available: https://www.datahub.io/

[29] Cerif. Accessed: 2020-07-10. [Online]. Available: https://eurocris.org/services/main-features-cerif

[30] Kdsf. Accessed: 2020-07-10. [Online]. Available: https://kerndatensatz-forschung.de/index.php?id=version1

[31] Wordnet. Accessed: 2020-07-10. [Online]. Available: https://wordnet.princeton.edu/

[32] Babelnet. Accessed: 2020-07-10. [Online]. Available: https://babelnet.org/

[33] Wiktionary. Accessed: 2020-07-10. [Online]. Available: https://www.wiktionary.org/

[34] Omegawiki. Accessed: 2020-07-10. [Online]. Available: http://www.omegawiki.org/

[35] Swoogle. Accessed: 2020-07-10. [Online]. Available: http://swoogle.umbc.edu/

[36] Sindice. Accessed: 2020-07-10. [Online]. Available: https://www.dataversity.net/end-support-sindice-com-search-engine-history-lessons-learned-legacy-guest-post/

[37] A. Langer, C. Göpfert, and M. Gaedke, "URI-aware user input interfaces for the unobtrusive reference to Linked Data," *IADIS International Journal on Computer Science and Information Systems*, vol. 13, no. 2, pp. 62–75, 2018.

[38] A. Langer, C. Göpfert, and M. Gaedke. Conceptquerier prototypical implementation. Accessed: 2020-07-10. [Online]. Available: https://gitlab.hrz.tu-chemnitz.de/vsr/researchinputform

[39] H. Albrechtsen and E. K. Jacob, "The dynamics of classification systems as boundary objects for cooperation in the electronic library," *Library Trends*, vol. 47, no. 2, pp. 293–312, 1998.

[40] P. Rafferty, "The representation of knowledge in library classification schemes," *Knowledge Organization*, vol. 28, no. 4, pp. 180–191, 2001.

[41] M. Satija, "Library classification : An essay in terminology," *Knowledge organization*, vol. 27, no. 4, pp. 221–229, 2000.

[42] E. T. Mitchell 2, *Library Linked Data: Early Activity and Development.*, 2016, vol. 52, no. 1.

[43] M. Hallo, S. Luján-Mora, A. Maté, and J. Trujillo, "Current state of Linked Data in digital libraries," *Journal of Information Science*, vol. 42, no. 2, pp. 117–127, 2016.

[44] D. Shumaker, *Embedded librarian: innovative strategies for taking knowledge where it's needed.* Information Today, 2012.

[45] A. Pfeifer, "More efficient research with Atomic Research," 2018, accessed: 2020-07-19. [Online]. Available: https://usertimes.io/2018/06/20/effizienter-forschen-mit-atomic-research/

[46] C. Bizer, "Quality-driven information filtering in the context of web-based information systems," Ph.D. dissertation, 2007, accessed: 2020-09-10. [Online]. Available: http://dx.doi.org/10.17169/refubium-14260

[47] N. A. Rakhmawati, J. Umbrich, M. Karnstedt, A. Hasnain, and M. Hausenblas, "Querying over federated sparql endpoints —a state of the art survey," 2013.

[48] O. Hartig, C. Bizer, and J.-C. Freytag, "Executing SPARQL Queries over the Web of Linked Data," accessed: 2020-09-10. [Online]. Available: http://olafhartig.de/files/HartigEtAl_QueryTheWeb_ISWC09_Preprint.pdf

[49] R. Parundekar, C. A. Knoblock, and J. L. Ambite, "Discovering concept coverings in ontologies of linked data sources," in *The Semantic Web – ISWC 2012*, P. Cudré-Mauroux *et al.*, Eds. Berlin, Heidelberg: Springer Berlin Heidelberg, 2012, pp. 427–443.

[50] M. Salvadores *et al.*, "Using SPARQL to query bioportal ontologies and metadata," *Lecture Notes in Computer Science (including subseries Lecture Notes in Artificial Intelligence and Lecture Notes in Bioinformatics)*, vol. 7650 LNCS, no. PART 2, pp. 180–195, 2012.

[51] K. Viljanen, J. Tuominen, E. Mäkelä, and E. Hyvönen, "Normalized access to ontology repositories," *Proceedings - IEEE 6th International Conference on Semantic Computing, ICSC 2012*, pp. 109–116, 2012.

[52] R. Navigli and S. P. Ponzetto, "BabelNet: The automatic construction, evaluation and application of a wide-coverage multilingual semantic network," *Artificial Intelligence*, vol. 193, pp. 217–250, 2012.

[53] R. Speer and C. Havasi, "Representing general relational knowledge in conceptnet 5." in *LREC*, 2012, pp. 3679–3686.

[54] N. Karam *et al.*, "A Terminology Service Supporting Semantic Annotation, Integration, Discovery and Analysis of Interdisciplinary Research Data," *Datenbank-Spektrum*, vol. 16, no. 3, pp. 195–205, 2016.

Using RESTFul API and SHACL to Invoke Executable Semantics in the Context of Core Software Ontology

Xianming Zhang
Aviation Industry Development and Research Center of China
Beijing, China
e-mail:forzxm@163.com

Abstract—**It is known that executable semantics can be constructed for tasks in the context of some ontologies for computational domain (here, it is Core Software Ontology), but it cannot support that the constructed executable semantics be invoked to launch an actual computing process for returned values. The goal of this paper is to put forward a framework in which Representational State Transfer Application Programming Interface (RESTFul API), Shapes Constraint Language (SHACL) and Core Software Ontology can work together to invoke constructed executable semantics and finally get the result. Firstly, a link between RESTFul API and Core Software Ontology is necessary and conceptually established. With such a link, we can see that the former will energize and refine the latter. Secondly, this paper investigates how to take advantage of SHACL to invoke RESTFul API for returned value. Thirdly, with the help of SHACL, we can see how RESTFul API energizes Core Software Ontology, namely by invoking the executable semantics in the context of Core Software Ontology to get the result. With an example in this paper, we can use this framework to get the returned value and prove the feasibility of this framework.**

Keywords-Executable Semantics; Core Software Ontology; DUL Ontology; SHACL; RESTFul API.

I. INTRODUCTION

DOLCE Ontology is a well-known foundation ontology that provides a few design patterns providing a substantial foundation for building multiple core ontologies and domain ontologies [1] [11]. One of these ontologies is the Core Software Ontology (CSO). It must be acknowledged that CSO diligently achieves the goal of describing computational domain, particularly portraying aspects of computing object (software, data and their realizations) and activity (execution of software) semantically, all of which implement executable semantics. With SPARQL QUERY, it is easy to catch sight of semantic aspects of a computing configuration, including its I/O, execution plan, and execution situation and so on. By combining SPARQL CONSTRUCT with execution plan, execution situation embodying computing objects and activities to portray computing configuration can be constructed. But the execution situation still cannot be used to invoke the included computing objects (software) and the initial hope of building software is to launch a computing/execution and return a value, so it is clear that the current state of CSO fails to achieve that.

Today, more and more RESTFul APIs are put into use as computing resources; their emergence means that software can be regarded as computing resources published on the Web. Both users and running codes can access them and get result via their open URLs. It is known that a typical ontology is based on the Resource Description Framework (RDF), and the RDF provides a format basis in which URLs are encapsulated to represent multiple entities, either types or instances. While navigating ontology, users can access these URLs that are often pointers to html files, texts and multimedia files, contents of which can be either directly downloaded or viewed on the Web browsers. But RESTFul APIs often focus on computing, which means that their URLs should not be simply accessed and need some values as input and then the subsequent returned values should be interpreted semantically and used for further computing tasks. It is simple to directly fit RESTFul APIs as URLs into the context of CSO for content management, but that cannot enable executable semantics, including these RESTFul APIs, to be invoked to launch computing in the context of CSO.

Shapes Constraint Language (SHACL) provides SHACL JavaScript Extensions (SHACL-JS) engine that can access and invoke JavaScript code on the Web by its URL, with which SHACL Specification based on SPARQL (SHACL-SPARQL), can be used to infer new triples containing values coming from invoking JavaScript code. From this perspective, SHACL can help to invoke executable semantic in the context of CSO if JavaScript file URLs are fitted into it. However JavaScript cannot support important intermediate data, often stored in databases or data files, for returning the final result and too complex algorithms such as Matrix or Calculus. As result, it is less necessary and applicable to have JavaScript files fit into the context of CSO than RESTFul APIs.

This paper presents a framework in which the problem above can be solved.

- a) Fitting RESTFul API into the context of CSO enables the URL of RESTFul to become part of the context of CSO as computing resource, which testifies the rationality that with the help of RESTFul API, the applicability of CSO makes a great progress. It is not easy to access RESTFul APIs as computing resources only by their URLs because the fault of CSO is that the first paper on CSO is before the emergence of RESTFul API.
- b) Breaking the hurdle between the SHACL-JS engine and RESTFul API to enable the former to invoke the latter to get the result, which can be done by investigating the running mechanism of the SHACL-JS engine and taking advantage of it to

make a devised scenario in which the engine invokes a specific RESTFul API as JavaScript code.

- c) With a , b and SHACL-SPARQL Construct, RESTFul API can fit into the context of CSO very well and the constructed executable semantics can invoked for desired purpose.

This paper is structured as follows. Section 2 presents the related work, mainly why to choose SHACL. Section 3 introduces a framework to achieve the purpose of this paper. Section 4 presents a use case of computing lift coefficient of airfoil, where readers can get sense of the motivation. Section 5 is how to apply the framework to the use case and get the desired result to verify the framework. Section 6 is the conclusion.

II. Related Work

In the past years, a large number of RDF-based applications have been developed for various domains. In order to take advantage of semantic feature of RDF, several query and rule languages, such as SPARQL [10], Jena rule [14] and SWRL [13], have been developed and adopted widely with a number of inbuilt functions [15][16] for users to execute various computations during either querying or reasoning.

Unfortunately, due to computing complexity in the real world, such as matrix calculation, linear operation and those requiring external data source, the execution above is insufficient to accomplish such computing tasks.

In order to solve such problems the paper [12] turns to SPARQL Inferencing Notation (SPIN) [17]. In SPIN, SPARQL queries can be stored together with RDF data models in RDF graphs to define executable semantics of classes and their members. SPIN provides a special framework (SPINx) that allows user-defined function to link an external JavaScript file to RDF data by RDF property, performs this user-defined function for executing computing by invoking this linked JavaScript file [18]. The paper [12] investigates the mechanism of SPINx framework and devises a method to link RESTFul API with RDF data, and invoke RESTFul API while either querying or reasoning. It must be pointed out that this paper opens a new window in Semantic Web technology.

SHACL is strongly influenced by SPIN and can be regarded as its successor [19]. SHACL includes basically all features of SPIN, and more. Most importantly, SHACL is an official W3C Recommendation, which makes it far more likely that other vendors will support it [19].

As result of this, this paper adopts SHACL rather than SPIN.

III. Introduction to the Framework

This paper puts forward a framework working as basis for invoking executable semantics, in which the following ones are cooperating with each other to achieve the goal: Core Software Ontology (CSO), Shapes Constraint Language (SHACL) and RESTFul API. It must be addressed that how SHACL-JS invoke a RESTFul API.

A. *Introduction to Core Software Ontology*

In this paper, a lightweight, easy-to-apply foundational ontology known as DOLCE+DnS Ultralite (DUL) [1] [5] is used as basis for CSO. Due to space limit of this paper, only some aspects concerned are discussed here. For more details, readers can refer to [1]-[4].

1) *Software and Data*

The programs that manipulate the data are usually referred to as CSO: Software, a special kind of DUL: InformationObject. CSO: Data also can be considered as a special kind of DUL: InformationObject. The difference to CSO: Software is that CSO: Data does not DUL: express a DUL: Plan.

CSO: ComputationalObject as a special kind of DUL: InformationRealization can be the appearance of algorithm in memory or disks. Just like the fact that DUL: InformationRealization DUL: realizes DUL: InformationObject in DUL, CSO: ComputationalObject DUL: realizes CSO: Data as well as CSO: Software.

CSO: ComputationalActivity as a special kind of DUL: Activity is the correspondence of the execution of a CSO: ComputationalObject. This is the form of software, which manifests itself in a sequence of activities in the computing domain.

2) *Task, Input and Output*

We use CSO: ComputationalTask, a special kind of DUL: Task, to represent invocations, and the actual executions of CSO: ComputationalTask can be CSO: ComputationalActivity. A set of CSO: ComputationalTask are grouped and linked via the DUL: follows and DUL: precedes associations in a DUL: Plan.

It is also needed to model the CSO: Input and CSO: Output for CSO: ComputationalTask. The CSO: Input and CSO: Output are required to represent the input and output for computing task, and they are special kinds of DUL: Role, which are both DUL: isRoleOf CSO: Data and DUL: definedIn a DUL: Plan. The relationships between CSO: Input (CSO: Output) and CSO: ComputationalTask are modeled by CSO: inputFor (CSO: outputFor).

CSO: executes is also introduced to formalize that a CSO: Software is used to complete a CSO: ComputationalTask. That means that CSO:Software begin to CSO:executes a CSO: ComputationalTask in the DUL:Plan and then a DUL:Situation regarded as a computing configuration holding DUL:satisfies association with the DUL:Plan, comes into being, where a DUL: CSO:ComputationalObject that DUL:realizes this CSO:Software holds a DUL:hasParticipant association with a CSO: ComputationalActivity that also has DUL:executesTask association with the CSO: ComputationalTask(see D1).

CSO:executes(x, y) =def CSO:Software(x) ∧
CSO:ComputationalTask(y) ∧
∃co,ca,p(CSO:ComputationalObject(co) ∧
CSO:ComputationalActivity(ca) ∧ DUL:Plan(p) ∧
DUL:realizes(co,x) ∧ DUL:express(x, p) ∧ DUL:

defines(p, y) ∧ DUL: executesTask (ca, y) ∧ DUL: hasParticipant (ca, co)) (D1)

B. Simple Introduction to RESTFul API

A RESTFul API is an application program interface (API) that uses existing HTTP methodologies defined by the RFC 2616 protocol. They use GET to retrieve a resource; PUT to change the state of or update a resource, which can be an object, file or block; POST to create that resource; and DELETE to remove it [9].

RESTFul APIs for a website are codes that allow software programs to communicate with each other. The RESTFul API spells out the proper way for a developer to write a program requesting services from an operating system or other applications.

With RESTFul APIs, networked components are resources the user requests access to -- a black box whose implementation details are unclear. All calls are stateless; nothing can be retained by the RESTFul service between executions [9].

C. Introduction to SHACL,SHACL-SPARQL and SHACL-JS

SHACL is a W3C recommendation [6] [7]. A SHACL processor takes a shapes graph and a data graph as input. The shapes graph defines so-called shapes, which are a collection of constraints. A shape also tells the engine for which nodes in the data graph it applies to (using sh: targetNode).

SHACL-SPARQL is one extension mechanism for SHACL to express constraints in SPARQL, allowing shape definitions to point at executable SPARQL queries to perform the validations [8].

SHACL-JS engine is an advanced extension mechanism for SHACL, allowing users to express SHACL constraints and the advanced features of custom targets, functions and rules with the help of JavaScript. The principle of calling JavaScript function is to download JavaScript file contents via HTTP to the engine, and then engine resolves the contents to execute the code specified by the function name. The figure below shows that how SHACL-JS invokes a RESTFul API.

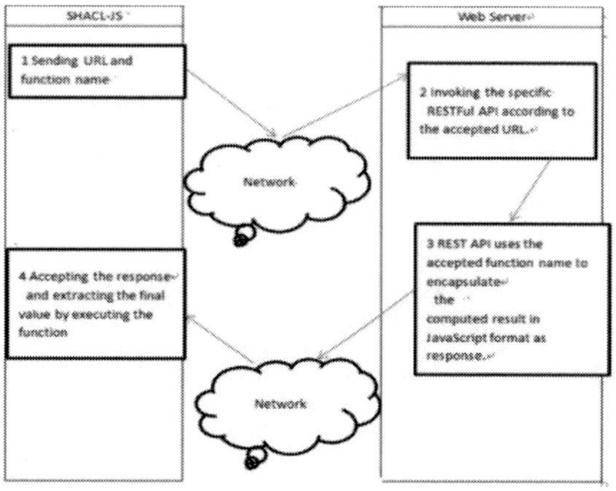

Figure 1. How to use SHAL-JS to invoke a RESTFul API.

Figure 1 above is explained in detail. A computer with SHACL-JS is called as client and a computer with RESTFul API running on it is called as Web Server.

1) A user operating the client submits data in RDF that contain URL of a RESTFul API and a function name into SHACL-JS, SHACL-JS sends the URL to Web Server after parsing. In this case, the URL is http://ip/lift-coefficient?attack-angle=13; function name is called as func.

2) Web Server runs the received URL and then gets 1.51, the returned value.

3) Web Server encapsulates the value as the string "function func () {return 1.55 ;}" in JavaScript code format, and then feedbacks to the client.

4) The client simply runs the string, and returns 1.51 to user.

IV. Introduction to A Use Case of Computing Lift Coefficient of Airfoil

The dedicated function of an airfoil on an airplane is to provide lift during flight and it is necessary to computing varying lift with continuously changing attack-angle. The lift-coefficient formula is as follow.

Lift-coefficient=f(attack-angle) (F1)

In F1, there is no explicit formula (or calculation script) to accurately calculate lift coefficient from attack angle. Typically, the actual lift-coefficient is a list of data through a limited number of experiments that record the data under different attack angles, as shown in Figure 2.

Attack Angle	Lift Coefficient
-5	0
0	0.6
5	1.1
10	1.4
15	1.7
20	1.6
22	0.6
23	0

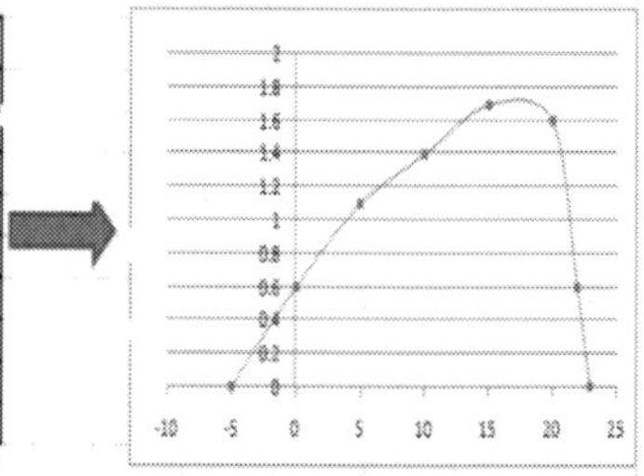

Figure 2. The feft part is a list of attack angles and corresponding lift coefficient, the right part is the curve graph reflecting the left part

Here these experiments are conducted independently, which means these data are locally stored in a Web server not freely accessible to others. A dedicated RESTFul API can be developed and deployed on the Web server. The RESTFul API implements numerical approximation, such as least square and interpolating to allow users to query for any given attack-angle. In this paper, the URL for this RESTFul API is below:

http://ip/lift-coefficient?attack-angle={value}

In order to work out lift coefficient while attack angle being 13, the access URL is

http://ip/lift-coefficient?attack-angle=13

V. Applying Framework to the Use Case

In this section, the framework is applied to the use case, and we can freely get the returned value of lift coefficient for a given attack angle. In this paper, a temporary ontology is created in the context of CSO for this use case, known as S-C ontology.

A. *Modeling the Basic Entities and Properties of S-C Ontology for Use Case In the Context of CSO*

A few of entities and properties can be extracted from this use case and be aligned to predefined concepts in CSO.

1. The s-c: attack-angle and s-c: lift-coefficient can be regarded as an instance of CSO: Data, due to their goals are to be manipulated by the software as input and output respectively.
2. The s-c: computation1 can be regarded as an instance of CSO: Software, which is responsible for computing lift-coefficient with an attack-angle.
3. The s-c: computation1-computational-object can be regarded as an instance of CSO: ComputationalObject, which DUL: realizes s-c: computation1 and rdfs:seeAlso "http://server:8080/lift-coefficient?Attack-angle={value}".
4. The s-c: activity1 can be regarded as an instance of CSO: ComputationalActivity, which identifies the execution of a certain CSO: ComputationalObject/CSO: Software.
5. The s-c: run is rdfs:subProperty of DUL: hasParticipant, which associates a CSO: ComputationalActivity with a CSO: ComputationalObject and means giving rise to an actual execution of a software.
6. The s-c:in is rdfs: subProperty of DUL: hasParticipant, which associates a CSO: ComputationalActivity with a CSO: Data as input for computing.
7. The s-c:out is rdfs:subProperty of DUL: hasParticipant, which associates a CSO: ComputationalActivity with a CSO: Data as output for computing.

B. *Modeling Plan and Situation in S-C ontology*

The s-c:computation-plan is an instance of DUL: Plan, the design of computing configuration , which includes entities as follows: s-c:input-attack-angle, s-c:output-lift-coefficient and s-c:task1.The s-c:input-attack-angle can be regarded as an instance of CSO:Input and DUL:isRoleOf s-c:attack-angle outside the plan. The s-c:output-lift-angle can be regarded as an instance of CSO:Output and DUL:isRoleOf s-c:lift-coefficient outside the plan The s-c:task1 can be regarded as an instance of CSO:ComputationalTask, which has CSO:inputFor association with s-c:input-attack-angle, CSO:outputFor association with s-c:output-lift-angle and CSO:executes association with s-c:computation1.

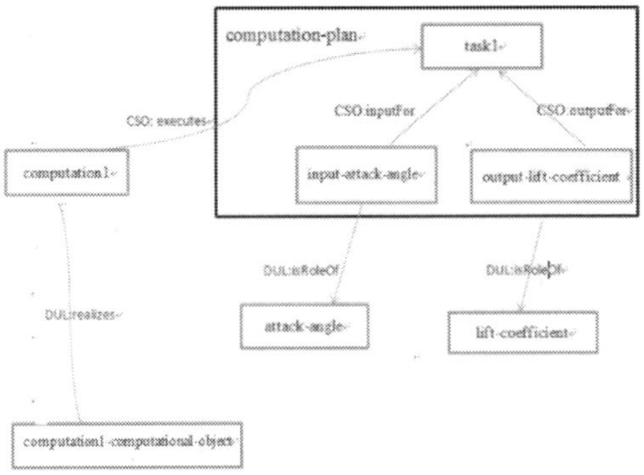

Figure 3. The structure of s-c: computation-plan and its association with software and data

Although s-c:computation-plan is the design of computing configuration, and the design does not coming into use until the situation known as s-c:computation-situation (an instance of DUL:Situation) holding DUL:satisfies association with it, includes s-c:attack-angle,s-c:lift-coefficient,s-c:activity1, s-ccomputation1-computational-object.In s-c:computation-situation, s-c:attack-angle s-c:in s-c:activity1,s-c:lift-coefficient s-c:out s-c:activity1 and s-c:computation1-computational-object s-c:run s-activity1. According to D1 (section 2), s-c: computation-situation will be constructed by s-c: computation-plan and associated CSO: Software and CSO: Data outside the plan.

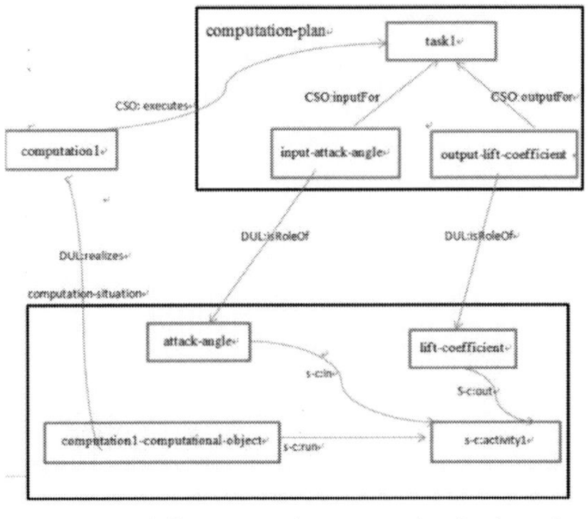

Figure 4. The structure of s-c: computation-situation and association with s-c: computation-plan

C. *To Inference Situation from Plan*

The s-c: computation-plan is the design of computing configuration, and according to CSO the actual computing configuration (executable semantics), which return values should be s-c: computation-situation, the special kind of DUL: Situation In this paper, the CONSTRUCT clause of SPARQL Update is used to construct s-c: computation-situation from s-c: computation-plan with associated CSO: Data and CSO: Software. The SPARQL statement is below.

```
construct {
  ?software_computational_object s-c: run s-c: activity1.
  ?inData s-c: in s-c: activity1.
  ?inData DUL: hasDataValue ?value.
  ?outData s-c: out s-c: activity1.
  ?software_computational_object rdfs: seeAlso ?url.
 }
where {
 GRAPH     <http://semantic-computing/#computation-plan>{
      ?inRole cso: input-for s-c: task1.
      ?outRole cso: output-for s-c: task1.
 }
 GRAPH <http://semantic-computing/#software-plan>{
   ?software cso: executes s-c: task1.
   ?inData  DUL: hasRole  ?inRole.
  ?outData DUL: hasRole   ?outRole.}
  GRAPH <http://semantic-computing/#software-data>{
?software_computational_object DUL:realizes ?software.
  ?software_computational_object rdfs: seeAlso ?url.
   ?inData DUL: hasDataValue ?value. }
}
```

There are several graphs in this statement: <http://semantic-computing/#computation-plan> contains triples of s-c: computation-plan; <http://semantic-computing/#software-plan> contains triples representing associations between CSO: Data/CSO: Software and entities in s-c:computation-plan; <http://semantic-computing/#software-data> contains triples representing associations among CSO:Data, CSO:Software. The constructed result is below, it is noted the s-c: computation1-computational-object (an instance of CSO: ComputationalObject) links a RESTFul API via rdfs: seeAlso.

```
  s-c: computation1-computational-object s-c: run s-c: activity1.
  s-c: attack-angle s-c: in s-c: activity1.
  s-c: attack-angle DUL: hasDataValue 13.0.
  s-c: lift-coefficient s-c: out s-c: activity1.
s-c: computation1-computational-object rdfs: seeAlso <http://ip/lift-coefficient?attack-angle=>.
```

D. Using SHACL to Invoke Executable Semantics

The s-c: computation-situation forms executable semantics, and now its goal is to create a triple of "s-c: lift-coefficient DUL: hasDataValue ?value",

Using the triples of s-c: computation-situation to create a model named Shape-Function, triples of which meet standard of SHACL-JS to form a function that will be further used to invoke RESTFul API. The SPARQL Construct statement to use is below.

```
 prefix sh: <http://www.w3.org/ns/shacl#>
 construct {
 s-c: dynamicFunc sh: jsFunctionName "dynamicFunc".
 s-c: dynamicFunc sh: jsLibrary <http://jsLibrary/temp>.
 s-c: dynamicFunc sh: returnType xsd: double.
 s-c: dynamicFunc sh: parameter <http://parameter/temp>.
 s-c: dynamicFunc rdf: type sh: JSFunction.
 <http://parameter/temp> sh: datatype  xsd: double.
 <http://parameter/temp> sh: path s-c: number.
 <http://jsLibrary/temp> sh: jsLibraryURL ?dynamicFuncURL.
 }
 where{
  ?software_computational_object s-c: run s-c: activity1.
  ?inData s-c: in s-c: activity1.
  ?inData DUL: hasDataValue ?value.
  ?software_computational_object rdfs: seeAlso ?url.
  BIND(('http://IP/RESTTemplate/access?url='+STR(?url)+
 '? value='+STR (?value)) as ?dynamicFuncURL).
}
```

The constructed model named as Shape-Function, also can be regarded as a shape according to SHACL, is below.

```
 s-c: dynamicFunc sh: jsFunctionName "dynamicFunc".
 s-c: dynamicFunc sh: jsLibrary <http://jsLibrary/temp>.
 s-c: dynamicFunc sh: returnType xsd:double.
 s-c: dynamicFunc sh: parameter <http://parameter/temp>.
 s-c: dynamicFunc rdf: type sh: JSFunction.
 <http://parameter/temp> sh: datatype xsd: double.
 <http://parameter/temp> sh: path s-c: number.
 <http://jsLibrary/temp>
sh:jsLibraryURL
'http://ip/RESTTemplate/access?url=http://ip/lift-coefficient?attack-angle=13'.
```

It is noted that there are two RESTFul APIs that should be discussed. They are 'http://ip/RESTTemplate/access?url=" and http://ip/lift-coefficient?attack-angle=. The function of the former is to invoke the latter and encapsulate the return value in JavaScript format with "dynamicFunc" as function name, below is the concise code.

In addition to the Shape-Function complied with SHACL-JS, another model named Shape–Construct complied with SHACL-SPARQL is needed to work with the Model-Function to achieve the goal. The Shape –Construct is below.

```
 @prefix s-c :< http://semantic-computing/#>.
 s-c:rule1
  a rdfs: Class, sh:NodeShape ;
  sh:targetNode s-c:activity1 ;
  rdfs:label "to run sc:activity1" ;
  sh: rule[
 a sh:SPARQLRule ;
 sh: construct """
 CONSTRUCT {
 ?outdata DUL: hasDataValue ?value.}
 WHERE {
 ?outdata s-c: out ?this.
 BIND    (<http://semantic-computing/#dynamicFunc>()
AS ?value).
      }
                """ ;
  ].
```

Figure 5 below shows the process and result.

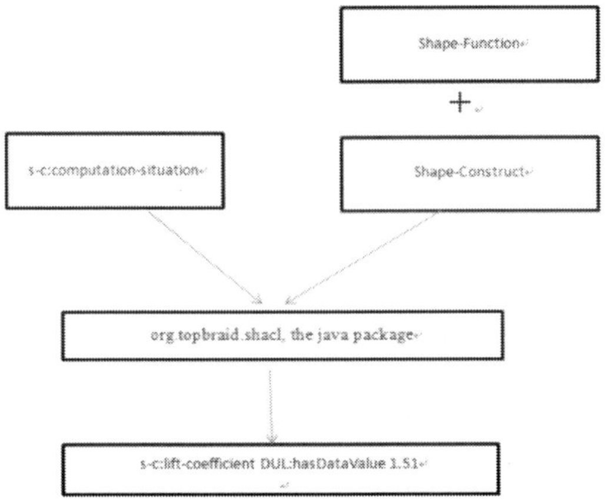

Figure 5. The process and method of creating the new triple

In Figure 5, after interference a new triple is generated, content of which is "s-c: lift-coefficient DUL: hasDataValue 1.51".

VI. CONCLUSION

With the abundance in IT infrastructure today, the number of RESTFul APIs is growing and applications of ontologies for computational domain should be constructed by fully taking advantage of this situation. This paper discusses that usefulness and feasibility of using SHACL and RESTFul API to invoke executable semantics. It can be said that the paper's achievement is useful in development of ontology-based knowledge system.

In our opinion, the study of this paper can make the Semantic Web models, here Core Software Ontology, have powerful computing capacity. Of course, the coordinating asynchronous requests, latency, availability and security must be taken into account. These problems should be solved effectively (at least in part) as the technologies for RESTFul API, exemplified by SPRING BOOT, has made much effort to solve them from birth.

REFERENCES

[1] A. Gangemi et al., "Sweetening Ontologies with DOLCE", EKAW 2002, pp. 166-181 ,2002

[2] A. Gangemi and P. Mika, "Understanding the Semantic Web through Descriptions and Situations", ODBASE 2003, pp. 689-706, 2003.

[3] A. Gangemi,"Task taxonomies for knowledge content. Metokis Deliverable D07",2004.

[4] D. Oberle et al.,"Towards Ontologies for Formalizing Modularization and Communication in Large Software Systems" , Journal of Applied Ontology, vol. 1, no. 2, pp. 163–202, 2006

[5] https://www.w3.org/2005/Incubator/ssn/wiki/DUL_ssn.[retrieved: November, 2020]

[6] https://www.w3.org/TR/shacl/.[retrieved: November, 2020]

[7] J. Corman et al.," Semantics and validation of recursive SHAC",ISWC 2018, pp. 318– 336,2018.

[8] https://w3c.github.io/data-shapes/shacl-js/#introduction.[retrieved: September, 2020]

[9] https://searchapparchitecture.techtarget.com/definition/RESTful-API. [retrieved: November, 2020]

[10] https://www.w3.org/TR/sparql11-query[retrieved: November, 2020]

[11] S. Borgo and C. Masolo," chapter Foundational choices in DOLCE", Handbook on Ontologies , 2009.

[12] X. Zhang,"An approach to enabling RDF data in querying to invoke REST API for complex calculating",International Conference on Dublin Core and Metadata Applications 2018,pp. 34-42, 2018.

[13] http://www.w3.org/Submission/SWRL. [retrieved: September, 2020]

[14] J. Carroll et al, "The Jena Semantic Web Platform: Architecture and Design", HP Laboratories Technical Report HPL-2003-146,2003.

[15] https://github.com/dotnetrdf/dotnetrdf/wiki/DeveloperGuide-SPARQL-XPath-Functions. [retrieved: November, 2020]

[16] http://jena.apache.org/documentation/query/library-function.html. [retrieved: November, 2020]

[17] https://www.topquadrant.com/technology/sparql-rules-spin. [retrieved: November, 2020]

[18] http://spinrdf.org/spinx.html. [retrieved: September, 2020]

[19] https://www.spinrdf.org/spin-shacl.html. [retrieved: September, 2020]

Toward a Semantic Representation of the Joconde Database

Jean-Claude Moissinac

LTCI, Télécom Paris
Institut polytechnique de Paris
19 Place Marguerite Perey,
91120 Palaiseau
France
Email: moissinac@enst.fr

François Rouzé

Independant researcher
France
Email: francois.rouze@gmail.com

Piyush Wadhera
and Bastien Germain

Réciproque
12 Rue Saint-Maur, 75011 Paris
France
Email: {piyush.wadhera,bastien.germain}@reciproque.com

***Abstract*—The Joconde database is a French database, which describes about 600,000 works from French art collections. In the *Data&Musée* project, we process data from museums and monuments. We have chosen to model the data using a knowledge graph approach. We enrich the data of the project partners with data from other sources. In this article, we present the semantic representation that we have adopted for the Joconde database and the methods used to obtain this representation. Our semantic representation of the Joconde database is available as Open data as the SemJoconde dataset. We believe that the SemJoconde data can become useful references for work on the use of semantic techniques in the cultural field.**

Keywords–RDF; semantic web; culture; SemJoconde; cultural heritage; LOD.

I. Introduction

This paper introduces a novel dataset named SemJoconde that contains a large number of artworks. This dataset is published as Open Data. This dataset is produced from the Joconde database, of which we have generated an enriched semantic version. We present the dataset and the methods used to obtain this representation. We define a semantic model based on CIDOC-CRM -Conceptual Reference Model- and interlink as many entities as possible to Wikidata [1]. Wikidata is a large semantic dataset about world things, linked to Wikipedia pages. Links with Wikidata are created for creators, domains, places, etc.

This work is part of the *Data&Musée* project [2], in which we process data from museums and monuments. The goal is to reply to questions like: is not a visitor to the Louvre also a visitor to the Eiffel Tower? Better still, a visitor who is satisfied with his Middle Ages journey at the Louvre, isn't he a future visitor to the ramparts and the old town of Carcassonne? So, beside collecting data about the visitors, we are collecting knowledges about the artworks and cultural institutions in France. Building the SemJoconde dataset is part of this process.

This paper follows some works related to semantic representation of data in the cultural heritage domain [3][4], which are generally limited to represent the collection of an unique collection, except Europeana [5]. Our contribution is the dataset itself rather than novel methods, which are mainly simples ways to get entity linking [6][7]. In this article, we present the model, and the process to translate from the JSON version of the database to the semantic interlinked version. We think that it will be useful for communities in the graph technologies domain -graph embedding, reasoning, etc.- and in the cultural heritage domain. Section II presents related works. Section III presents sources used to build SemJoconde. Section V presents the methods used to build SemJoconde and some insight to evaluate the quality of the results. Section VI gives an idea of the technical structure of the dataset. Section II-C presents related datasets. Section VII concludes and suggests future works.

II. Related works

A. *Entity Matching and Entity Linking*

Several part of our work deal with entity matching: we search for entities in text [6][7]. The problem is composed of entity recognition, entity disambiguation and entity linking. In our case, the searched entity is known by its label (e.g., Claude Monet) and, sometimes, some complementary data (e.g., period of the work) and we expect to produce a link/URI - Uniform Resource Identifier- in some Linked Data dataset. It is a well-known problem with different approaches proposed depending on each context.

In our work, the problem is simplified by the fact that we do not need to recognize the entities and the entities types in a text: we need only to search for identifiers corresponding to labels for which we know the type. We tried different approaches to produce the links and the simple approach presented in this article gives good results.

B. *Production and applications of Cultural Heritage datasets*

In this section, we will present previous works about the build process of semantically structured datasets in the cultural heritage domain.

The Getty Foundation has a knowledge graph about its collections. The Foundation described in detail the choices about vocabularies and ontologies used by the Knowledge graph and the process of building it [3]. The Getty Foundation proposes a list of vocabularies and entities using these vocabularies [3]: specifically Art Architecture Thesaurus (AAT) and Union List of Artist Names (ULAN). Both AAT and ULAN are thesauri containing structured terminology for art, architecture, decorative arts, archival materials, visual surrogates, conservation, and bibliographic materials. A very interesting document explains how the foundation build the vocabularies (see below).

The foundation uses the Open Data Commons Attribution License. These vocabularies comply with thesaurus construction standards (NISO- National Information Standards Organization and ISO-International Organization for Standardization), and are developed through contributions from the user community, complied and disseminated by the Getty Vocabulary Program and Getty Digital, and released finally in XML, JSON,RDF N-Triples and via a Sparql endpoint.

In 2012, the Amsterdam Museum published a work on the use of linked data. They start from XML data and present the process of converting the data to linked data with "man in the middle" [8].

In [9], the authors present their approach to build a service for converting legacy data into linked data. They focus on the problems resulting from heterogeneity of the sources, which is not a problem for SemJoconde: we have only one source.

Rijks Museum is one of the first major museums to publish data about its collections according to the principles of Linked Open Data [4]. The Rijks Museum has published a Linked Open Data -LOD- dataset with more than 350000 objects in the version of March 2016. In [4], the authors explain their approach, which is the result of several successive projects. So, the result benefits from a progressive consolidation.

JocondeLab [10] is a French project, which worked on a semantic model to get semantic representation of the Joconde database. To our knowledge, the representation obtained by JocondeLab is not available in Open Data, nor based on CIDOC-CRM.

Globally, we observe that more and more cultural institutions are considering Linked Open Data as a value for the future of their collections and their visitors.

C. Other related datasets

In this section, we present some significant datasets for our projects. As SemJoconde, several are based on CIDOC-CRM. Others are sources of inspiration or candidates for useful links, in the spirit of Linked Open Data.

The Europeana project [5] produces an aggregation of different sources of European cultural content - librairies, archives; audiovisual collections, theme-based content, as well as regional and national aggregators. Europeana follows the rules of Linked Open Data (LOD). As for SemJoconde, the schema is largely layered over the CIDOC-CRM model and includes concepts from ORE and Dublin core as well. The EDM -Europeana Data Model- is a flexible data model that combines object-centric, contextual and event-centric approaches to data representation. It uses URIs for addressing accessible resources.

The British Museum dataset [11] is organised using the CIDOC-CRM model, with the objective of harmonising with other international cultural heritage data. Although based on a linked data service, dataset licensing combines Creative Commons, and BM Licensing for 3D and HD content. Linked data is available in RDF and via a SPARQL Endpoint.

Paris Musées Collections [12] is a dataset of artworks curated by the members of the Paris Musées consortium. The dataset enrichment was an OpenData project executed in 2019-2020, but no Linked Data enrichment is available. Most data is open access (Creative Commons CC0), there is licensed HD and 3D content, as well as some specific licensed content. Data is available through an API, and dissemination on Wikimedia commons and Europeana is in the process. This dataset, as Joconde, is a source for our project Data&Musée. We have modeled part of these works with the CIDOC-CRM model.

DataTourisme [13] is a French LOD project regarding touristic offer and points of interest. The ontology supports Schema and Dublin Core vocabularies amongst others. It is a source of useful links, mainly for practical data about museums and monuments, but also about point of interest around them.

Geonames [14] proposes a massive list of geographical entities with their coordinates using the WGS84 latitude longitude system (World Geodetic System, 1984) and some other data about these entities: administrative links, country, etc. The dataset is collaborative and allows contributions using a wiki interface. It is available under a Creative commons licence. The data is accessible in a zip file and through webservices.

DBPedia [15] is a large dataset of entities based on Wikipedia data. It is a community effort to extract structured information from Wikipedia and to make this information available on the Web. DBpedia allows you to ask sophisticated queries. DBPedia is interlinked with a lot of other datasets. A RDF dump is available, and queries can be send to a SPARQL endpoint. DBpedia-Fr is similar and build from the french Wikipedia.

Wikidata [1] is a large dataset of world things linked to Wikipedia pages. Wikidata is a project of the Wikimedia foundation. As Wikidata offered the best coverage of the museums and monuments partners in the *Data&Musée* project, we privilege links with Wikidata. Wikidata allows you to ask sophisticated queries and to link other datasets on the Web and to Wikipedia. Similar to Wikipedia (creative commons) RDF, SPARQL as well as semantic web sitemaps are available to obtain the data. The RDF data is structured in N-Triples.

Yago [16] is a semantic knowledge base derived from Wikipedia, WordNet and GeoNames. Its specificity comes from the accuracy scores that have been manually attached to the data. The data and resources are available in many formats including RDF and TSV.

III. Sources

In this section, we describe the data sources that allowed us to build SemJoconde.

A. Joconde database

The Joconde database describes 589,278 works of art from French collections. It is established by the French Ministry of Culture. An extraction was made available in Open Data via the Open platform for French public data [17]. It is available in several formats including JSON. It is the extraction in this format that we used. An open license allowing free reuse is associated with this data.

Each Joconde database record has 14 fields

- 'STAT': status of the work: owner, place, etc.; for example: "propriété de la commune ; achat ; Château-Thierry ; musée Jean de La Fontaine",
- 'EPOQ': eras associated with the work; for example: "Paléolithique" or "Qing (1644-1911)",

- 'DOMN': fields associated with the work; for example: "dinanderie" or "Néolithique" or "photographie",
- 'INV' : an inventory number,
- 'TECH': techniques used by the work; for example: "matière plastique (moulé, imprimé)" (plastic (molded, printed)),
- 'DIMS': dimensions of the work; for example: "H. 27 ; l. 6.1 ; P. 4.2",
- 'LOCA': place of conservation and / or exhibition of the work; for example: "Grenoble ; musée Stendhal",
- 'DENO': object types; for example: "silex" (flint) or "tombeau" (tomb),
- 'TITR': title associated with the work (a simple string),
- 'AUTR': creators of the work; for example: "RODIN Auguste"
- 'DECV': elements concerning the discovery of the work; not used in this article,
- 'COPY': always '© Direction des musées de France',
- 'REF' : a unique identifier for the work; for example: 'AE037477',
- 'PERI': periods associated with the work; for example: 2e quart 20e siècle

B. Analysis

For some fields, we analyze the dataset. The goal is to find the values used for these fields and the count of works associated with each value of each field. Table I shows in the 'Dataset' column the count of values for the fields: AUTR, DOMN, DENO, LOCA, EPOQ, PERI.

C. Wikidata alignment and ground truth

In this work, we favor a mapping between Joconde vocabulary and Wikidata.

Thanks to the project WikiProject Vocabulaires Joconde [18], we have a ground truth. In this project, volunteers try to link manually the Joconde vocabulary with Wikidata. They use some tools to help humans to produce and validate such links. Links are notably available for creators, domains, places, epochs, periods, techniques.

TABLE I. GROUND TRUTH (14/7/2020).

Category (field)	*Validated*	*Dataset*	*%*
Creators (AUTR)	2560	37828	6.7
Domains (DOMN)	168	168	100.
Object types (DENO)	77	5766	1.3
Places (LOCA)	35	3593	0.9
Epochs (EPOQ)	500	831	60.1
Periods (PERI)	60	346	17.3

Table I shows the state of the ground truth at 14/7/2020. Corresponding files are available on github (and other files related to this article) [19].

IV. SEMANTIC MODEL

We have chosen to rely on the CIDOC-CRM model for our different representations. The CIDOC Conceptual Reference Model (CRM) [20] is a theoretical and practical tool for information integration in the field of cultural heritage. This model is massively used in the cultural heritage domain [21]. For example, Europeana (see Section II-C) uses CIDOC-CRM as a base for its Europeana Data Model (EDM).

Figure 1 shows the model used to represent the works. Properties starting with P and concepts starting with E followed by a number and text, such as P65_is_shown_by and E65_Creation, are properties or concepts defined by CIDOC-CRM. Properties starting with DMP -for Data Musée Property- followed by a number and text, like DMP2_has_description, are defined in our vocabulary. Entities starting with "dmgs:" have a defined URI in our domain where dmgs: is a prefix whose expanded value is "http://datamusee.givingsense.eu/".

As shown in Figure 1 and Section V-C, we need several linked entities to represent a work. An entity A represents the act of creating the work; this entity A is linked by the property P108_has_produced to the physical object P result of the act of creation; entity A is also linked to a conceptual object C by the property P94_has_created. The object P is linked by the property P43_has_dimension to an entity describing the dimensions of the physical object.

V. SEMANTIC TRANSLATION METHOD

Each field of the original data requires interpretation to enter the proposed semantic model. In this section, we present the process used to obtain a semantic representation from these fields.

A. General approach

As each field contains one or more labels for a specific type of data, we have no need for entity recognition, but just parsing each field to split the values for the field. Then, we need to undertake entity linking with a level of disambiguation. The main method for disambiguation is based on prior knowledge: we know that the field LOCA contains a place and the place is in France, the field AUTR contains one or several persons or organizations, etc.

Our strategy is the same for each field:

- we analyze the Joconde dataset to produce a list of possible values (strings) for each field,
- we count the number of works associated with each value (some works have several values),
- for some field, we need to parse the value to produce more useful data (see below in each field)
- we can use any algorithm to match a value against an entity of Wikidata; a simple algorithm is presented in Section V-B,
- humans check the link for the most used values (values covering the most works); in this way, we are able to guarantee good links for the most used values,
- when available, we check the obtained links against a ground truth; so, we have an idea of the quality of our data beyond the human checked links.

We will now see how this strategy is applied for some fields.

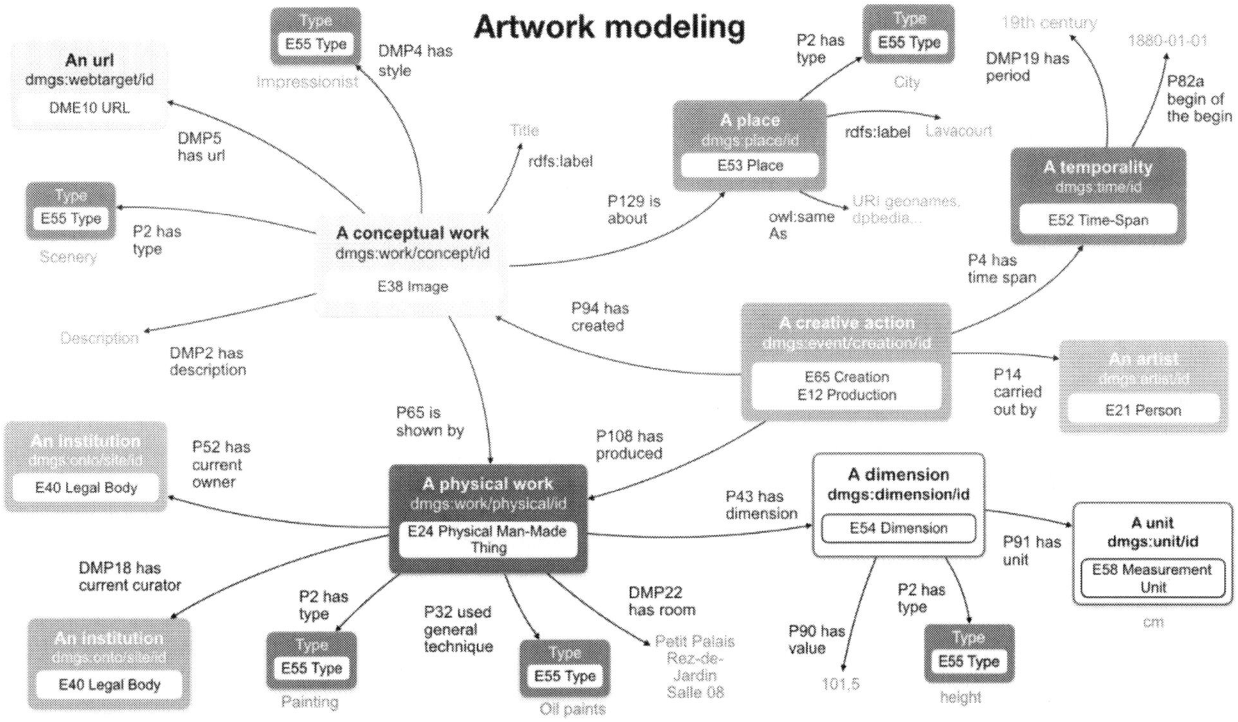

Figure 1. Artwork modeling.

B. *Entity matching and simple algorithm*

Several algorithms have been tried, like using DBpedia Spotlight [22] to get links with DBpedia or Aïda to get links with Yago [23]. The results presented here are obtained with a very simple algorithm based on the search service of Wikidata to get links with Wikidata. The search service gives us some entities corresponding to a label and some variants:

Algorithm:

- produce variants of the label: the label, the label in lowercase, the label in uppercase, the label in title case (each word with the first char in uppercase), and finally, if the label has several words, we attempt to move the first word to the last position,
- check the Wikidata search service for each variant,
- filter the results by some types,
- if only one entity is found, we keep that one; if several entities are found, we keep only the one which matches the label in lower case or none (a better disambiguation must be used in a future release)

For example, the Wikidata query template used to get the creators is in the github repository, file wikidataQueryTemplateForWord2UrisCreators.rq. The search service of Wikidata is combined with the knowledge that we search for some types of creators:

- painter "http://www.wikidata.org/entity/Q1028181"
- sculptor "http://www.wikidata.org/entity/Q1281618"
- drawer "http://www.wikidata.org/entity/Q15296811"
- artist "http://www.wikidata.org/entity/Q483501"
- visualartist "http://www.wikidata.org/entity/Q3391743"
- photographer "http://www.wikidata.org/entity/Q33231"
- engraver "http://www.wikidata.org/entity/Q329439"
- ceramicist "http://www.wikidata.org/entity/Q7541856"

See Section /refcreators for results.

Similar strategies are used for the other fields.

C. *URIs and REF field*

The original data presents a unique identifier for each work. We will use this identifier to build several URIs needed for our model. Each work gives rise to the creation of at least 4 entities: the creative act, at least one physical object, a conceptual object, several URIs for the dimensions of the physical object.

Here are the rules to build each URI, where {REF} must be replaced by the value of the REF field in the source:

- URI for the creative act: http://datamusee.givingsense.eu/event/creation/{REF}
- URI for the physical object: http://datamusee.givingsense.eu/work/physical/{REF}
- URI for the conceptual object: http://datamusee.givingsense.eu/work/concept/{REF}
- URI for the dimensions of the physical object: http://datamusee.givingsense.eu/dimension/{REF}_X, where X is a number generated for each dimension

D. *Domains: field DOMN*

As this field is completely covered by the ground truth, we use directly the proposed links.

E. Object types: field TECH

9697 terms are used for the 'TECH' field. The hundred most used cover more than 88% of the works. Many values used for this field are artistic techniques - drawing, painting, mosaic, etc- in particular in the most used values. We searched for corresponding entities in Wikidata. A useful class is "http://www.wikidata.org/entity/Q11177771", with the label "artsistic technique". So, with the property P31 (instance of) or P279 (subclass of), we were able to find all the artistic techniques known by Wikidata. We found 306 of them (result obtained on July 13, 2020). Then, we search for corresponding techniques values in Joconde. We did the same with the instances and subclass of "http://www.wikidata.org/entity/Q3300034", with the label "painting material". We found 116 of them. Then, we found 45 exact match in the Joconde data for one class or the other; we checked all of them. These 45 techniques covers 254630 works (43% of the works). Note: the SPARQL queries used to do it on Wikidata Query Service are available on the github repository referenced above.

In the ground truth, there is no association for the TECH field. So, some more work must be done to complete and to assert the quality of our results for this field.

F. Object types: field AUTR

The field AUTR gives a string naming the creator of a work. Some works have no known creator (99194 works; 16.83%). Many (63199; 10.72%) have the creator named 'anonymous'. But for the others (426885), we will try to find a matching entity in Wikidata. Creators are persons or organizations.

We are particularly interested in the most productive creators. We have chosen a threshold of 10 or more works per selected creator. There are 5217 creators in this category. They produced 98.07% of the works attributed to a creator.

We have benefited in particular from the work carried out by the Wikidata-Joconde project [18]. This project associates terms used in the Joconde database with Wikidata entities, with a human validation process. As of 5/30/2020, 2560 associations were validated for creators. 1325 are in our target of productive creators. They cover 25.04% of the attributed works.

Our algorithm V-B allows to find 1173 Wikidata entities associated with the designation of the creator by the AUTR field in Joconde, of which 1168 correspond to the entities validated by the Wikidata-Joconde project.

To evaluate our results, we use precision, recall and F1 measures.

Ncw = number of creators validated by the Wikidata Joconde project and targets of the evaluation

Nct = number of creators for which our algorithm finds a Wikidata entity

Nce = number of exact links found

Pc = precision relative to creators = Nce/Nct

Rc = recall relative to creators = Nce/Ncw

$F1c = 2*Pc*Rc/(Pc+Rc)$

We also considered the 100 creators with the greatest number of works except 'anonymous'. Of these 100 creators,

TABLE II. RESULTS FOR CREATORS

Measure	*Value*
Ncw	1315
Nct	1180
Nce	1177
Pc	99.74
Rc	88.83
F1c	93.97

a Wikidata link was found for 59 of them. Of these 59, 28 were among the links already validated by the ground truth. We proceeded to a human validation of the other 31 links: all of them were exact. On these 59 links, an accuracy of 100% was therefore obtained. The recall cannot be evaluated, since for creators not found, we do not have a method to tell if the creator is not in Wikidata or if our algorithm failed to find it. Assuming that all creators are listed in Wikidata, we get a lower bound of the recall: 59%; and a lower bound for the F1 measure: 74.21.

We have manually checked 10 links for creators among the most productive, covering 47029 works (11.01% of attributed works). The list is: RODIN Auguste (13231 works), MOREAU Gustave (6816), CHASSERIAU Théodore (5010), DELACROIX Eugène (4136), COROT Jean-Baptiste Camille (4114), INGRES Jean Auguste Dominique (3202), STEINLEN Théophile Alexandre (2916), LE BRUN Charles (2882), PICASSO Pablo (2496), HEBERT Ernest (2226). Ten correct links are found by our algorithm for these 10 creators.

For the 5127 productive creators, we found 2199 links by our algorithm. A simple extrapolation from the results obtained on the ground truth, with $Pc = 99.74$, suggests a result of around $2199*Pc/100 = 2193$ correct links, which is 878 new links beyond the ground truth.

G. Localisation: fields LOCA and STAT

The LOCA is generally composed of a city name, followed by an institution or organization name, separated by a semicolon.

We will skip the entity linking of the city, because it is a very classical problem with good results using a lot of available tools. So, our focus will be the organization or institution. Each institution has the same city coupled with her in each occurrence of the institution in a LOCA field value. So, the count of institutions is the count of different values in the LOCA field: 3593. No link to Wikidata is available in the ground truth.

For our algorithm, we selected the following types:

- museum "www.wikidata.org/entity/Q33506"
- glam ".../entity/Q1030034"
- cultural institution ".../entity/Q5193377"
- cultural organization ".../entity/Q29918292"

And we add a filter against the city: the institution found must be in the good city.

We selected institutions with more than 100 works in Joconde, the 'richest' institutions. So, 304 institutions were selected. They are covering 580035 works (98.43%). For these institutions, we found 155 links. We undertook manual check on the first quarter of the list (first 76 museums). We found 42

TABLE III. RESULTS FOR A SELECTION OF LOCALIZATION

Measure	*Value*
Searched museums	76
Found links	42
Exact links	42
Precision	100
Recall	55.26
F1c	71.18

links for these museums; all found links have been checked manually: all are exact. So, on this sample, we have:

The STAT field is similar to the LOCA field in the sense that it contains mainly a city and an organization/institution. So, the STAT field is processed similarly to the LOCA field.

VI. SEMJOCONDE DATASET

In our triple store, Fuseki, we have a dataset named SemJoconde. The main components of this dataset are the following RDF graphs:

- one graph contains the works,
- one graph contains the creators,
- one graph contains the institutions and organizations,
- one graph contains the cities.

These graphs are linked together and are linked with Wikidata. These graphs are available with a Creative Commons licence in the github repository [19]. It is evolving on daily basis and will soon have a description with VOID triples [24].

For entities not found in Wikidata by the previously described methods, we produce our own URIs and, in the future, expect to complete these URIs by owl:sameAs links to other Knowledge Graphs, like Getty, BNF, Europeana, British Museum, Wikidata, DBpedia, Yago (see Section II-C), etc.

In addition, the github repository includes JSON files which list the domains, the authors and the techniques encountered in the database, with their frequency of use. It includes queries to Wikidata Query Service, which contributes to the process of building this dataset.

VII. CONCLUSION AND FUTURE WORKS

In this paper, we introduce a new LOD dataset. With close to 600000 artistic works described by triples. A work to produce links over Wikidata entities is presented. A good coverage of works interlinked with Wikidata by at least one property is our goal and we see some preliminary results as links for 59% of the creators with a precision of more than 99% and similar results for the institutions.

In the future, we expect to improve the coverage and consolidate our results by exploiting the context more intensively. For example, we can use the PERI field (period) to improve the selection of a creator or improve the links with institutions by knowing the creators presented in them.

Also, we intend to use the SemJoconde graph in recommendation projects using graph embedding methods.

ACKNOWLEDGMENT

This work is conducted as part of the *Data&Musée* project selected in the $23rd$ call for projects of the Fonds Unique Interministériel (FUI) and certified by Cap Digital and Imaginove.

REFERENCES

[1] "Wikidata," 2020, URL: https://www.wikidata.org [retrieved: October, 2020].

[2] "Data&Musée," 2020, URL: http://datamusee.fr [retrieved: October, 2020].

[3] "Getty Research: Editorial Guidelines," 2018, URL: http://www.getty.edu/research/tools/vocabularies/guidelines/index.html [retrieved: September, 2020].

[4] C. Dijkshoorn et al., "The rijksmuseum collection as linked data," Semantic Web, vol. 9, no. 2, 1 2018, pp. 221–230.

[5] "Europeana project," 2020, URL: https://www.europeana.eu [retrieved: October, 2020].

[6] J. Hoffart et al., "Robust Disambiguation of Named Entities in Text," in Conference on Empirical Methods in Natural Language Processing, EMNLP 2011, Edinburgh, Scotland, 2011, pp. 782–792.

[7] J. Volz, C. Bizer, M. Gaedke, and G. Kobilarov, "Silk–a link discovery framework for the web of data," Proceedings of the 2nd Linked Data on the Web Workshop, 01 2009.

[8] V. de Boer et al., "Supporting linked data production for cultural heritage institutes: The amsterdam museum case study," in The Semantic Web: Research and Applications. Berlin, Heidelberg: Springer Berlin Heidelberg, 2012, pp. 733–747.

[9] E. Mäkelä, E. Hyvönen, and T. Ruotsalo, "How to deal with massively heterogeneous cultural heritage data - lessons learned in culturesampo," Semantic Web, vol. 3, 01 2012, pp. 85–109.

[10] "CIDOC-CRM: Conceptual Reference Model," 2020, URL: http://jocondelab.iri-research.org/jocondelab/about/ [french; retrieved: September, 2020].

[11] "British Museum dataset," 2020, URL: https://info.datatourisme.gouv.fr [retrieved: October, 2020].

[12] "Paris Musées Collections," 2020, URL: https://apicollections.parismusees.paris.fr [retrieved: October, 2020].

[13] "DataTourisme," 2020, URL: https://old.datahub.io/dataset/british-museum-collection [retrieved: October, 2020].

[14] "Geonames," 2020, URL: https://www.geonames.org [retrieved: October, 2020].

[15] "DBpedia," 2020, URL: https://dbpedia.org [retrieved: October, 2020].

[16] "Yago," 2020, URL: https://www.mpi-inf.mpg.de/departments/databases-and-information-systems/research/yago-naga/yago [retrieved: October, 2020].

[17] "Data Gouv," 2020, URL: https://www.data.gouv.fr/en/datasets/collections-des-musees-de-france-extrait-de-la-base-joconde-en-format-xml/ [retrieved: October, 2020].

[18] "Wikidata:WikiProject Vocabulaires Joconde," 2020, URL: http://www.wikidata.org/wiki/Wikidata:WikiProject_Vocabulaires_Joconde/en [retrieved: September, 2020].

[19] "Repository for SemJoconde," 2020, URL: https://github.com/datamusee/semjoconde [retrieved: September, 2020].

[20] "CIDOC-CRM: Conceptual Reference Model," 2020, URL: http://www.cidoc-crm.org/ [retrieved: September, 2020].

[21] V. Alexiev, V. C. Ivanov, and M. Grinberg, Eds., Practical Experiences with CIDOC CRM and its Extensions (CRMEX 2013) Workshop, 17th International Conference on Theory and Practice of Digital Libraries (TPDL 2013), Dec. 2013.

[22] J. Daiber, M. Jakob, C. Hokamp, and P. N. Mendes, "Improving efficiency and accuracy in multilingual entity extraction," in Proceedings of the 9th International Conference on Semantic Systems, ser. I-SEMANTICS '13. New York, NY, USA: Association for Computing Machinery, 2013, p. 121–124. [Online]. Available: https://doi.org/10.1145/2506182.2506198

[23] J. Hoffart, "Discovering and disambiguating named entities in text," in Proceedings of the 2013 SIGMOD/PODS Ph.D. Symposium, ser. SIGMOD'13 PhD Symposium. New York, NY, USA: Association for Computing Machinery, 2013, p. 43–48. [Online]. Available: https://doi.org/10.1145/2483574.2483582

[24] "Describing Linked Datasets with the VoID Vocabulary," 2011, URL: https://www.w3.org/TR/void/ [retrieved September, 2020].

The Semantic Web in the Internet of Production: A Strategic Approach with Use-Case Examples

Johannes Lipp
(i) Chair of Databases and Information Systems
RWTH Aachen University, Aachen, Germany
(ii) Fraunhofer Institute for Applied Information Technology
Sankt Augustin, Germany
orcid.org/0000-0002-2639-1949
email: lipp@dbis.rwth-aachen.de

Katrin Schilling
Laboratory for Machine Tools
and Production Engineering (WZL)
RWTH Aachen University, Aachen, Germany
email: k.schilling@wzl.rwth-aachen.de

Abstract—**The semantic interoperability of data, models, systems, and knowledge in general is a core element of the Internet of Production, i.e., a cross-life cycle and interdisciplinary networking of all levels in manufacturing technology. Semantic Web technologies are a good choice for the implementation of such applications, but, despite numerous academic research projects, its true potential is still rarely used in practice. One reason is the lack of knowledge among practitioners about both the technology itself and possible application areas, as manufacturing engineers usually are no Semantic Web experts and vice versa. In this paper, we present five essential application areas for Semantic Web technologies in production engineering, and give five examples of how we use these in practice in the Internet of Production. Our two-folded presentation intends to clarify potentials within application areas, and at the same time support the ramp-up of practical applications based on our examples.**

Keywords*—*Semantic Web; Internet of Production; Use-Cases.

I. Introduction

The Semantic Web [1] and its community proposed multiple recommendations and standards to improve semantic interoperability in the interconnected World Wide Web. It addresses, among others, the tasks of knowledge sharing, validation, and reasoning. Users can tackle these tasks via combinations of a broad range of solutions, including Persistent IDentifiers (PIDs), ontologies, data shapes, and reasoning rules. Semantic Web solutions in general do not intend to replace other solutions like relational databases or machine learning, but aim to cooperate closely with them.

In the field of production technology, the idea of the Semantic Web got attention in various, mostly academic, research projects. Unfortunately, these technologies have not yet reached a broad acceptance or implementation in industry. This is mainly due to lacking ontology knowledge among employees, missing tool support, imprecise problem statements in industry use-cases, and unclear benefits like the return on invest for the extensive modeling effort. These issues in industry range among multiple levels and domains, and effect engineers, domain experts, ontology engineers, and C-level managers. For these reasons, even though some interesting concepts and the technical feasibility were analyzed in demo implementations, hardly any application was properly realized in a productive system or product. Most applications in production did never leave an experimental stage.

There indeed are strong reasons to continue the research on Semantic Web technologies for production engineering. Following the achievements in the vision of "Industry 4.0" in the recent years, a proper infrastructure – a basic prerequisite for a networked production – has been created. Nowadays, the latest generation of products in automation technology are equipped with the necessary interfaces and communication protocols to enable distributed, data-driven applications. In particular, this means that "data" is now available outside the devices and applications with low effort. Availability and accessibility of data alone however are not sufficient to match the vision of the Internet of Production [2], which requires the networking of all systems and data-based optimization along in the entire production process. For example, with a higher level of maturity for knowledge-based applications like artificial intelligence, lifting simple data to proper knowledge is a crucial factor. This need for semantic technologies is supported by the increased attention for protocols like OPC Unified Architecture (OPC UA) [3] as they add semantics to data interactions and also support interoperability. We argue that the development of these solutions did not fully take into account the previous achievements by the Semantic Web and thus tend to partially re-invent the wheel.

Both aspects, the better availability of data through an advanced infrastructure of production systems, and the increasing demand for semantically described data for new applications, show that a Semantic Web in action is required by the Internet of Production. In this paper, a state of the art overview is in Section II, before, in Section III, we demonstrate the benefits of the Semantic Web for both ontology experts and non-experts in order to convince all above-mentioned users in a handy way. We subsequently in Section IV present concrete use-cases that we observed in the research project *Internet of Production* and thus support industry and institutes in planning their use-cases, before we conclude our work in Section V.

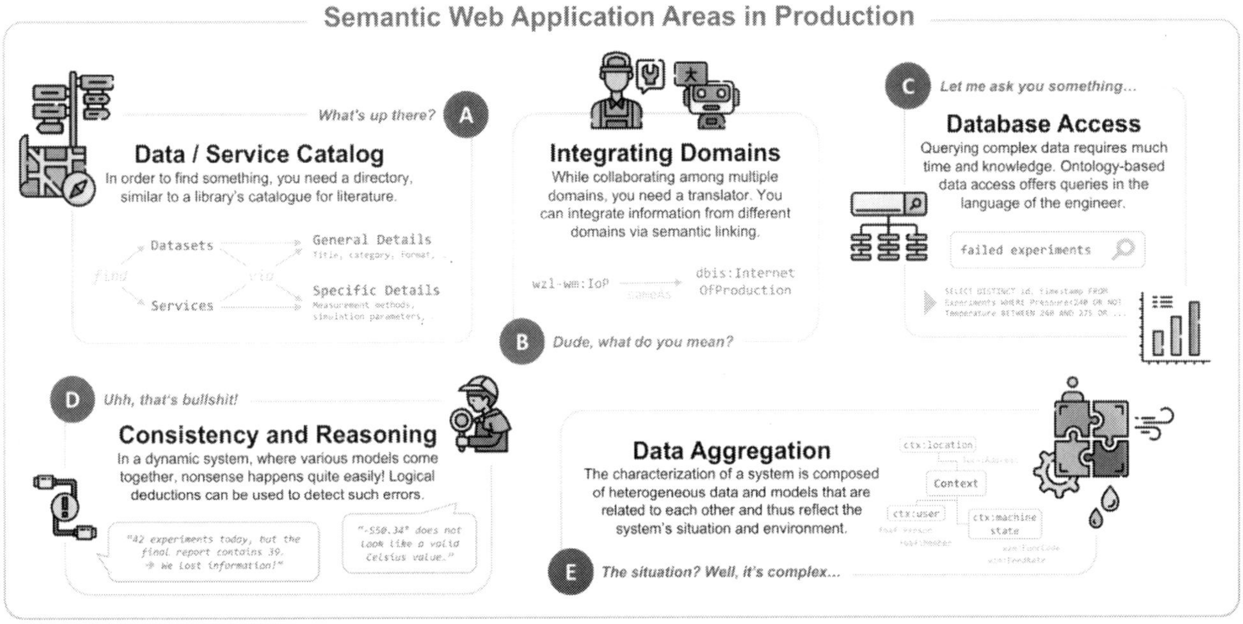

Fig. 1. Illustration of the main application areas for the Semantic Web in the context of production. This figure supports demonstrate the benefits to both experts and non-experts. These include, but are not limited to, the five areas data/service catalog, integrating domains, database access, consistency and reasoning, and data aggregation.

II. State of the Art

The potential of the Semantic Web idea in the context of production technology has been discussed in research projects. Upper ontologies for manufacturing, such as DOLCE [4], Cyc [5], SUMO [6] or MASON [7], as well as specific domain ontologies, were developed. An overview and comparison can be found in [8]. In particular, the challenge of breaking up silos and linking information across value chains is essential in the "Industry 4.0"; the concept of the administration shell is a concrete example [9]. It is still difficult to find these ontologies and reuse that work.

Semantic Web technologies have also been applied to solve a wide range of concrete research questions: From dynamic processor orchestration [10], over worker assistance [11], up to visualization via augmented reality [12], just to name a few examples. Furthermore, initiatives such as the Open Services for Lifecycle Collaboration (OSLC) try to establish the application in (engineering) tools through industry cooperations.

Unfortunately, all this knowledge and experience is still not well known outside these participating disciplines. Especially classical engineering disciplines, which have had little contact with software engineering and information modeling, often face difficulties in transferring the often abstract paradigms to problems in their own domain. Our goal is not to replace any established or advanced technologies of these experts with Semantic Web technologies. Rather, the intention is to support the use of Semantic Web technologies as a "glue" to connect the specific technologies and expert domains by providing a descriptive set of application areas.

III. Application Areas in Production

This section presents possible application areas for the Semantic Web in production and it is intended to give a high-level overview for all relevant people. The following explanations refer to the graphical overview shown in Figure 1 and which we use as a one-page flyer to advertise this at partners.

A **Data / Service Catalog** (A) probably is the mostly used application and is well-known among most people. It is a directory of any data sources of interest, such as datasets, services, programs, people, projects, or sensors. Such a catalog enables people to find information based on given search details. Prominent examples are open data portals such as [13] or [14], where users typically can apply a wide range of parameters to their search, including keywords, usage rules, and both spatial and temporal ranges. Another frequently applied example is the dynamic management of semantically described functions for a service-oriented / skill-based management of production processes, described in [10], [15].

A catalog usually is deployed independent from the data itself, which means that it can be easily applied to any existing data management system. Note that, as depicted in Figure 1, it supports searching for general filters as well as specific details. The former represents domain-independent information that can be applied to most catalogs and thus can and should be shared among these. Concretely, this means that catalog developers should reuse existing (de-facto) standards such as the Data CATalog Vocabulary (DCAT) [16] to enable smooth interoperability on this level between different catalogs. The latter, namely specific details, stands for information that is particular for a certain domain. Defining these requires much communication between both disciplines Semantic Web and the domain, as only the annotated pieces of information can be included in search requests afterwards.

The area **Integrating Domains** (B) supports human understanding as well as interoperability on machine level. Since it is not useful to re-invent the wheel for each small area one works on, people tie together knowledge from different domains in order to represent their particular use-case best. Combining pieces of different knowledge sources such as ontologies usually leads to intersections or overlaps, which often are not clear for humans and machines. With methods from the Semantic Web, we can solve these issues by introducing relations like `sameAs`, `broader`, or `narrower` between concepts from different domains.

Ontology Based Data Access (OBDA) provides the potential of simple **Database Access** (C) on a semantic level. By defining basic concepts such as "failed experiments" for a specific scenario, the domain expert (without extensive database knowledge) is enabled to easily articulate even complicated queries. The goal is to separate a user-friendly wording of the queries from the concrete database structure.

The potential to check semantically described data for **Consistency** and to derive insights through **Reasoning** (D) is beneficial in the complex ecosystem of production technology: Errors can rapidly occur during the transition between different applications, systems from multiple manufacturers, and various standards along the product's life cycle. But even logical conflicts within the data sets can be identified.

The **Aggregation of Data** and models (E) enables the mapping of complex situations and environmental conditions based on heterogeneous information sources. Semantic relationships of potentially very different aspects characterizing a situation allow an abstraction of concepts (such as location, states, persons) with their individual representation, even if they are represented in different structures.

IV. Application Examples in the Internet of Production

This section presents five use-case examples we identified in the research project *Internet of Production* and which we will fully implement in the near future. They all originate from open research questions in different domains, and aim to improve existent processes in terms of usability, stability, speed, or precision. These concrete examples are intended to be used by researchers as models for any application area in the future, and might even be translated into archetypes. Figure 2 clearly illustrates which application areas from Figure 1 are covered by the five example applications. All examples cover one or two areas, and all areas are covered by at least one example.

Example 1: An example of an application for area (A) is the creation of a cross-disciplinary catalogue that provides a searchable overview of the various research activities and the data generated in the project. The catalogue makes it easier for researchers in computer science, mechanical engineering, economics and social sciences to find links between

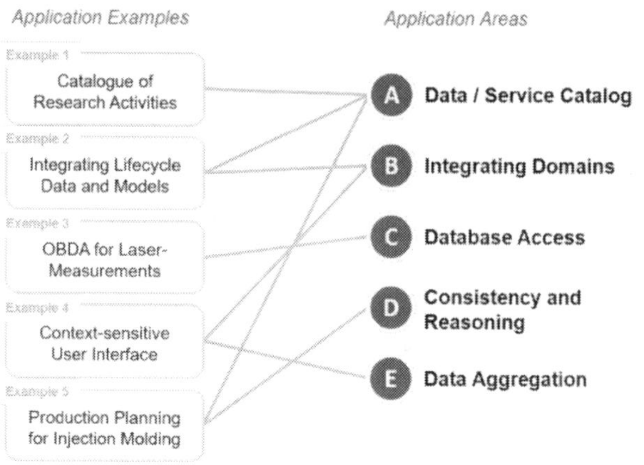

Fig. 2. Allocation of the use-case examples presented in Section IV to the application areas from Section III. Note that some examples cover multiple areas, and that all areas are covered.

(sub-) projects, solutions for similar problems or potential research partners. A concrete implementation plan includes both a distributed file system that stores the data, and Apache Jena Fuseki [17] metadata system that provides metadata management and a convenient query interface via the SPARQL Protocol and RDF Query Language (SPARQL) [18]. The catalogued information includes, but is not limited to, a vast amount of datasets consisting of sensor values collected from production machines or simulations. Required annotations and search filter in this example include responsible person, temporal characteristics, accrual periodicity, domain and file format. Note that providing data to others requires the data steward to add most of the above-mentioned annotations manually, as only some fields can be filled automatically. It is not a trivial task to motivate data providers to execute this step properly.

Example 2: The second application is the integration of different engineering models and to relate these with each other, which combines areas (A) and (B). In the product development process, a wide variety of models is created and their relations are mostly implicit knowledge only. Our partners asked for techniques to explicitly annotate important relations between models and query these afterwards. Please note that the models are very heterogeneous in terms of domain, file format, and level of detail. The file format, for instance, ranges from simulation scripts over 3D sketches to rich Computer-Aided Design (CAD) models. We tackle area (B) in this use-case by introducing a minimal ontology, which is depicted in Figure 3 and is aligned with DCAT. This ontology is used to properly relate models with each other, which includes to tell that (i) two models represent the same thing, (ii) an element in one model represents the same thing than one from another, or (iii) an element in a model or a complete model is more specific or general than another. The first realized concrete axioms state that a particular engine within a CAD model of a Audi A4 car represents the same as a blender 3D visualization's part that depicts the engine of a Volkswagen Amarok. Since we did not only link models to each other via these properties, but also catalogize them in a model catalog, this use-case combines areas (A) and (B) and enables a holistic integration of individual (sub-)models along the life cycle.

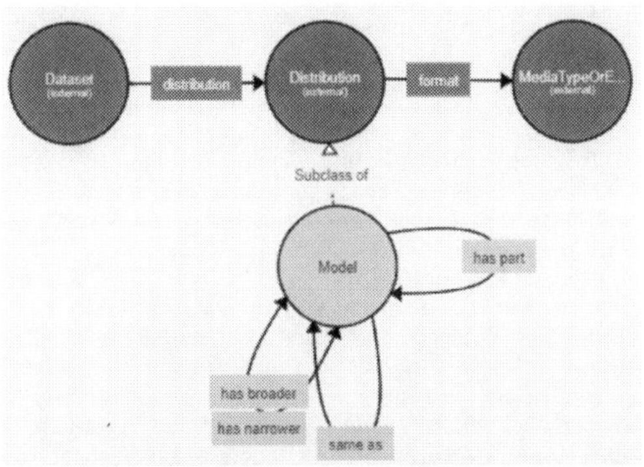

Fig. 3. The minimal ontology we created for the model catalog use-case. It is aligned with DCAT and represents any model as a distribution that has a file format (dark blue above). In this WebVOWL [19] screenshot, the light blue properties below show possible relations between models and elements within these, which are linked via the property *has part*.

Example 3: Another promising use-case is an implementation of the OBDA approach (C) for Ultrashort Pulse Laser Processing (USP). In this process, we record time series of a laser's three-dimensional position as well as temperature data of four locations, and store it in a relational database. Analyzing the data requires the USP domain experts to design complex Structured Query Language (SQL) queries, which however is not part of their expertise. We avoid the time-consuming and error-prone individual process via OBDA mappings and a minimal ontology, which are both designed cooperatively by the USP domain experts and ourselves. The current demonstrator can be queried locally via the Ontop plugin for Protégé and allows the engineers in particular query failed experiments, crucial temperature developments, stable runs etc. in their own wording via SPARQL. A full implementation of this use-case includes to identify and understand all existing SQL queries, create new ones where required, and specify proper OBDA mappings that are easy to understand for the end users.

Example 4: An example for the data aggregation (E) as well as the integration of domains (B) is a context-sensitive user interface that adapts the user's position to show relevant information regarding the nearest, dynamic environment. For this purpose, a predefined information object is labeled with contextual tags (e.g., a location, device category, user role, machine state). Depending on the user's devices (e.g., tablet or glasses) the localization can be determined in different ways: An indoor tracking system such as Bluetooth Low Energy beacons refers to the referencing anchors; image recognition enables tracking based on visual significant features in the environment; augmented reality frameworks (e.g., Google ARCore) combine multiple technologies and define virtual anchors. A semantic description of the spatial references links them to the concrete information object via the concept of localization. This is applied in the same way to other tags such as machine state or the user role.

Example 5: The last use-case we present models production planning, logistics, and control for injection molding in plastics processing. It combines areas (D) and (A), as we construct and manage both reasoning rules and instances, respectively. In this example, we together with the experts from plastics processing fully model the required complexity of production planning in this domain. That are in particular dependencies and consequences between possible choices, and support to infer new knowledge from given the input in form of annotated instances. Possible outcomes of this use-case include the ability to produce optimal production plans from given inputs, as well as to derive new knowledge in that area, which can be shared among humans and machines. In order to complete this, all necessary information on the machines' availability, incoming orders, and matching rules need to be extracted in a semi-automatic way from an Enterprise Resource Planning (ERP) system.

This section presented five exemplary use-cases that we observed, and which are intended to support future researchers in their tasks to leverage the Semantic Web in their projects. As shown in Figure 2, these examples cover one or two application areas from Figure 1 each, and all areas are covered. The presented examples tackle practical problems occurring in different domains, ranging from data access and management to analysis and reasoning. In the concrete implementation, domain experts work together with Semantic Web experts to build target-oriented solutions for practical use.

V. Conclusion and Future Work

In this paper we argued that, especially in the recent years, the push of the Semantic Web matches well with the pull from the ever growing amount of networked information sources in the Internet of Production. This leads to an increased need for an actual application of Semantic Web technologies within various domains including production. We grouped the major strengths of the Semantic Web in the production domain into five areas that are intended to support motivating these to different people in research and industry.

With five exemplary use-cases that we observed in the project *Internet of Production*, we demonstrate possible solutions and their effectiveness to future researchers. These use-cases show that a strong collaboration of experts from both the Semantic Web and the application domain is essential indeed. Our paper is a good step towards bridging these domains, as we showed important matches between possibilities on the one side and requirements in use-cases on the other side.

Future work includes to further design, implement, and document these five use-cases. Further leveraging the strengths of the Semantic Web and its community in production will enable a semantically interconnected Internet of Production. The importance of collaboration between experts from both fields remains, and is crucial to drive both domains semantics and production.

ACKNOWLEDGEMENT

Funded by the Deutsche Forschungsgemeinschaft (DFG, German Research Foundation) under Germany's Excellence Strategy – EXC-2023 Internet of Production – 390621612.

REFERENCES

[1] T. Berners-Lee, J. Hendler, and O. Lassila, "The Semantic Web," *Scientific American*, vol. 284, no. 5, pp. 34–43, 2001.

[2] J. Pennekamp et al., "Towards an Infrastructure Enabling the Internet of Production," in *2019 IEEE International Conference on Industrial Cyber Physical Systems (ICPS)*, May 2019, pp. 31–37.

[3] T. Hannelius, M. Salmenpera, and S. Kuikka, "Roadmap to Adopting OPC UA," in *2008 6th IEEE International Conference on Industrial Informatics*. IEEE, 2008, pp. 756–761.

[4] A. Gangemi, N. Guarino, C. Masolo, A. Oltramari, and L. Schneider, "Sweetening Ontologies with DOLCE," in *International Conference on Knowledge Engineering and Knowledge Management*. Springer, 2002, pp. 166–181.

[5] D. B. Lenat and R. V. Guha, *Building Large Knowledge-based Systems; Representation and Inference in the Cyc Project*. Addison-Wesley Longman Publishing Co., Inc., 1989.

[6] I. Niles and A. Pease, "Towards a Standard Upper Ontology," in *Proceedings of the international conference on Formal Ontology in Information Systems-Volume 2001*, 2001, pp. 2–9.

[7] S. Lemaignan, A. Siadat, J. Dantan, and A. Semenenko, "Mason: A proposal for an ontology of manufacturing domain," in *IEEE Workshop on Distributed Intelligent Systems: Collective Intelligence and Its Applications (DIS'06)*, 2006, pp. 195–200.

[8] N. Khilwani, J. A. Harding, and A. K. Choudhary, "Semantic Web in Manufacturing," *Proceedings of the Institution of Mechanical Engineers, Part B: Journal of Engineering Manufacture*, vol. 223, no. 7, pp. 905–924, 2009.

[9] I. Grangel-González, L. Halilaj, S. Auer, S. Lohmann, C. Lange, and D. Collarana, "An RDF-based Approach for Implementing Industry 4.0 Components with Administration Shells," in *2016 IEEE 21st International Conference on Emerging Technologies and Factory Automation (ETFA)*, 2016, pp. 1–8.

[10] M. Loskyll, J. Schlick, S. Hodek, L. Ollinger, T. Gerber, and B. Pîrvu, "Semantic Service Discovery and Orchestration for Manufacturing Processes," in *ETFA2011*, 2011, pp. 1–8.

[11] D. Gorecky, M. Loskyll, and C. Stahl, "Semantic Digital Factory – Using Engineering Knowledge to Create Ontologies for Virtual Training," *IFAC Proceedings Volumes*, vol. 47, no. 3, pp. 7825 – 7830, 2014, 19th IFAC World Congress. [Online]. Available: http://www.sciencedirect.com/science/article/pii/S1474667016428454

[12] I. Mizutani, M. Kritzler, K. Garcia, and F. Michahelles, "Intuitive Interaction with Semantics Using Augmented Reality: A Case Study of Workforce Management in an Industrial Setting," in *Proceedings of the Seventh International Conference on the Internet of Things*, ser. IoT '17. New York, NY, USA: Association for Computing Machinery, 2017. [Online]. Available: https://doi.org/10.1145/3131542.3131550

[13] "GOVData," https://govdata.de, accessed: 2020-10-21.

[14] "EU Open Data Portal," https://data.europa.eu/euodp, accessed: 2020-10-21.

[15] C. Brecher, E. Kusmenko, A. Lindt, B. Rumpe, S. Storms, S. Wein, M. von Wenckstern, and A. Wortmann, "Multi-Level Modeling Framework for Machine as a Service Applications Based on Product Process Resource Models," in *Proceedings of the 2nd International Symposium on Computer Science and Intelligent Control*, ser. ISCSIC '18. New York, NY, USA: Association for Computing Machinery, 2018. [Online]. Available: https://doi.org/10.1145/3284557.3284714

[16] R. Albertoni, D. Browning, S. Cox, A. G. Beltran, A. Perego, and P. Winstanley, "Data Catalog Vocabulary (DCAT)-Version 2," *W3C Recommendation*, vol. 3, 2019, [Accessed 2020.09.15].

[17] The Apache Software Foundation, "Apache Jena Fuseki," https://jena.apache.org/documentation/fuseki2/, 2011, [Accessed 2020.09.15].

[18] E. Prud'hommeaux and A. Seaborne, "SPARQL 1.1 language to query and manipulate RDF graph content, W3C Recommendation, 21 March 2013," https://www.w3.org/TR/sparql11-overview/, 2013, [Accessed 2020.09.15].

[19] S. Lohmann, V. Link, E. Marbach, and S. Negru, "WebVOWL: Web-based Visualization of Ontologies," in *International Conference on Knowledge Engineering and Knowledge Management*. Springer, 2014, pp. 154–158.